Ann
Brimacombe
Elliot

Charming the Bones

A Portrait of
Margaret
Matthew
Colbert

The Kent State University Press
Kent, Ohio, and London

© 2000 by The Kent State University Press, Kent, Ohio 44242
All rights reserved
Library of Congress Catalog Card Number 99-048584
ISBN 0-87338-648-5
Manufactured in the United States of America

06 05 04 03 02 01 00   5 4 3 2 1

Library of Congress Cataloging-in-Publication Data
Elliot, Ann Brimacombe, 1937–
    Charming the bones: a portrait of Margaret Matthew Colbert / Ann Brimacombe Elliot.
        p. cm.
    Includes bibliographical references and index.
    ISBN 0-87338-648-5 (cloth: alk. paper) ∞
    1. Colbert, Margaret. 2. Artists—United States—Biography. I. Title.
    N 6537 C589 A4   2000
    709'.2 — DC21
    [B]   99-048584

British Library Cataloging-in-Publication data area available.

Artists are the eyes of paleontologists, and paintings
are the window through which nonspecialists can see
the dinosaurian world.

—*Dale A. Russell*

◡∴ Contents ∴◡

~: *Preface* :~

It has been said that artists skilled in restorations of extinct animals are "the eyes of paleontologists." They provide scientists with a concrete idea of what a fossilized beast might have looked like in life and enable them to infer activities, behavior, and relationships.

The work of restoration artists also stirs the imagination of the general public and has been behind the creation of dozens of stories and books—from Sir Arthur Conan Doyle's *Lost World* (1912) to Michael Crichton's *Jurassic Park* (1990). At the end of *Jurassic Park,* Crichton acknowledges the artists who inspired him. One of those artists is Margaret Matthew Colbert, whom he describes as one of the "new generation of illustrators . . . whose reconstructions incorporate the new perception of how dinosaurs behaved."

In paleontological circles, everyone knows Margaret's husband. Edwin (Ned) Colbert is revered among his peers as the "Grand Old Man" of dinosaurs and other early reptiles. Margaret has been the quiet, supportive partner in his home and in his work. It is time that her own contributions to the science of paleontology and to art are recognized.

Margaret chose to be conventional—to marry and have children—and to be a "good wife" to Ned so that he could focus all his energies on his work. At times she wished that she, too, had a "good wife" so that she could make full use of her abilities. Through the first half of her married life, art was squeezed into interludes snatched from wifehood and motherhood. But she was grateful that she was spared the anxieties and pressures that go with earning a living as an artist. Because of the support and security her partner provided, she was free to take risks and thus free to explore different media and techniques.

At a stage in life when most of her peers were folding their wings and settling down to roost, Margaret at last found the time and opportunity to devote herself more fully to her art. And she flew. Since reaching the age of sixty, she has been enormously productive.

Margaret is responsible for excellent model restorations. Her illustrations have graced many books and magazines, and she has important museum murals to her credit. Although most of her production has been restoration in various forms, she has also turned out a quantity of work that has nothing to do with long-dead creatures and everything to do with sensitivity, a fine intelligence, and—often—a wonderfully quirky sense of humor.

But Margaret Matthew Colbert is not merely an artist. She is a wise and literate woman, a philosopher, a poet, a linguist. She has accompanied Ned on his travels in pursuit of fossils to the far corners of the world. Her adventures and experiences have added brilliant color to her life, both as an artist and a person. Indeed, this enterprise began as an account of her journeys. However, it was soon evident that a travelogue could not do justice to her life.

This book is Margaret's own story. She has spent hours of precious time submitting to my inquisitions and further hours checking that I have not distorted facts. For me, the process has been one of unalloyed pleasure. I hope this exploration begins to do justice to a remarkable woman.

✌ *Acknowledgments* ⁀

First, I thank Margaret Colbert herself. She is a private person who has nonetheless allowed me to question, dig, and pry. She has made me welcome in her home and her family. I cherish the special relationship that has grown out of this enterprise.

Ned Colbert, too, helped me in more ways than I can list. He painstakingly read more than one version of the manuscript and checked my accuracy and science. He also gave me his friendship.

Ghost Ranch, Abiquiu, New Mexico, and Lynett Gillette gave me not only encouragement but also board and lodging for a week, so that I could spend concentrated time with Margaret in a wonderful setting.

Bill Matthew, Philip Colbert, and Denis Colbert wrote me long, interesting, and intuitive letters about Margaret. Hamish Campbell wrote from Bangkok, Thailand, with his memories and report of the Stephens Island, New Zealand, adventure. Miriam Schlein and Birgitte Urmann spared me their valuable time and provided their perceptions. James Collinson and my husband, David Elliot, helped me sort out geological conundrums, and Kate Elliot read some chapters and offered constructive criticism.

Charlotte Dihoff gave me help, recommendations, and support in her professional capacity as an editor and as a friend. Charles Wooley, M.D., and Sonia Aycock both read the manuscript; I am very grateful to both for their insights and advice.

I thank the members of my family—David, James, Kate, and Simon—and my many good friends for their support and patience over the years of this project.

Finally, my special thanks go to the staff of The Kent State University Press. Julia Morton, Joanna Hildebrand Craig, Christine Brooks, Susan Cash, and—in particular—Erin Holman have led me gently, efficiently, and professionally through the maze of the publishing world. I have enjoyed them and, indeed, the whole process.

~ 1 ~

Introduction

Under a clear blue sky, a slow-moving river meanders through rolling country and open forests of giant conifers, past stands of tree ferns and cycads. The vegetation is strange in form and scale. The animals that wander across the landscape are also unfamiliar. Creatures that resemble enormous crocodiles grin from the water, baring impressive racks of teeth. Large pig-like beasts with beaks and tusks look up from their grazing with comically benign expressions beneath noble brows. A tiny gliding reptile launches itself from the top of a conifer. A herd of small striped dinosaurs, lithe and agile, cavorts at the edge of the river. . . . The painting is a large one; it measures 24 x 7 feet.

The interior design of the New Mexico Natural History Museum in Albuquerque impels the visitor through a logical progression of geologic periods and their representative fauna and flora. This mural dominates a second-floor gallery devoted to the Triassic; the fifty-seven creatures and the plants the painting depicts are restorations of late Triassic fossils excavated from the Chinle Formation of northern New Mexico.

The mural was unveiled at the opening of the museum in January 1986. The artist, Margaret Matthew Colbert, was seventy-four years old when she completed the work.

I first met Margaret Colbert in August 1971. Her husband, Ned, and my husband, David Elliot, had spent the winter of 1969–70 together in Antarctica, where they had found an important fossil and forged a friendship. We were traveling that summer in the Southwest, and Ned invited us to the Colbert home in Flagstaff, Arizona.

We came from the north. We had crossed the blazing moonscape of the Painted Desert and skirted the flanks of the San Francisco Peaks—the sleeping volcanoes that form the backdrop to Flagstaff. Our eyes were gritty, our camping shorts and shirts full of dust, and the station wagon was crammed to its roof with tents, toys, cooking equipment, bedding. As the sound of the motor died, the front door of the house opened, and Margaret and Ned Colbert appeared. In silence, they watched us emerge: three small children, two frazzled adults, one dog. I gathered the children to prepare for formal introductions.

Ned wore neatly pressed twills and a checked shirt. He placed a broad-brimmed straw hat on his bald pate and stepped briskly out of the shade. He warmly greeted David. Margaret, in slacks of a soft gray-green, a rose-and-gray-patterned blouse, a silk scarf knotted at her throat, extended a cool hand to shake our hot and sticky ones. She pretended not to notice our disarray.

Ned fidgeted, impatient. Then, pivoting on his heel, "Well, come along," he said. "Come inside and have something cold to drink." He led the way. Margaret moved more slowly but, strangely, arrived at the same time as he.

I followed her to her kitchen. Ned was in the next room area and could be heard pushing chairs around and organizing. Margaret prepared a tray of drinks and goodies quietly and deliberately. She cocked her head at the bustling activity: "Ned and I," she said, "are like a chipmunk married to a snail. We work at different revs." Grandson Denis Colbert has put it differently: "Grandfather hurtles," he wrote, "and Grandmother glides. Grandmother knows how to gracefully glide from one sequence of life to the next. She has what we soldiers call 'Grace under Pressure.'"

In the high-ceilinged living room, Ned and David were off and running on war stories of ice and snow. Gratefully I sipped my drink and allowed my eyes to roam over the beauty of the room, taking in Navajo rugs, Scandinavian furniture, books and more books. On a shelf were two life-sized terra-cotta heads of children. Margaret anticipated my question: "Our grandsons," and Ned broke in with the information that Margaret was the sculptor. I had not known she was an artist, but I was not surprised; to make a room so right takes talent.

Later, Ned offered to show me more examples of Margaret's work. We scampered the quarter mile to the research center of the Museum of Northern Arizona, and charged down a corridor lined with pictures of prehistoric creatures—pen-and-ink and scratchboard drawings, acrylic and gouache paintings—nearly all Margaret's. Ned rattled off Latin names and millions of years. Then he opened the door to the library (the Edwin H. Colbert Library, I noted, impressed and out of breath), and we stopped in front of a large bronze bust, sculpted by Margaret, of a handsome man with a high brow and humorous mouth: William Diller Matthew, distinguished paleontologist, Margaret's father. Ned gazed at it with reverence.

Back at the house, Margaret was preparing soup. Feeling a little shy, I asked her about her career. Margaret has a distinct manner of speaking. She allows herself a moment to arrange her thoughts and her words. Her soft voice is precise and unequivocal, her speech patterns akin to her fossil bone drawings: no flourishes, nothing redundant. She said: "When people ask what I *do,* I'm a housewife. If they ask what I *am,* I'm an artist."

Restoration artists raise extinct beasts from their jumbled fossil fragments. They give them form, substance, color, and set them moving and dancing in appropriate landscapes. The artists may use imagination in composition and in color; indeed, paintings, drawings, and sculptures of ancient creatures are often fine works of art. But if a work is not based on study and sound knowledge of anatomy; if it is not backed by information from paleozoologists, paleobotanists, paleoclimatologists, paleoecologists; if it is not state-of-the-art; it is not valid. It is useless to science.

Why would an artist—for whom imaginative freedom and invention is normally de rigueur—choose a demanding profession in which creativity is kept within bounds, and submission to rigid discipline is obligatory? For Margaret Colbert, these very restrictions have posed an interesting and exhilarating challenge. In addition, her genetic heritage—a paleontologist father, an artist mother—can hardly be denied.

Margaret's mother, Kate Matthew, came from a family rich in artistic talent. Two of Kate's older sisters—Elizabeth (Bess) and Emma (Em)—were decorative artists, specializing in painted walls. Bess worked in the Hartford, Connecticut, area. Margaret said, "She could paint a garden around a room." Some of her work may still be in existence, but most of her lavish fruits and flowers were hidden by coats of paint when plain white walls became the fashion. Em was painting equally stunning murals at the 1890 World's Fair in Chicago at the age of sixteen. Kate herself showed an unusually creative and imaginative aptitude for needlework and opted for a career in dressmaking and sewing, perhaps partly to thumb her nose at the gods. No occupation could be more taxing on the eyes, and Kate had spent nine of her childhood years functionally blind. She was born in 1876 in Troy, Pennsylvania, to Edgar and Jane Lee, one of eight children and the youngest of four daughters. She learned to read very early and at the age of six was sampling Shakespeare and Dickens. Then her corneas developed painful blisters; she had to spend her days in a darkened room because she could bear no glimmer of light, and if she went out, her eyes were bandaged. Her parents and siblings did everything possible to prevent her from feeling isolated or abandoned, and Em—two years older than Kate—made the education of her young sister a personal mission. Daily, Em sat cross-legged on the floor outside the doorway of the dark room and shared her school lessons. In the evenings, the family gathered outside Kate's room and took turns reading to her. She learned and absorbed eagerly; perhaps being deprived of the stimulations and distractions of normal childhood made her especially hungry for knowledge.

When Kate was fifteen the Lee family moved to Brooklyn to be close to a doctor who had cured similar cases of blindness. He prescribed drops for Kate's eyes, and in a few short weeks, she emerged from the darkness. Her bubbling humor and general good health were intact, although she had badly scarred corneas and was very nearsighted. However, as Margaret wrote about her mother, "heavy glasses and an insatiable appetite for visual delights compensated." Her handwritten memoir describes Kate as "barely five feet tall, but strong like a Shetland pony. She wore her hair parted in the middle, fluffed out on both sides with 'rats' made of hair combings, and with a small knot behind. Her eyes were large and blue, although her glasses made them appear small. She had tiny feet—the only feature of which she was a little vain."

The Lees attended St. Luke's Episcopal Church in Brooklyn. Its minister was the Reverend Jacob William Diller and Kate made good friends of the young Dillers—Frank, Alfred, Helen, and Angela. She also became acquainted with a frequent visitor to the Diller ménage: William Diller Matthew, a cousin from New Brunswick, who was working at the American Museum of Natural History in New York.

Born in 1871, Will was the second of eight children. His father, George Frederic Matthew, was a customs officer in Saint John, New Brunswick, but his passion was the study of fossils. In spite of his amateur status, his papers were published by reputable zoological societies. He was also a charter member of the Royal Society of Canada. From a young age, Will accompanied his father on fossil-hunting excursions. He was a clever and precocious child, who graduated from high school at the age of thirteen. He worked then in a Saint John law office until he was sixteen and old enough to enter the University of New Brunswick in Fredericton, where he obtained a bachelor's degree in two years. At eighteen, he journeyed south to New York to enroll in the doctoral program at Columbia's School of Mines. He intended to become a mining geologist, but contact with Columbia paleontologists soon diverted him. One of these, Henry Fairfield Osborn, took a particular interest in Will and in 1895 helped him obtain a position in the paleontology department at the American Museum.

Will was a "slightly built young man of fair complexion, with rosy cheeks, sandy hair, and brown eyes behind steel-rimmed spectacles" (from Edwin Colbert's biography *William Diller Matthew*). He was shy and unsure in the company of young women and therefore took his time, but in 1904 he proposed marriage to Kate Lee and was accepted. The wedding took place in Brooklyn on July 15, 1905. They spent their honeymoon camping and canoeing in the New Brunswick wilderness, then settled in Manhattan. Their first child, Elizabeth Lee, was born in Saint John in August 1906. (Kate had spent the summer with her parents-in-law, awaiting the birth while Will hunted fossils in South Dakota.)

Will Matthew and a group of his Columbia friends formed a cooperative, bought a parcel of land in Hastings-on-Hudson, New York, and divided it between them. The Matthews found themselves the owners of an acre of land high above the river. In April 1907 they moved into a rental property in Hastings and prepared to build their house. They engaged architect William Sanger, who lived nearby. His wife was Margaret Sanger, whose crusade for education about birth control and family planning was highly unpopular with the establishment. Kate and Margaret Sanger became close friends—a friendship cemented in February 1908 when the Sanger home burned to the ground. Kate and Will supplied emergency food, clothing, and money and housed the Sangers in their own home for several weeks.

The new house on Edgar Lane was completed and occupied well before the arrival of the Matthews' second child. Born on April 18, 1911, in a Brooklyn hospital—chosen so that Kate could be close to her own mother for the event—the infant was named Margaret, for Margaret Sanger.

Margaret Mary Matthew, aged three, informed her parents that she planned to be an artist when she grew up. Already, her chief joy was drawing; she could think of no better way to spend her time. Her thrifty mother supplied her with drawing paper in the shape of the stout paper dividers from boxes of Shredded Wheat cereal; these were plentiful in the Matthew household because Kate ate three Shredded Wheat biscuits for breakfast every morning.

At the same time, the American Museum of Natural History was a second home to the child. She was comfortable and familiar with fossils, and restorations of extinct animals. Paleontologists, restoration artists, and fossil preparators were some of the people whom she knew best.

∿ 2 ∾
Childhood

The house at 65 Edgar Lane, Hastings-on-Hudson, was built into a slope and designed to make the most of a prospect of the river about a quarter of a mile downhill and of the Palisades across the water. The three entrances (the "front" door, "back" door, and "side" door) were all on the north side so that from inside the grand view was unimpeded The house had three floors, a yellow stucco exterior and a tiled roof, and it was designed to provide lots of outdoor space with balconies, porches, and decks at all levels. Greenery covered the house; concord grapes and wisteria clawed their way to the third floor, and honeysuckle hung thick and fragrant over the front entrance. By the back door was a peach tree. Margaret said, "Every member of the family believed that he or she was the one who had planted that tree because we all dropped our peach pits there."

Edgar Lane curved around two sides of the house at a level higher than the windows, and passersby could look right in. Kate Matthew said to one of her friends: "I'll bet you can look in those windows and see what we're eating." The friend responded: "I can see what you're *thinking*!"

Elizabeth and Margaret shared a bedroom decorated for them by their aunt Emma Lee. Em made stencils based on the John Tenniel illustrations for *Through the Looking Glass* and painted them in color. At the end of the room were cabinets with mirrors on the doors. Alice went in one side of the mirrors, and from the other side emerged the Red Queen, while Jabberwocky, Tweedledum and Tweedledee, and the other famous characters and creatures, cavorted around the room.

Will Matthew's joy was to work in the grounds and the gardens; he spent hours terracing, digging, and planting. He laid out two big kitchen gardens

Margaret Mary Matthew,
age 5, 1916.

on terraces on the north side of the house, one below the other. A third, which the family called the sunken garden, was on the site of what had been a pond fed by an intermittent stream. This dribble ran off into the dell, where there were bulbs, wild flowers, small trees and shrubs, and ferns. On the north side of this was a level area dubbed the tennis court, although it was never made up to be such. A stone barn dating from the Revolution and owned by next-door neighbors invaded the northwest corner of the Matthew land. The later purchase of a half-acre on the northern edge of the property abutting the sunken garden added hardwoods, more wild flowers and weeds, and a flourishing crop of poison ivy. The property was bounded to the west by the Croton Aqueduct, which carried water from the Croton Reservoir to Manhattan; this was preserved as a grassy right-of-way.

Hastings-on-Hudson was an ideal environment in which to grow up. The children roamed freely and safely in the woods surrounding their home and the suburban "village." They gathered bouquets of wild flowers without worrying that they might exhaust the bounty. The night sky was clear and free of "light pollution," and the Matthew children learned to know the stars, as Margaret put it, "with easy friendliness." They knew the local

birds, and adopted "outdoor pets" like snakes, salamanders, frogs, and tur-
tles; from an early age, Margaret was comfortable and intrigued by reptiles
and other nonmammalian creatures.

On September 18, 1914, Elizabeth and Margaret acquired a brother. In
her position as the oldest child—with a five-year age gap between Margaret
and herself—Elizabeth generally identified more with her parents than with
her siblings. She felt that she must keep the youngsters in line, an attitude
that caused difficulties at times. Margaret did not become close to her sister
until they were both almost adult. However, Margaret and her brother, christened William Pomeroy, became great friends as soon as he was old enough.
In a 1993 letter, Bill Matthew recalled that Margaret "would generally include me on her various adventures and projects while we were under the
same roof. She was a great one for getting me out on the top deck of our
Hastings house to watch a thunderstorm in progress, or to go sledding in the
winter by getting up at 5 o'clock in the morning while it was still dark, and
no one else would be sledding."

Not that their relationship was always harmonious. With some indignation remaining even after seventy-five years, Margaret recalled playing tug-
of-war with Bill and a broomstick. Margaret let go, and the stick recoiled
onto Bill's head, where it raised a sizeable goose-egg. His wails of grief brought
their mother running. Sobbing furiously, Bill maintained that Margaret had
whopped him on purpose. An aggrieved Margaret was sent to bed, from
whence, through her open window she heard a school friend: "Where's
Margie?" And Bill's complacent voice, "She can't come out. She's *bad*."

In those days even people with modest incomes could afford servants.
The Matthews employed several people from a local Hungarian enclave,
including Rosa, hired to care for Elizabeth and Margaret, and a succession of cooks. The cook Margaret remembered best was "Little Fat Mary,"
as she was known to all. Margaret recalled: "She was very belligerent about
our coming into 'her' kitchen. She'd say ferociously, 'Vot you vonting?'
But she was friendly too—she'd give us pieces of uncooked dough and do
little dances for us. She taught us to count to ten in Hungarian, and I can
still do that."

Little girls of that era were dressed in white piqué, the boiling, starching,
and ironing of which was the realm of Sophie—warm, loving Sophie, whose
husband Frank helped Will in the garden. Grass stains were a source of
Sophie's ire. The girls had no "play" clothes; irreversibly stained dresses
were worn for running around in the woods, but comfortable, casual clothes
for children were not yet invented.

With this much household help, Kate Matthew was able to start a small business with two friends. They made stenciled curtains, appliquéd bedspreads, and small decorated items and costumes. Kate had prodigious energy: in addition to the business endeavor, she was doing regular dressmaking and knitting. From "Miss Lozier's," a thrift store in the city, she bought secondhand clothing and made it over—and over again—as hand-me-downs for herself and for her daughters. Margaret wrote in her reminiscences of her mother:

Late summers saw a flurry of canning. She put up produce from the garden until the shelves that lined a room in the basement were filled with jars or cans. Year round—unless we were elsewhere for summer vacations—Sundays saw largish family gatherings for dinner and an afternoon around the piano or walking the Croton Aqueduct. And there were visitors from around the world—my father's confreres—from time to time.

Besides Mother's part in all this, she engaged in village and neighborhood activities: the vote-for-women fight; P.T.A.; the Women's Club; the Literature Club, which staged tableaux at least once a year; Red Cross nursing during World War I. It makes me tired just to list these.

Mother grew up in an era when modesty was obligatory, when clothing was one's armor against the outside world: necklines were high, gloves met sleeves, skirts were long, and shoes laced high. Once, when her artist sister Bess persuaded her to pose for her in the nude, Bess remarked, "Kit's eyes perspired." Even in later years, she always put her undergarments on or off under the tent of her "nightie."

The need to belittle her appearance or accomplishments, combined with a natural thirst for praise, made her, in a curious extension of her modesty, beg for praise by running down her obvious merits. When politely contradicted, she would say, "Oh, do you really think so?"

To people outside the family, Will Matthew sometimes appeared stiff and unapproachable—a naturally shy person's common defense against the world. However, as a girl Margaret sat in his lap, inhaling the smoky aroma of his clothes. (He was an inveterate smoker of cigars; the smell of cigar smoke conjured his presence long after he was no longer alive.) And she rode on his back: "We used to have him be our horse when we were little kids." He was a caring parent who listened to his children with respect. "The dinner table was a place for discussion, or rather, argument *as* discussion. The ideal was not to win the argument, but to bring out the facts through discussion with various people." Margaret found this a helpful technique. She believed she was rather combative as a child, and was always hearing, "Don't *talk* so loudly!" But she felt she was free to do as she pleased, and then to find out by results whether her actions were right or wrong. Margaret was a perfectionist. She found early that if something must be done perfectly, it often does not get done at all. "Dad helped me get things done by saying, 'There are a lot of things that need to be done that needn't be done well.'"

Will worked in the garden every spare moment he had. In the months when it got light early enough, he spent an hour gardening when he got up. "Then he'd come in and take a shower, and come down to breakfast with his hair wet and standing on end." He would walk the half mile to the station and take the train to 125th Street and then walk the three miles downtown, across Central Park, to the museum. When the weather or the time of year precluded gardening and walking, he would stand in front of an open window, even if a blizzard raged outside, and whirl Indian clubs for an hour. He was serious about physical fitness, and in those days this was considered quite unnatural. Kate Matthew was approached by many friends and relations, who warned, "You shouldn't let him do it! He'll strain himself."

Margaret wrote:

Mother and Dad had a close and utterly devoted relationship as we children saw it, and I don't think we could have been wrong. Here's what might have passed for a quarrel between them:

Dad: "Don't worry, she's going to be all right."

Mother: "I will too worry. If mothers hadn't always worried, you'd none of you be here."

Or again:

Mother: "I just can't seem to work in all that I plan for the day."

Dad: "Well, you'd be pretty stupid if you couldn't think up more to do than anyone can actually accomplish in a day!"

Mother always claimed that my father married her "for a complete intellectual rest." She tried reading his newly published *Carnivora and Insectivora of the Bridger Basin* but put it down half read, saying, "Billy, I'll cook your meals and darn your socks, but I won't read your darn books!"

She disciplined us three most lovingly, although as tots we were sometimes resentful of punishment. Once when I was shut in a closet for obstreperous behavior, I told myself through bitter tears that I was going to climb up on the closet shelf, and then the pigs would eat me. Then my parents would be sorry!

Mother literally raised us by hand—bare hand on bare bottom, after the reason was clearly stated. Or we might be shut in a closet or sent to bed. For minor infractions, ghastly threats, which none of us took seriously, might be: "I'll skin you alive!" or "I'll pin back your ears and swallow you whole!" It seems unfair that Mother administered all the punishment, but perhaps it was better so than: "Just wait until your father gets home!"

She taught us songs and poems by the dozen from a seemingly limitless store in her memory. She taught us hand-sewing as we dressed our dolls. We made Christmas presents for rather long lists of relatives and friends: cloth napkin rings, stenciled, buttonhole-stitched, and fastened with a loop and bead; painted boxes; knitted mittens and caps; and so on. Mother taught us the fundamentals of color use in oils at the age of about eight, but use of the sewing machine was reserved until a (supposedly!) responsible eleven.

The "factions" developed for joking or teasing: Dad and Elizabeth—the Canadians—versus the rest of us. Then Mother, born and raised in Pennsylvania, found herself to her surprise transferred to the Canadian side. She had been voting after women gained that privilege for a couple of years when someone at the polls challenged her American citizenship. Sure enough, she had lost it by marrying a Canadian. After that, she had to come back from trips abroad as a "Non-Quota Immigrant Alien," to her great chagrin.

Kate never bothered to reestablish her U.S. citizenship. Apparently she considered her time better filled with other matters. She was probably right. When much later Elizabeth—Canadian because she had been born in Canada—decided to seek naturalization after her marriage to an American, it took her five years of hassle, lawyers, and aggravation to persuade the authorities that she would be a suitable member of the citizenry.

Because they were Canadian, World War I started for the Matthew clan in 1914. Will and five of his siblings—Bess, George, Harrison, Charles, and Jack—were living south of the border, but, as Edwin Colbert writes in *William Diller Matthew*, they "could not remain mentally neutral, as could many of their American friends and relatives. They . . . felt the threat to the Empire—a sinister cloud that hung over their daily lives." In 1916 they received the news that Will's brother Robin had been killed at Ypres on August 12. Margaret was too young to remember him, but she recalled the bitterness and sadness that permeated the household.

When the United States entered the war, Will joined the Home Guard. His duties took up much of his spare time—that is, his gardening time—and those years, the shelves in the storeroom were not as heavily laden as usual. Shortages of various commodities had to be endured by nearly everyone.

The winter of 1917–18 was so cold that Will was able to pull eleven-year-old Elizabeth and six-year-old Margaret across the frozen Hudson on a sled. During that winter, the whole family came down with Spanish 'flu, the vicious influenza that was decimating populations around the world. With both parents very sick, the family was in a difficult situation that could have proved desperate, had it not been for the ministrations of Dr. Tyler—a retired physician from upstate New York, the father of the wife of Will's brother Charles. He appeared on the Edgar Lane doorstep and moved in; he cooked meals and fed the sufferers, washed them, dressed them, dosed them. As the invalids began to recover, Dr. Tyler propped them up in front of the open fire; because of the severe coal shortage, the furnace was out more often than not. The strain of virus was particularly prone to attack lungs and lead to fatal pneumonia. Will's lungs were in a poor state from earlier illness, compounded by the heavy cigar-smoking habit. To every-one's surprise, he survived. But Kate and Will lost a child; a third daughter had been born to them early in 1917. Little Christine, only eighteen months old, died in the summer of 1918 from late complications. She was buried in Canada beside several generations of deceased Matthews in the crypt of the church at Gondola Point, on the Kennebecasis River.

Grandfather and Grandmother Matthew came to Hastings from New Brunswick in the spring of 1918 to celebrate their golden wedding anniver-sary. A grand party was hosted by Will and Kate on April 1, and many Matthews and Dillers and other relations crammed into 65 Edgar Lane. The highlight of the evening was the premiere presentation of "Rip van Winkle," an operetta composed by Edward (Ned) Manning, the husband of Will's sister Bess. It was performed by the assembled relatives, including Elizabeth, Margaret, and four-year-old Bill—who was a sensational dwarf.

For the Matthew family, the party and the operetta were cheering after a somber winter. One of the guests had brought a pot of hardy orange mari-golds as a gift. The grandparents could not take them back to New Brun-swick, so Will planted them on one of the Hastings terraces. They multiplied and rampaged all over the Hastings garden, an annual remembrance of the occasion.

The third floor rooms of 65 Edgar Lane had been designed as quarters for domestic help but were easily converted into a comfortable self-contained apartment for the Matthew grandparents in 1921. In 1923, the whole family, one after the other, contracted "yellow jaundice"—hepatitis. Sadly, both grandparents succumbed to the disease. Their deaths left the apartment empty.

In 1924, Grandmother Lee and her oldest daughter, Mame, moved in. Margaret said, "We forget about poor old Aunty Mame. She took care of Grandmother. She wasn't bright like the other sisters, but she made up for it by being very kind. She was just a comfortable, soft person, a little bit of a clown, and we loved her."

At about the same time that Jane Lee and Mame joined the Matthew household, the walls of 65 Edgar Lane expanded even further to include a Japanese lodger. Will's cousin Helen Diller was teaching "English to Foreigners" at Columbia Teacher's College; among her students were mature men who needed English for their careers. She realized that many of these students from overseas were living under lonely and unpleasant conditions in the city. She conceived the idea of finding suburban homes willing to take in foreign lodgers. Living with families would broaden her students' education and experience and would be much more congenial. It would do the host families no harm either.

Thus Mr. Sogo came to live at the Matthew home. He was an executive of Nipon Yusen Caisha, a Japanese shipping firm with a branch in New York. The Matthew children were intrigued. They learned a word or two of Japanese, which made them feel cosmopolitan. It was also interesting to learn Japanese manners—how to hold a cup gracefully with both hands, how to use chopsticks. Margaret recalls the cultural exchange:

> At first Mr. Sogo nearly starved because when Mother offered him a second helping of food he would say, "Sssh," (a rapid indrawing of breath), "No, thank you." And Mother would move away with the dish. Finally, eyes bugging with hunger, he was forced to explain that in Japan it was expected that a guest refuse the first offer. The hostess had to say, "Oh, but please have a second helping!" We worked it out that he should say firmly, "American no!" if he really meant it; or, shyly, with a slight upward inflection, "Japanese no?" if he would indeed like more.
>
> He brought us little Japanese dolls as gifts, and one night he took us all to a dining establishment in New York that was just for Japanese. We had dinner there in a lovely room with about fifteen people. It was elegant—the Japanese ladies all dressed in traditional costume. Bill was only nine or ten years old, and they found him very appealing. He sat next to the hostess and she plied him with little bits of this and that with chopsticks. He gobbled everything down happily. We all liked the food very much—except that poor Mother took a large mouthful of what she believed was mashed potato, and which turned out to be

horseradish. She struggled to retain her composure as her eyes streamed, her face turned scarlet, and she gasped for breath.

Japanese men in those days slicked their hair back with something that smelled extremely strong. It was quite a nice spicy smell, but rather insistent. You could always tell if there was a Japanese man in a room, even a very large room. Then, as now, the Japanese did a lot of bowing. And one thing I clearly remember was the quite frequent "Sssh!"—the juicy indrawn breath that expressed nervousness and insecurity.

One day Mother took us children, Mr. Sogo, and a bunch of his friends from New York out to the Children's Village, a home for delinquent boys in Dobbs Ferry. Mother had known the directors of the establishment since her Troy days. They housed the boys in little cottages and tried to simulate family life to give them a new start. We toured the village and, when we had seen it all, the Japanese men lined up, jumped in the air, and threw their arms up. They shouted in unison, "Banzai!" One of the men turned to Mother: "If I were a boy in New York City, I would be a bad boy!" he said.

∴ 3 ∾

Schools, Saturdays, Summers

She has graduated from white piqué; her dress now is a demure blue, high of waist, low of hem. She wears long black socks; her high black shoes have to be fastened with a buttonhook, and with these she has help from Rosa or Sophie. Margaret Mary Matthew, not yet three, dawdles along the Croton Aqueduct on her way to school. Elizabeth, aged eight, coaxes her—or, rather, drags her—because they are approaching a point on the path where they frequently encounter Margaret's nemesis—a "nasty little Boston bull terrier." It erupts yipping from its home, heads straight for Margaret, delivers a spiteful nip to her heels, then snuffles its way home again. It spoils Margaret's days—she does not want to go to school because she does not "want to have to cope with that darn dog."

Miss Trube's School catered to children from preschool through fourth grade. Pronounced *Troo-bee's*, it was named for the older of two sisters from Germany. Both women taught, with the help of a few other teachers. The large, old-fashioned frame house was furnished with low tables and child-sized chairs and few modern amenities. It was in Dobbs Ferry, the next town north of Hastings, and was just beside the aqueduct. Thus, the Matthew children were able to walk alone to school from a very young age. "I started there at two and a half—I suppose that was the age when I could be relied upon to stay dry!" said Margaret. "But I was not properly socialized—I had my hands tied together because I grabbed my neighbors' belongings. I also had my mouth washed out with soap for saying 'Gee!'"

Bull terriers and soap notwithstanding, Margaret enjoyed her six years at the school. Classes were small and the children learned, and learned to

15

concentrate. They were drilled in mental arithmetic and times tables, and were required to memorize reams of suitable verse and poetry. As would be expected of a German school, neatness and organization were obligatory. Margaret remembered pulling off galoshes on wet days and clipping them together with a clothes pin.

In the garage, the children practiced various arts and crafts. In these, Margaret reveled. She remembered painting plain wooden beads, decorating and then stringing them—this when she was very small. One day in her later years at the school she found a discarded rocking horse in the woods on the other side of the aqueduct. Her craft compulsion to the fore, she took the hide off the horse—it was real horse skin—and fashioned from it a pair of moccasins for Charlie Wink, a schoolmate and the older of two brothers. "They were aggressive little boys. Charlie tried to kiss all the girls." Apparently Margaret did not much object to his attentions.

The early classes were conducted in German because the Misses Trube believed that as the sound of the language became familiar, words would infiltrate young brains naturally and easily. Margaret learned enough German to get by. The fourth-grade language teacher was French and claimed to speak no English. Margaret picked up French much more easily than she had German and learned to love reading in the language.

This formal and intense early schooling was undoubtedly important in Margaret's development, but the American Museum of Natural History— the "Natch"—probably had a stronger influence. Several years before Margaret was born, Will Matthew had been appointed curator of vertebrate paleontology at the museum. He took one or another of his children to the Natch on Saturday mornings when he was not away on field expeditions.

Margaret was impatient for her Saturdays. She walked with her father to the Hastings station and they took the train and the elevated railway to the Natch. While he worked in his office or laboratory, she was free to roam the great building. Sometimes she appeared at the office doors of Walter Granger or William King Gregory—eminent paleontologists and personal friends of the Matthew family—and was invited in for visits. She wandered through the exhibition halls; over the years, restorations and mounted skeletons of long-extinct beasts became familiar friends.

Partially closed off from the mammal exhibition hall was a diorama of wolves coming across the snow. Margaret often went in there for a frisson of terror: "It was lovely because I knew I was perfectly safe."

After this self-imposed fright, she usually made a beeline for the sixth floor, where the museum scientific illustrators were concentrated. She watched the artists measure fossil bones with calipers, make minute adjustments to drawings, measure again. They were very patient as the child hovered and breathed down their necks. Lindsay Morris Sterling, whose pen-and-ink drawings of skulls and other bones are still considered among the finest, was one of the artists. Other well-respected illustrators were Hazel De Berard, and German-born Lisa Fulda, whom Margaret called Tante Lisa. (Tante Lisa's brother was Carl Rungius, whose paintings of living fauna still hang at the Bronx zoo.) And she watched Louis Agassiz Fuertes, who was an exceptional ornithological artist, named after the nineteenth-century Swiss biologist Louis Agassiz.

On the roof of the museum was an area where Mr. S. Harmstead Chubb macerated flesh to remove it from the bones of carcasses as a first step in the preparation of mounts of modern skeletons. It was a smelly process, especially when the animal was a large one. Breathless, Margaret ran down to her father's office one day: "Dad! *Dad!* Mr. Chubb is *masticating* a horse!"

She watched Carl Akeley create dioramas. Akeley was an African explorer and collector of beasts. He had devised a new and inventive way of mounting animals. Instead of simply stuffing their skins and setting them in static poses as was customary in most museums of the time, he sculpted meticulously correct action models and arranged the animals' skins over the sculptures. The animals were running, turning their heads to snuff the wind, scratching their ears, infinitely more lifelike than mounts prepared in the traditional fashion.

Sometimes Charles R. Knight was at work on murals in the exhibition halls. He was a freelance artist who spent much of his life working at the Natch. Margaret's father called Knight "Nature's sweet restorer." He was one of the first artists to paint lifelike restorations of extinct animals. Particularly known for his dinosaur paintings, he also painted ancient mammals and was responsible for all the murals in the Hall of Early Man at the American Museum. His restorations are still recognized as masterpieces. Scientifically authentic, they are also fine works of art.

Another of Margaret's favorite haunts at the Natch was the paleontology laboratory. There, skilled preparators—including Charles Lang, Otto Falkenbach, Bill Thompson, and Carl Sorensen—extracted and sorted fossil bones from their jumbled condition in blocks of sedimentary rock. They carefully chipped and brushed away the matrix, often resorting to instruments as fine as dental picks. Margaret watched them "put the bones back into their shapes—such beautiful shapes!"

In January 1921, Margaret had her first taste of public school. It was hard at first. The large classes and lack of individual attention were in marked contrast to Miss Trube's. Thinking back on her teen years, Margaret wondered if she might not have been slightly manic depressive at that time; her highs were very high, her lows a misery. "It was no fun. I dared not enjoy the manic part, because I knew I would be even lower next time I was down."

After some months at Hastings High School, Margaret made a pact with a friend to "get out of all this childishness and get on with *life*." The two girls took on extra course work and helped each other with assignments. They completed high school in three years.

Good learning habits instilled by the Misses Trube, the Natch experiences, and the sharpening of wits the Matthew children continuously experienced at home made up for deficiencies in the public schools. The family made a habit of gathering in the evening; dinner became a kind of ceremony. Afterward, a member of the family read aloud from a book or article he or she had enjoyed, and lively discussion and argument ensued. Or someone would go to the piano and play, and the family would sing together.

Margaret said, "I had more musical education than I could profit by, because I've always been a musical duffer." The public schools provided some music: "In elementary school we had singing lessons, and one year our school choir went down to Yonkers for an interschool competition, and we won a silver cup. There were three silver cups, and three contestants—we won the third award!"

When she was twelve and thirteen, Margaret attended Saturday morning classes in music theory and appreciation at the Diller-Quayle music school. This establishment had been founded by Angela Diller. Angela herself taught the Saturday classes. "Aunt Angela was a very exacting teacher. I was the oldest and the dumbest in the class, but I got a lot out of it. I had always liked music—and the classes put more sense into it." At that time, most songs considered appropriate for children tended to be about butterflies, bunnies, or birdies. Angela believed children to be worthy of more than that. She revived a lot of folk music from around the world and published it in simplified "easy-read" form.

Margaret took piano lessons with her aunt Bess Manning; these she looked forward to because she enjoyed any time spent with Bess. In a thumbnail sketch, Margaret describes this favorite aunt:

She was third in the family of eight children. Christened Elizabeth, she was always known as Bess. I picture her as a grave sweet child in the "serviceable" dress appropriate to a middle-class family in the city of Saint John, New Brunswick, in the 1870s and 1880s, going to the local grammar school and Episcopal church, and focusing more and more on music.

I really know nothing of her education, nor how she met Edward Betts Manning, her husband and lifelong companion. From as far back as I can remember, they lived in a gas-lit apartment on 115th Street, not far from Columbia University. Uncle Ned, a violinist and composer, taught in Columbia's music department under Edward McDowell, and in the New York public schools. He had previously taught at Oberlin College, and before that had some kind of fellowship for study in Germany under Humperdinck. They were newly married in 1910 when Bess went down to the ship to see him off on this trip. They found parting altogether too difficult, so she simply stayed aboard and spent the year with him in Europe. They must have sharpened their talents for economy as well as music.

Ned Manning was a talented composer. "His music was tuneful and lively —wonderful to sing to—and his verses were clever. But his work was old-fashioned and dated, and it never caught the imagination of the general public. His operetta 'Rip van Winkle' was staged on Broadway but did not fly." Because he was constitutionally unable to go along with dictates from his superiors if he did not agree with them, he lost his jobs at Oberlin, at Columbia, and in the New York City school system. To keep bread on the table, he taught violin to private students, and Bess supplemented their income by teaching piano.

In summer when school was out, the Matthew children either went to New England or to New Brunswick to escape the heat and humidity of New York. When they were small, Kate went with them. Later, because of her business, she would be with them for only part of the summer, if at all. During those months, Will Matthew was almost invariably engaged in field work in distant parts of the country, collecting fossils for the museum and for his own research.

The New England venue was the summer home of Bess and Ned Manning. Bess had taught piano to the children of a man named White. A wealthy idealist, Mr. White had bought a large tract of land south of Litchfield, Connecticut, which he intended to turn back to nature—to make it into a game reserve. Roads ran through the property, but no automobiles were allowed. White demolished all the houses on the land except for one cottage; this he spared and offered to the Mannings one summer. He let them have it again the next year, and the next; ultimately, the cottage was their summer haunt for twenty years. It was not maintained apart from repairs Uncle Ned managed in the summers, and one year, the Mannings arrived to find that all the plumbing had vanished—stolen, presumably, for the lead content of the pipes. After many hours of toil, Uncle Ned fixed it. He emerged from the basement and reported solemnly that he was a "solder and viser" man. "Uncle Ned was a man of rather insistent good cheer," said Margaret.

Both Mannings loved the outdoors. Ned knew the wildlife of the area, and Bess's specialty was botany. It was Bess's pleasure to walk in the woods and fields gathering edible wild plants to supplement her dinner menus.

When Margaret was not painting or drawing at the cottage, she read. The Mannings had obtained great numbers of paperbacks on their European sojourn. They had found all kinds of books inexpensively available there, at a time when the paperback market was still virtually nonexistent in the States. For Margaret, their collection was a treasure trove to add to books she borrowed from the Litchfield library. She read voraciously but selectively. One summer it was all Stevenson; another year, Conrad. The summer after her fourth-grade year with the French teacher at Miss Trube's, she tackled the Mannings' French paperbacks. She could not understand every word but comprehended enough to keep her interested. Sometimes she curled in a chair to read, or lay on her stomach on a rug. But her favorite retreat was a comfortable crotch high in the cherry tree behind the Mannings' cottage. She stuffed her book in her belt and shinned aloft. People rarely look upward; she could remain there undisturbed for hours. If cherries were ripe and within reach, so much the better—although the books sometimes suffered. Through an open window, Brahms intermezzi and rhapsodies drifted toward her—Aunty Bess practicing. One reason that Bess and Ned Manning loved the little house was that they could play music or sing there at any time of the day or night, as loud and as long as they liked, without bothering neighbors. A robin tuned up from the top of Margaret's tree one morning. Uncle Ned went to the piano and, with no fumbling for the right key, accompanied the bird in full harmony.

When the Matthews summered in New Brunswick, they went by sea—first a boat from New York to Boston, and then a change of vessels for the trip to Saint John. Margaret hated these trips because she was miserably seasick. Her mother and her siblings loved them and had a somewhat cavalier attitude toward her sufferings. On arrival, however, Margaret recovered quickly and forgot all about seasickness until she had to walk up the gangplank for the return voyage.

Summer cabins and cottages belonging to Matthew relatives were strung along the banks of the Kennebecasis River. The line of Matthew dwellings —including Amkuk, Margaret's grandparents' cottage—stretched for about a mile, so all were within easy reach of each other. From the age of three, Canadian summers meant for Margaret gaggles of cousins of all ages. (Her ancestors had been healthy as well as prolific, and the branches of the family tree spread sideways, unwieldy and twisting, yielding a plethora of relations.) And there was the river.

Kennebecasis is an Indian word meaning "little snake." A tributary of the Saint John River, it is tidal up to fifteen miles inland from Saint John and the Bay of Fundy. The water is brackish, cold, and very deep. It winds almost like a fjord through towering tree-covered bluffs. "The brackish water was just wonderful to swim in," said Margaret. "Its saltiness was the same as your eyes, so you could comfortably open them under water—not too salty, as the sea can be. And yet it was salty enough to bear you up."

The Matthew children stayed with Christine Matthew—"Tante Tina." (Margaret's grandfather George Frederic Matthew and his brother Robert had married the Diller sisters, Katherine and Christiana. Thus, Tina— daughter of Robert and Christiana, was Will's double cousin.) The children stayed at Edgewater, Tina's house; or they stayed in a cabin on the property called "Three Bears Camp." In spring, a freshet caused by meltwater and the bottleneck at the mouth of the Saint John River sometimes tipped Three Bears off its foundation. Only the wood stove acting as an anchor prevented it from floating out to sea.

The cousins, including the Hastings Matthews, entertained a romantic notion that Christiana was not really Tante Tina's mother. Tina had very dark skin and kinky hair that seemed out of place in the family. Alternatively, "we attributed her coloring to her enthusiasm for drinking coffee," said Margaret. Wherever she came from, Tina was a colorful personality, eccentric and extravagantly slow. But, "she had an amazing mind and a phenomenal memory. She could read a page of text and recite it back, word perfect. She was a great storyteller, a fine pianist, and also quite a linguist." For several years, she lived in New York, employed at the Natch in various capacities related to her linguistic abilities.

Tina's loves were boats and the river. One of her greatest joys was to launch a canoe in a fierce northwester. She would paddle against the storm for hours at a time. When she returned she would be exhausted and exhilarated. She loved the river as if it were alive, and she treated it with the respect due a wild and unpredictable force. She was strict with the children, her primary premise being to teach them this same respect. Before they could be trusted in boats, they had to learn to swim. She started them young, before they were old enough to know fear. Tina rowed Margaret out into deep water, tied a rope around her middle, and had her jump out of the boat. The icy water took the child's breath away, but the natural reaction was to dog-paddle to the surface. Very quickly, she was at home in the water.

Tante Tina insisted the children be involved in the annual chore of preparing family rafts, rowboats, and canoes for the season. All the craft— even the thirty-foot sailboat—had to be scraped and painted before they were launched. Tina gave lessons in the correct ways to row and to paddle canoes. A "rookie" child would be shown how to paddle a canoe out into the Kennebecasis, to tip it over, and to "swim" it safely to shore. Only when she was certain of a child's respect and responsibility for a boat and for the river would Tina give her or him free rein.

A piece of land across the road from Edgewater was also owned by Tante Tina. On that land, she grew fine lush vegetables because the large enamel pot from the Edgewater outhouse was carried daily across the road to the top of the garden and emptied into a trench out of which its contents leached and fertilized the garden. (When Margaret's sister married, she spent part of her honeymoon in the garden cabin. She was mortified when Tante Tina gave her brand-new husband the task of emptying and cleaning the out-house pot.) After she stopped working in New York, Tante Tina opened a little restaurant at Edgewater called "The Goose Hangs High." It was sup-plied from her garden and from local tradespeople. Tables were set on a glassed-in veranda that hung over the beach. Customers had to wait and w-a-i-t before their meals showed up, for Tina was a perfectionist. The menu promised fresh vegetables, and she gathered them then and there right from the garden. Then she stoked up her little wood stove and cooked them— fresher they could not be. She trained Margaret, aged about ten, to wait tables: "I learned the correct way to do things according to Tina's lights—I served from the left, took empties from the right, and so on. She had Mother make a chef's costume for Bill—he was about seven—and he made quite a hit with the patiently waiting clientele, keeping everyone entertained."

When her father died, Tina inherited Ashbrook, a site on what is now called Matthew Cove. It had been owned jointly by the two brothers, George

Frederic and Robert Matthew, and the house on the property had burned years earlier. A steep bluff came right down to the Kennebecasis, and sandy beaches at its foot were fine landing places for canoes. A spring that emerged in the cove supplied what Margaret described as "the most delicious water ever." Margaret found deposits of red clay at the edge of one of the beaches, and it was the best modeling clay. "It felt so good. Water clay is delicious because your fingers slide in it just the right amount."

From a 1993 letter from Margaret's brother Bill: "Margs was always creating something such as clay pots and candlesticks made from the natural red clay . . . and baked in the wood-stove oven." Today she uses the image of collecting the clay as a kind of mantra to soothe her in times of stress: "In my mind I paddle a canoe from Three Bears to the cove, the canoe slipping through the water lilies that fill the little bay. As I approach the shore under the bluff with its hemlocks and pillows of moss, minnows skitter away on each side. I pull the canoe up, walk to the place where the clay is, dig up a handful, clean the stones away, and start modeling."

One summer, Margaret and Bill decided the log cribbing that held up Three Bears would look better painted. "We made paint from the red clay. We had no regular brushes—only toothbrushes—and the project took us the whole summer. The paint all washed off in the next spring freshet, but we did enjoy doing it!"

On Sundays, all the Matthew families went to church at Gondola Point. They attended two services—matins and evensong—and the children also went to Sunday school because it was expected by the local inhabitants. The windows of the little church commemorated several Matthew ancestors, and Margaret sat in her Sunday best dress, gazing up at the colored glass and silently reading off the names of her forebears to stop herself going to sleep during sermons. Tante Tina played the harmonium for the services. "When the congregation prayed," said Margaret, "everyone went along with the minister, except Tina. She was simply born in low gear and she'd wind up long after everyone else. But she'd have that prayer down perfectly. The minister would wait politely for her to finish and then go on." Tina's feet pumped valiantly through the dismal setting of a hymn that filled Margaret with horror: "Oh what the joy and the glory must be, / Those endless sabbaths the blessed ones see." Heaven would be nothing but *Sundays?*

When she was ten years old, Margaret saved a child from drowning. Distant relatives from Trinidad, named Morton, were spending the summer at one of the Matthew cabins. They had two small children. Margaret and a few other cousins had been playing with these little ones. After a bit, they decided they would like to go out on the Gondola Point pier that jutted into the river. The older children asked Mrs. Morton if this would be all right. She was doubtful at first because neither of her chicks could swim. "I can swim," said Margaret, "I'll take care of them." And so permission was granted.

Sally Morton, aged three, was on the sloping ramp that accommodated the pier to the tides. She was holding a fishing rod. She dropped it, and it rolled into the water. When she reached for it, she overbalanced and fell in. Margaret heard the splash. She turned around and saw in a moment that burned itself indelibly into her memory, the cloud of blonde hair floating to the surface. The other children were frozen in horror. Margaret simply jumped into the water. She was in a long sweater that reached below her knees, its pockets heavy with all sorts of treasures and trophies, but she was able to swim to Sally, grab her from behind, and haul her back to the pier. When she took Sally, tearful but safe, back to her parents, the Mortons "got all excited and thought I'd done a wonderful thing. But it was nothing! It was only about a five-foot swim."

Margaret walked home, dripping. Kate met her at the door. "What happened to you?" she asked. Margaret told her and she said, "Well, why didn't you take off your sweater?" Margaret could not think why.

The *Daily Telegraph* of Saint John reported the matter on Thursday, July 28, 1921 in colorful terms:

A most thrilling rescue was achieved at Gondola Point on Monday last by Margaret Matthews [sic]. . . . Sally Morton, aged three, daughter of Rev. A. S. and Mrs. Morton of Trinidad, and granddaughter of Hon. J. G. Forbes, toppled over the wharf at the Point, and was carried a considerable distance from the shore by the strong current which was sweeping up at the time of the accident. Little Miss Matthews, who was near, immediately plunged into the water, without stopping to remove any of her clothing, and struck off after the infant. Miss Matthews soon had the younger girl in a position where she could prepare for the return to the wharf. Taking the child's clothing in her teeth, she struck out for the shore, and, being a splendid swimmer, soon had the little one safely on the beach. Grown-ups who soon arrived at the scene were warm in their praise of the pluck and resourcefulness shown by Miss Matthews, and enthusiastic over the demonstration of the value of teaching young people to swim.

"It's a much better tale as they tell it," Margaret said. The local Hastings-on-Hudson newspaper also reported the event—proudly and inaccurately.

A squib about the rescue even appeared in the august pages of the *New York Times* of July 29.

The Honorable J. G. Forbes, Sally's grandfather back in Trinidad, gave Margaret a gold signet ring with her initial engraved upon it, and he reported the event to the Royal Canadian Humane Association. In the following January, the association presented Margaret with a large bronze medal commemorating the rescue and commending her bravery. Margaret is nonchalant about the affair, but she still has the medal and the ring in a leather box, along with the press clippings.

∽ 4 ∽

Watershed

In 1926, Margaret's parents took a trip around the world. Will departed in January, and Kate and a friend, Virginia Fulenwider, joined him in China in July. Elizabeth—who had become "Betty"—graduated that spring from Sweet Briar College, in Sweet Briar, Virginia. She took a job in New York and was now out in the world and independent. In the fall, Margaret would be a high school senior, and Bill would still be in junior high school. As their parents were to be away until March of the following year, the two younger siblings needed somewhere to be "at home" during their parents' absence. It was decided to send them to the Charles Matthew family (the "Charliematts") in Portsmouth, Virginia.

Of Uncle Charlie—Will's second to youngest brother—Margaret said: "He was sweet-natured and genial. He was no scholar and had little ambition, but he always found work that paid enough to keep his family just the right side of poverty." His wife, Peggy, was the strength behind the Charliematts. Uncle Charlie brought home money and she managed it, him, and their four children. She was very resourceful and treated the family's financial circumstances as a personal challenge.

Margaret and Bill had spent the summer with the Mannings. After Kate departed on her travels, Aunt Peggy and her younger children came to fetch them from Litchfield in her open car. It took them two days to make the trip to Portsmouth. In Margaret's words:

The first night out Aunt Peggy gave me a quarter and asked me to run into a store and get some wienies. I didn't know what wienies were. I started slowly out of the car, thinking—Do I make a fool of myself in front of my cousins, or in front of the shopkeeper? I settled on the shopkeeper and just went in and asked boldly for a quarter's worth of wienies and waited to see what he would bring out. And then, we were driving along and suddenly Aunt Peggy braked and jumped out of the car. She had noticed a fresh road kill. She picked it up and took it home to cook for dinner. Our cousins showed no surprise—they were quite used to this."

As the car approached Portsmouth, Peggy sniffed the air happily. "Mmmm!" she said, "Puff mud!" Margaret looked at her in astonishment. Her own nose was wrinkling in disgust at the growing odor of stagnant salt water and rotting seaweed. To Aunt Peggy, it was home. Several times in the coming months, Peggy drove Margaret and Bill to visit the oldest Charliematt cousin, Mary, who was at William and Mary College in Williamsburg. "When we'd get back close to Portsmouth, it was always the same. My aunt's nostrils would flare, and a smile would spread across her face. 'Puff mud!'"

The other three Charliematt cousins were Douglas, who was four years older than Margaret and had been a Siamese twin—his brother had not survived the separation, and Douglas himself had a malformed right arm about which nobody made a big deal; Tyler, a few months Margaret's senior, with whom she had a less satisfactory relationship ("He could hardly stand that I was younger than he, and I was a senior, and he a junior—and I a *girl* to boot!"); and Betsy, four years her junior, with whom she shared a room in Portsmouth.

The last member of the household was Dr. Tyler, Aunt Peggy's father, who had nursed the Will Matthew family through the influenza epidemic. He was resident on the third floor of the house, lively and kind as ever.

Each day in Portsmouth started the same way: "We ate our breakfasts and then we knelt by our chairs. Aunt Peggy said a prayer for the whole bunch of us. She would include a list of all our peccadilloes from the day before: 'Please Lord, forgive us . . .' she prayed, and then would play a hymn on the piano. After that we could all go off to school."

School was about three-quarters of a mile away. The children walked to and from school whatever the weather; there was no money for streetcar fares. Often, as the year rolled toward winter, it rained. When she got home, Margaret would put her cold, wet feet on the potbellied stove in her room. She soon began to suffer from chilblains—her toes and heels became red and swollen and itched abominably. (Margaret remarked, "My present doctor does not believe chilblains exist. He is wrong.")

The house was in the city, close to the waterfront. It was a frame building with no basement, built up off the ground on three-foot-square brick
pillars. The floor was so full of cracks and holes that when the wind blew,
the rugs rippled and waved. The potbellied stoves in each room were the
sole sources of heat. Hot water for the bathtub was supplied by a "geyser,"
which consisted of a water tank above the tub, with a gas flame under it. A
person wanting a bath would first walk around the house calling, "Bath!" to
warn the household. If anybody ran water elsewhere, the water pressure
was insufficient to keep the geyser tank full, and it went dry and became in
danger of exploding. The prospective bather lit the gas with a match, then
jumped back as the flame leaped out with a roar.

"We used to go out crabbing," said Margaret. "We rented a boat and
rowed out into the Roads. We lowered a chunk of stale meat on the end of
a piece of string into the water. When a crab took hold, we gradually pulled
it up, and the crab came along. Then we scooped him out with a net. If
enough of us were involved, we'd get a big pile of crabs. We'd cook them,
put them on a tray in the middle of the dining-room table, and sit around
picking crabs and having a great feast.

"Sometimes auctions of goods that had been salvaged from wrecks or
washed up on shore were held in Norfolk. Aunt Peggy attended whenever
she could. Often the sea goods were not even damaged. But one day she
bore home in triumph five huge cans of peanuts. She opened the first one,
and her face fell. The nuts were rancid. She opened the second, and the
third—they were all rancid. So we all went out in the alley, and had a
glorious peanut fight."

At Christmas time, Peggy gathered her family and the visiting cousins
and told them, "You can each spend ten cents on a present. Then we'll sit
around the table and you will wrap your present and enclose a verse or tag for
the person to your left; you will hand the present to that person, and they will
wrap it again and add a tag for the next person, and so on." The wrapped,
rewrapped, and wrapped-again gifts were piled under the Christmas tree. On
Christmas day, each person had a package; as they unwrapped each layer,
they read out the enclosed verse. Her idea generated much laughter, fun, and
love, while taking next to nothing out of the family exchequer.

At irregular intervals, Margaret received mail from her parents from dif-
ferent points on the globe. The letters indulged her delight in the visual.
The following is from one of her father's letters, written on board the S.S.
Malwa, en route from Hong Kong to Malaya on September 21, 1926:

Here we are at sea and expect to land in Singapore tomorrow. There we have to change to another steamer for Calcutta. We are really in the tropics here— Singapore is nearly on the equator, and it is almost oppressively warm with the sun about over our heads in the middle of the day. On shore it would be h-o-t, but on the ocean it keeps cool enough to be comfortable as long as there is a wind.

How you would love these Chinese boats with their high bow and stern, the four-sided cross-ribbed mainsail hung askew upon the mast and with a cord from the end of each rib all meeting together to make the mainsheet, a single hal-yard, the ribs slender bamboo poles, a rather heavy boom and gaff, that is all the rigging. A small jigger aft of something the same shape and rig. To reef, they just roll up part of the sail and I suppose tie in the rib in some way. They have a lee-board, and steer with a big sculling oar. Simple rig, but they certainly know how to manage it, and make pretty good speed on the wind or before it; they are slow at tacking into the wind. The sails are not white but usually a red-brown, and most of them ragged to an unbelievable degree. The crew put up a little mat shelter under semicircular hoops or tent-poles, and they eat and sleep and live most of their lives on these boats. Thousands upon thousands of them that we have seen in the little bit of China that we've been through. I imagine there must be millions altogether. You see the rivers and canals and the sea are the great highways of traffic and transportation in China. Roads are few and un-speakably bad, and railroads are only a recent introduction.

Most of the country is very closely cultivated except the bare hills and moun-tains. The fields are small, no fences, only stone landmarks to divide them and the plowing is done by donkeys or by men or women hitched to the plow. The farm-houses are clustered together in villages, often walled, never scattered out like ours. The walls are of mud or underbaked bricks or some kind of very poor ce-ment, and they crumble rapidly in the rainy season and have to be repaired each year. The houses are mostly mud-walled, tiled roofs in North China, thatched in South China, and they too crumble and tumble down in a few years if not kept in continual repair. Roads are just dirt tracks, and each dry season the wind blows dust out of them and onto the fields around until in time they get sunk far below the level. What such a road would be like in the rains you may imagine!

As for the people, the coolies go around in a very aged pair of cotton trou-sers, with or without a jumper, sometimes with wood or straw sandals, usually bare-headed with closely cropped hair (what you might call a "baby bob"). The better class Chinese wear a long gown, loose down to the ankles, open at each side to above the knees, and a little black skull-cap. The coolies and farmers often wear broad brimmed straw hats. In south China these come up to a little button or knob in the centre, and the women wear a little edging of flounced cloth hanging down all around the hat about 3 inches wide.

Well, we have about left China and the Chinese ways, and the next we meet are the Malays. Got our first glimpse of their ways on this boat, the sailors being mostly Lascars (= Malay sailors) and very picturesque and piratical looking, but slim pipestem chaps by comparison with the big powerfully built Chinese of North China. You never see the northern Chinese in the U.S.; all our [Chinese] are Cantonese, much smaller and slenderer men. I saw a great many Chinese around Peking who were as big as any men I have ever seen. One giant nearly eight feet tall and powerfully built is doorkeeper of the Zoological Park. Of course he is exceptional, but there is a large proportion of six footers.

And Kate wrote, on October 26, 1926, from the Hotel Grand, Calcutta, India:

I just wish you could sit here by me, now and look out of this fourth story window of the Grand Hotel. (It isn't really very *grand* though it is simply enormous—all the rooms large, great long endless corridors, etc. but not [at] all beautifully furnished.) What queer people you would see—One man going by now dressed *very* simply in a draped trouser effect and the rest brown skin— shiny like a bronze statue. He is carrying a basket of vegetables on his head. In the middle of the sidewalk calmly stands a white sacred cow. Everybody walks around her and tries to keep from stepping on a sleeping dog a little farther on. A beggar woman with a little black rag on her head and a few odd rugs which half cover her sits on the corner in the position daddy uses when gar- dening, and as the people come by she puts her two hands together as if in prayer and chants an endless, monotonous chant. A man in white turkish trousers, bare feet, a regular American lavender shirt with the tails hanging out & a red fez on his head has just stopped to give her a coin. A rickshaw, with a coolie in front and an Indian lady inside is going down the street, the bell on the rickshaw ringing with each jounce. Several "ticca gharries" (little sort of wooden boxes with side doors) are passing in different directions, drawn by horses almost as bony as the drivers who sit up on a seat as high as the top of the gharry. An automobile whizzes around the corner and groups of all sorts of people dodge out of the way—and so it goes on. And overhead a blue, blue sky with a few powder puffs of clouds, and below that heaps and heaps of crows and kites go whirling and flying. You never saw so many crows in your life—and the kites are enormous and lots of them. . . . It's lots of fun to watch them while we have our "chota hazri" which means tea & toast that they bring to our room about an hour before breakfast. It is a funny world, isn't it? And I can hardly believe that I'm in such a funny part of it.

Will and Kate returned to the United States on March 23, 1927. Margaret and Bill were to stay in Portsmouth until the end of their school years, but their parents came by train to see them soon after their return. There was time during the brief visit to share some of the highlights of the journey. Kate and Ginny Fulenwider had spent a lot of time traveling independent of Will and, among other countries, had visited Japan, China, India, and Egypt. Miraculously, they had managed to meet up with Will after each separation and more or less at the prearranged times and places; this was no mean feat in those days of slow and undependable communications.

Margaret particularly remembered Kate's tale of her meeting with Mahatma Ghandi in Ahmedabad. This encounter had been engineered by Ginny's sister, a journalist for a Birmingham, Alabama, newspaper. It was a disaster. To begin with, it was too uncomfortable for the ladies to talk to a man who received them in his underwear. Mrs. Fulenwider, usually a ready talker, stammered a few questions, but Ghandi was unresponsive. Ginny's last question was, "Do you have any message for the people in America?" Ghandi said coldly, "I think not."

Kate had been especially delighted with Darjeeling—its fresh, cool air; its small dwellings clinging to precipitate slopes; its people with their Mongolian features; the vivid green of tea bushes on every arable patch of land on every hill until the rampart of the Himalayan high peaks; and overall, the towering glory of Kanchenjunga.

The trip had given Will enough time and distance from New York and the American Museum to seriously consider an offer that he had received, and thus far rejected, from the University of California at Berkeley; it was to head a new department of paleontology. He felt his loyalties were tied to the American Museum of Natural History. Almost all the relatives lived on or near the eastern seaboard and it was no light matter to move so far away; the journey from east to west coast was a major undertaking in terms of both time and expense. It seemed unthinkable to abandon the Hastings-on-Hudson home and gardens. In addition, Kate's mother and sister Mame still had a claim to the apartment on the top floor of the house; while Grandmother Lee was alive, there was no question of moving. In spite of all this, the Berkeley offer was attractive. Will had always wanted to teach. The idea of being his own boss was appealing, especially as his relationship with his chief at the Natch, Henry Fairfield Osborn, had become strained.

Osborn was the scion of a wealthy aristocratic family. His father had been a nineteenth-century railroad baron. Henry Fairfield considered himself little less than royalty, and expected obeisance from all around him. He lived in a huge mansion—a castle in effect—on the east bank of the Hudson north of Hastings, facing the Palisades. (As a child, Margaret had sometimes been taken to visit the Osborn home. She puzzled over the west-facing windows of this mansion. They were stained glass and depicted the Palisades. No doubt the windows were gloriously executed—probably by Tiffany—but how could they compete with the real thing, which was obscured by all that dense color?) Osborn, then in his mid-thirties, had come to Columbia in 1891, to head a new biology department; in the same year he founded the paleontology department at the American Museum.

In spite of his arrogance and conceit, Osborn was kind and fatherly toward those beneath him and his era at the museum was one of genuinely good feeling. Scientifically, however, Will Matthew could not always agree with him. The specialty of both men was ancient mammals. Osborn was a fine paleontologist, but his view of evolution was colored by religious dogma, and as Matthew's national and international reputation grew, the philosophical rift between the two men became increasingly difficult to bridge. Will had been one of Osborn's first students, and the situation must have been as difficult for Osborn as it was for Will. When Osborn heard of the Berkeley invitation, he encouraged Will to accept. Thus the anticipated difficulty of breaking with Osborn and the museum immediately became less onerous.

Jane Lee and Mame had stayed in Brooklyn to be near other relatives while Will and Kate were traveling. In the fall of 1926, Mame died of the malaria from which she had suffered periodically for years. On January 22, 1927, while Will and Kate were in London, they received a telegram that Jane Lee, too, had died peacefully in her sleep. In spite of their sadness, they realized another obstacle to the Californian position had been removed in an almost uncannily timely fashion.

Will arranged to meet the university president at the end of March in Berkeley to discuss the matter, but by the time he and Kate arrived in Portsmouth to be reunited with Margaret and Bill, the die was essentially cast. They would go to California. Margaret received the news of the impending move with calm, but then took herself off alone to examine what it was going to mean. It was hard to accept that she would not return to the Hastings home—that indeed it would not be "home" again. The distance from beloved aunts, uncles, and cousins would be difficult, but she supposed she would find friends to make up for the loss of family. In any case, her life would reach a watershed when she graduated from high school in June. The West Coast was another world—different time zone, different climate, different seasons, different vegetation. There would be new things to see, to sketch, to paint. On balance, she accepted the idea of California with equanimity and even admitted to a stirring of excitement and anticipation.

Will Matthew was too occupied tying up loose ends of his career at the American Museum to help with the move; at the beginning of May he left for California. Betty helped her mother to sell the Hastings-on-Hudson house and to arrange the packing and shipment of furniture, household goods, and other belongings. They purchased an umbrella tent with a floor, sleeping bags, a Coleman stove, and Rand McNally road maps for the entire breadth of the country. Finally, they bought a 1927 Dodge sedan with cross-hatched rubber on its ponderous running boards—the family's first automobile. Because of their poor eyesight, neither Will nor Kate had learned to drive, so Betty hurriedly acquired a driver's license. She had decided to accompany the family to California and wait there for her fiancé, medical student Ira (Nick) Nichols, to qualify in his specialty of psychiatry. As soon as Margaret and Bill's respective schools were out, Betty drove with Kate to Portsmouth to collect them.

The journey to Berkeley took more than four weeks. A slow trip by modern standards, but in 1927, superhighways were not even a twinkle in an engineer's eye. West of Chicago, roads were not paved except through towns and cities. They were gravel at best, or dirt—mud when it rained. Flat tires occurred from time to time, but the Matthews knew how to change to the spare and would take the punctured tire to be fixed at the next service station. Betty essentially did all the driving; occasionally, if there was a long straight stretch, she allowed Margaret to take the wheel.

There were no motels and few enough inns. The heavily laden Dodge lumbered from one roadside camping spot to the next. As dusk fell, the family would pick a site with a flat area large enough to accommodate their tent. After about ten days, they were able to boast twenty minutes from turning off the car's motor to having the camp ready for occupation. Tent up, they would go to the nearest farm to purchase eggs, milk, and vegetables to augment staples purchased at grocery stores. Then they lit the Coleman camp stove to cook their evening meal. In the mornings, they became equally swift and organized at breaking camp.

The girls and their mother were dressed for the trip in contemporary outfits considered appropriate for sporting pastimes. They consisted of khaki bloomers—full loose trousers gathered just below the knee and pullover shirts to match; socks and sneakers or oxfords. Kate was in corsets. Climbing modestly into a corset in the confines of a small umbrella tent in mixed company was a trick. "It wasn't easy. It was simply necessary," said Margaret. The fabrics of the time must have caused some inconvenience on the road. No crease-resistant or quick-drying materials were yet available. Apart from the essential rinsing out of "smalls," laundry was forgotten until they reached Denver, where they camped in a regular campsite with communal shower and laundry facilities.

The Matthews planned their itinerary so that they could visit national parks and other points of interest that were not too far out of their way. The first stop was at Mammoth Cave in Kentucky, where Margaret learned the difference between stalactites and stalagmites. Thence, they drove westward along the Lincoln Highway. To keep them on the correct route, the Highway was indicated by distinctive colored bands around telephone poles along the road. Illinois. Missouri. Iowa. Nebraska.

At Ogallala, Nebraska, they turned onto Route 26 and followed the North Platte River to Mitchell in the far western part of the state. Will Matthew had made arrangements for his family to visit an American Museum field camp located in the rolling hills north of Mitchell. The camp's leader was Bill Thompson, a collector of mammalian fossils, who had worked with Will for years, and one of the preparators that Margaret used to watch on her Saturday mornings at the Natch.

The Dodge bumped along farm roads closed off by gates—which had to be opened ahead of the car, and closed behind—and at last reached the field camp. From a memoir Margaret wrote of the trip:

> We set up our tent, shared grub with the fossil hunters and caught up on the news. Mr. Thompson told Bill and me that we were free to look around. So we walked a little way off and climbed through a barbed-wire fence. And wow!—fossils were all over the place: ancient horse teeth, skulls of oreodonts (sheep-like early mammals), and assorted fragments were just lying around on the ground. We filled pockets and shirt-fronts and oozed back through the fence. It turned out that we had trespassed on the land of a rancher who had refused the museum party permission to prospect on his property. (Subsequently, Mr. Thompson put

it to the rancher that it made more sense to let folk from a reputable institution collect there than to have mere tourists make off with his treasures, and finally he relented.)

The following day, the Matthews drove on north to Agate, through more gates, more fences. In *William Diller Matthew*, Ned Colbert describes Agate:

> Agate is a lovely oasis, a green island in the high, sun-baked plains, where grass-covered rugged hills form an introduction to the high Rockies, fifty miles or so to the west. It is an island of lofty trees, among which wind the headwaters of the Niobrara River, at the beginning of its three hundred mile journey eastward to join the great, muddy Missouri. In the midst of this little park (for it is not very large) there is a rather plain, square, white house, bordered by the nascent river and shaded by tall cottonwoods.
>
> Agate, on the upper Niobrara, with its grove of trees and its wide expanses of lawns, is the creation of Captain James H. Cook, one of the remarkable men of western North American history. Captain Cook, cowboy, hunter, guide, scout, and ranchman, acquired this land in 1887 and brought to it his young wife and his baby boy, Harold. He built the house and planted the trees where no trees had grown and nurtured them during the crucial early years of growth. Harold Cook wrote, "I can remember seeing him after he had come in from riding or working in the corrals, dog-tired and weary, carrying buckets of water to each tree, individually, hundreds of them, to keep the seedlings alive and growing until their roots could push down to the water."

Captain Cook's book *Fifty Years on the Old Frontier*, a colorful and authentic story of the West, had been published four years before Margaret and her family met him. Continuing with Margaret's account: "Captain Cook regaled us with tales and quiddities, sitting cross-legged in his hammock on the sunporch. He showed us a drawer full of Indian arrowheads. Next morning, Bill and I explored the two nearby conical hills that have yielded such bonanzas of mammalian fossils—the fossil fields that have since been incorporated in Agate Fossil Beds National Monument."

After Agate, the Matthews retraced their path southeast to Ogallala, then drove south to Goodland, Kansas, to rejoin a highway. They pressed on westward. Fifty miles out of Denver the Rockies heaved themselves out of the haze on the horizon, and grew steadily as the Dodge approached the city. After the stay in the Denver campsite, where they were able to thoroughly wash their bodies and their clothes, the Matthews headed north to Wyoming, the Grand Tetons and Yellowstone National Park.

In Yellowstone, a bear visited them in the middle of the night. Kate woke to hear the beast snuffling and nudging at the tent canvas. She was at a loss to know what to do. All she could think of was her flashlight; she snapped it on, pointing it in the direction of the animal. Luckily it was a bear unused to sudden light in the darkness, and it lumbered away.

On a muddy road in Montana, they slid without dignity into a ditch and had to be pulled out by a horse, which strained and sweated to heave the vehicle from its soggy resting place. They drove on through Butte, Montana; Lewiston, Idaho; Pendleton, Oregon.

In reach of Portland and the sea, they had a bad fright. Betty was driving at their giddy top speed of about thirty-five miles per hour. She misjudged a bend on a gravel road, and the car skidded on the loose surface and lurched into another ditch, this time hitting a concrete culvert. Kate cracked her head into the windshield; she did not lose consciousness but bled dramatically from a gash in her forehead and was quite dazed and incoherent for several hours, much to the terror of her offspring. Margaret wrote of the experience:

> A kind farm woman took us in, laid Mother on a couch, bathed her brow, and called for a tow truck. A facet of Mother's character was brought out in a curious way by the concussion. She kept repeating over and over, "Are you children all right?" We were. "Oh, I'm so glad, and I so little hurt. Thank you, kind people." She had always said there were so many kind people in the world. Then she would start again: "Are you children all right?"
>
> It was scary for us—and scarier still when that evening in a Portland hotel the doctor who examined Mother said gloomily she'd either be all right in the morning—or she would not. She was—except for a bandaged forehead and two very black eyes.
>
> By the time we reached Berkeley, the bandage was gone, but the black eyes were still spectacular. Betty found her way to the Claremont Inn where Dad had located rooms for us all, and then we drove to Bacon Hall on the Berkeley campus where Dad was at work. After fond greetings he asked about the trip but avoided any personal remarks. Finally, Mother said, "Do you notice anything different about me, Billy?" and the story had to come out. Dad had been honoring a Matthew tradition that held that personal injuries were somehow shameful to the hurt person and therefore indelicate to mention.

◡ 5 ◡

California

For the first time in their married lives, Margaret's parents were feeling affluent. As part of the inducement to go west, Will had been offered the highest salary Berkeley had ever paid a professor. In addition, he was receiving a pension from the American Museum of Natural History. Thus, they were able to look for quite an upscale home. Several older beauties were considered, but in the end, they settled for a brand-new Spanish-style dwelling on the steep hill of Cedar Street, quite close to the northern edge of the campus. White stucco, with a red tiled roof, it was equipped with every modern convenience. The Hastings furniture slid into the new surroundings as if designed for them and made the house feel like home.

The house had three wings, built around a patio. Will no longer had the heart to create another garden—he had given his all in that direction in Hastings—and he engaged a Japanese gardener to tend the patio and the tiny back garden. Still a devotee of physical fitness and exercise, and deprived of both the gardening and the long walk to work he was used to in New York, Will Matthew took up jogging every day. This was very unusual at that time, and he attracted many curious stares.

The living room of the house was upstairs. It was close to thirty feet long, full of light. From the wall opposite the fireplace, French doors opened onto a balcony over the patio. Windows at one end commanded a view of San Francisco Bay and the Golden Gate. The other end begged for a grand piano, and Will bought a new Steinway. Margaret and Betty spent a lot of time playing that piano.

Berkeley saw the beginning of a new phase in Margaret's relationship with Betty. The five-year age gap between Betty and Margaret had been an

37

almost unbridgeable chasm in earlier years; it now was less important. Margaret wrote of her sister:

> Betty and Mother (and she and I) had considerable friction in our younger days, but by the time we were in Berkeley we were all very close. Betty was the scholar among us three children. She was a voracious reader with a good retentive mind. Dad had helped her with fourth-year high-school Latin since there were not enough students to form that class at school; they had some problems with pronunciation, but Betty passed the Regents Exams in Latin and everything else, and graduated with honors at age fifteen. She took four more years of Latin at Sweet Briar College and became quite proficient in French and German as well. She was strong willed and decided in her opinions, though essentially kind and generous. She developed her many talents—pianist, scientific assistant, librarian, homemaker, mother *extraordinaire*, social *doyenne*, etc., etc.—all her life. We were all proud of her and grateful.

One of the first things the sisters did together in Berkeley was to drag their father to a store to obtain a new overcoat. His old coat had done seventeen years of service in New York, and he was prepared to have it do seventeen more. Such a garment—fraying at the cuffs, shiny of seat, slightly green with age—would not suit, his daughters insisted, a department chair of an august university. They would brook no argument. A pair of gentle but determined viragos, they flanked him until he had completed the transaction and had left the store with a coat of which they approved.

Betty stayed in Berkeley for two years. She worked with Will in his laboratory and office in Bacon Hall, helping him with research and administrative duties. She swiftly found herself a circle of friends and acquaintances. Margaret was included in many of their activities: "Betty and her friends were so nice to me. . . . And that was when Betty taught me to smoke. One time I was caught smoking at art school. I was in an upper room catching up on some homework and the wife of the proprietor climbed the stairs and found me puffing away. She said, 'Miss Matthew, this is *not* a *Bohemian* art school!'"

That Margaret would go to an art school was never in question. The obvious choice now that the family lived in Berkeley was the California School of Arts and Crafts in Oakland, and there, in the fall of 1927, she began a four-year course of study to obtain a bachelor's degree in fine arts.

She decided to major in sculpture. Shape and form fascinated her; she recognized in herself a tendency to translate everything into three dimensions. When she listened to music, the sounds were mental shapes—soft curves, jagged edges, delicate filigrees. Language and poetry were also three-dimensional in her mind, which may account for the ease with which she burst into what she called her "versification"—although this had always been a tendency on both sides of her family.

As well as teaching her sculpture, the school honed her drawing and painting abilities, instructed her in the techniques of pottery and clay modeling, and introduced her to the mystiques of fiber and weaving. She also acquired more prosaic drafting and lettering skills. The required "academic" courses in art history, history of education, modern European history, and expository writing were badly taught, and Margaret found the subjects excruciatingly dull to study. But all in all, art school was a happy period in her life, especially the first three years.

"We did a lot of silly things as art students but, looking back, they seem pretty innocent. Once I painted a baby's face on my bare knee, hugged it to me, draped a sheet strategically around it and over my head, had someone take a photograph, and gave the picture to my mother.

"We used to go out on what were called sketching trips on the mothballed fleet of World War I ships that was in the Bay, near Alameda. We could climb from one ship to another. It was more exploring than sketching."

The students also took a ferry across San Francisco Bay to sketch in Muir Woods. The ferry was an adventure—today the only way to make the trip is by car—and the woods an almost holy experience. Emma came from back East to visit, and Margaret and her mother took her to Muir Woods. Margaret was not surprised to see her aunt put a reverent hand on a great cathedral redwood and stand silent, tears rolling down her cheeks.

Betty left California to marry her Nick in 1929. The couple did not want a fancy wedding. They were married in a swift civil ceremony in a New Jersey city hall with no immediate family present. Nick obtained a practice in Philadelphia, and they settled into a home there. Betty's departure meant that the family Dodge was available, so Margaret obtained her driver's license and started driving herself to and from school.

That fall she was attending an evening class. Recently there had been a rape on the Berkeley campus. "Please come straight home after class," her mother had urged, "I shall worry until you're here." Accordingly Margaret set off into the darkness intending to be home as soon as possible. A short stretch of the route passed through woods. It was unlit, with no buildings on either side and she felt a prickling of unease between her shoulder blades as she turned into it. An open unmarked touring car with no lights was parked on the left side of the road. She drove past it at the city limit of twenty-five miles per hour, uncomfortably aware of two male figures seated in it. As soon as she passed it, its engine gunned into life, its lights blazed and it tore after her. Thoroughly spooked, Margaret speeded up to thirty-five—her one thought to reach the comfort and safety of well-lit city streets. The powerful tourer passed her effortlessly and swung across the road, cutting her off. Helpless, she watched as one of the men got out and slouched toward her. Then she realized he was in uniform.

"Oh, thank goodness!" she cried, "You're a cop!"

He grunted and started writing out a ticket. "You're on campus," he growled, "Limit's fifteen—you were doing thirty-five."

"But I thought this stretch was city, not campus!" She explained her mistake and her terror. He shrugged, without mercy. "Tell that all to the judge," he said and handed Margaret the ticket.

Margaret was humiliated and very angry. Her father went with her to the court; they had to go down to Oakland three times before she finally had her hearing and her chance to tell all to the judge. The trial was listed in the court docket as "*People* against Matthew," which struck her to the heart. The judge listened, impassive, to what she had to say, and then asked the policeman for his version. The officer produced a different story, an unrecognizable tale that left Margaret open-mouthed with astonishment. The judge believed the police officer. He took away her license for six weeks. "Unfair!" she said, her cheeks pink with indignation as she recounted the event more than sixty years later. "*So* unfair!"

The chilblains she had suffered in the winter in Portsmouth came back to haunt her in California in a curious way. They must have caused some nerve damage, because from time to time her feet stamped all by themselves. It was a nuisance and an embarrassment when it happened in class. She would be sitting listening to a teacher or working on a project, and suddenly the involuntary tattoo would begin. At first she tried to ignore it, but her fellow students would turn and stare reproachfully. She would gather up her work and slink out of the room. It is possible that exercise such as walking could have corrected the problem, but Margaret was not yet fond of walking. As a child she had suffered from mild rickets, and her metatarsal joints hurt after a short time on her feet. Her chief form of exercise in Berkeley was horseback riding; feet are constrained aboard a horse, and riding may have even exacerbated the problem.

When Bill was not involved with school work, Margaret still sought his company. Always ready for an ambitious project, sister and brother went on scrounging forays in the neighborhood and gathered scrap lumber and shingles from houses that were being torn down, and in the pocket-hand-kerchief back garden of the Cedar Street house, they constructed a hut from these materials. They also played tennis; Bill said she would drag him out of bed at five in the morning in order to secure a public court for a game.

When the art school needed a model, Margaret press-ganged her brother into the job. He was posed as a baseball player making a swing with a bat, and also as a cyclist in the act of getting on a bicycle. "I can't remember ever getting so tired as I did in those five- or ten-minute pose cycles that seemed like hours," Bill recalled. He felt he truly earned the pittance he was paid.

Will Matthew still had work to do on mammal fossils collected under the auspices of the American Museum. Thus, he spent the summers of 1928, 1929, and 1930 in New York. In the summer of 1930, Kate, Margaret, and Bill followed him back East. Margaret's art school and Bill's high school were out at the end of May, so the three boarded the train in early June.

Kate decided they should take a side trip to the Grand Canyon. Two or three sleeping cars of the train were designated for this purpose and were shunted off at Williams, just west of Flagstaff. Kate also organized in advance a guided mule trip down into the canyon. They rode down the old Hermit Trail to the Hermit Cabins, situated at the top of the dark volcanic inner gorge. There they stayed overnight. Between supper and sunset, Margaret and Bill hiked down to the river. Next morning the three rode along the Tonto Platform and back up to the rim on the Bright Angel Trail. On the platform section, Margaret's shade hat blew off and spooked her mule. She was bounced off onto the ground. No harm was done, except to her pride, but her mother was highly indignant. "What if," she spluttered, "that had happened higher up—on those steep trails?" The muleteer took off his hat and scratched his head. "The mule has more sense than that," he said at last.

The eastern sojourn promised to be particularly pleasant. The family stayed with relatives, reaffirming old ties, and had a joyful visit with Betty and Nick in Philadelphia. Will and Kate were looking forward to the celebration of their twenty-fifth wedding anniversary on July 15.

But Kate was keeping rather a close eye on Will. In May, before leaving California, he had suffered severe headaches. These had been in abeyance for some weeks, but Kate could not rid herself of a nagging anxiety and made excuses to check up on him from time to time. Thus, one morning, after some city errands, she and Margaret dropped in to his fifth-floor office at the museum. Will delivered the necessary reassurance and accompanied them out of his office and along a corridor lined with storage cases. Halfway down, a young man in a laboratory smock was on a stepladder, rummaging in a case that contained, Will said, fossil elephant teeth. Margaret looked up at him as they passed and briefly their eyes met. She was aware of a high forehead, dark hair, widely spaced eyes. The young stranger looked worried. He climbed down from his perch and Will introduced him to the two women: "This," he said, "is the White Hope of Nebraska—Edwin Colbert."

Any interest Margaret might have felt in young men on stepladders was suppressed by the nightmare of the next weeks. Her father's headaches returned and became debilitating. Plans for celebrating the silver wedding were put aside. His face gray and strained with pain, Will visited a New York physician. He was advised to return immediately to California for treatment for advanced kidney failure. Thus, in early August, he and Kate boarded a westbound train. In San Francisco, an exhaustive and exhausting battery of tests and treatments, culminating in surgery to remove one kidney, failed to halt his deterioration.

It did not seem necessary for Margaret and Bill to accompany their parents while they wrestled with this medical emergency, so they did not change their own train reservations. But it was a strange time. Distance from worry affords some detachment, and Margaret even enjoyed herself, but fear for her father never left her. She and Bill continued their round of summer visits and went as planned to New Brunswick to stay with Tante Tina for a couple of weeks.

To their dismay, Tina was different. She had become censorious and demanding, but what it was she was asking them to do was very unclear. They felt they did not do the right thing once.

The date of their reservations finally arrived, and Tina set up the two young people with food and drink for the journey. "She prepared for us thin slices—*very* thin slices—of white bread, buttered," said Margaret, "and also what she called crème de menthe, which was sugar syrup flavored with mint to put in the water. Water on trains always tasted horribly of soot, and the mint helped some."

The four-thousand-mile journey began. After the first couple of days, Margaret's throat began to feel irritated and sore. She thought it was from the dust and the soot, but by the time they saw the first ramparts of the Rockies towering into the sky of western Alberta, she was feverish. When she made the reservations for them, Kate had arranged for a one-night stopover in Banff National Park. The train pulled into Lake Louise early in the morning. Margaret felt sick and uncomfortable, but decided, nonetheless, to hike with Bill up to the glacier. It would be the only chance they would have.

They set off on the trail around the edge of the lake. Margaret remembers the startling turquoise-green of the water, opaque from glacial flour; ranks of dark lodge-pole pines; brilliant wild flowers; talus slopes at the feet of vertical crags reaching up toward ice-capped peaks; the steep stony trail through vast moraines to the throat of the Victoria Glacier.

"And every time we were in the shade, I shivered with chills; every time we were in the sun, I was burning up. But in some curious way, it made that hike especially vivid and memorable.

"After we finished our hike, we went out on the lake in a rowboat and we came across a weird little whirlpool. How could such a thing be in the middle of a lake? We took a small piece of paper and dropped it into the whirlpool. It disappeared, swallowed up in an instant. We thought this was fun and shredded more paper and did it again. And again. Suddenly, the whirlpool stopped. We thought we had killed it. We rowed away in a hurry."

They spent the night in modest accommodation not far from the lake and the grand Victorian hotel—the Chateau at Lake Louise. Next morning, they boarded the train again. Margaret's fever had subsided—the day in the fresh air and the exercise had apparently done her no harm—but her throat stayed uncomfortably sore. The train clawed its way through tunnels, up and down steep grades, and the stupendous scenery whirled by. At last they reached Vancouver and transferred to a train to take them south to California. Detachment from reality slipped inexorably away.

Their father was still alive when Margaret and Bill reached Berkeley. He died in the hospital about a week later, on September 24. He was fifty-nine.

In her memoir, Margaret recalls her mother's demeanor after her father's death:

Two friends came home from the hospital with Mother, saw that she took the sedative the doctor had given her, and settled her for the night. The weeks following the funeral were difficult and painful, but Mother went about doing all that was necessary with habitual courage. Friends and neighbors flocked around, and some came great distances and stayed days or weeks: these included Mrs. Walter Granger, wife of Dad's colleague at the American Museum from New York; Père Teilhard de Chardin from China; and Sir Arthur Keith from Britain.

Margaret complicated the general disorder of the ménage when her throat flared again. The doctor advised immediate removal of her tonsils. The operation went without a hitch, but after she was home from Alta Beta hospital, she began to hemorrhage. When the bleeding slowed, the doctor peered into her throat and was alarmed. A throat swab indicated diphtheria bacteria. The doctor had the house plastered with quarantine signs and ordered further tests. Fortunately, these showed the bacteria were not of a highly virulent strain. Nobody else in the household contracted the disease, and Margaret slowly pulled around.

She still had another year of art school ahead of her, and the family decided to stay in Berkeley until she had finished. That year was torture. She could not get over the loss of her father and felt inadequate because she was unable to offer her grieving mother any real support. She floundered through her courses, distracted and miserable, health and energy level at a low ebb.

In spite of the conviction that it would never happen, the school year dragged toward spring, and she graduated quite satisfactorily in May 1931. In the middle of the Great Depression it seemed unlikely that a young female artist could find employment. And then Kate had the idea of writing to Walter Granger to find out if the American Museum could do with another illustrator in the paleontology department. A job offer came swiftly, and Margaret was thrilled. The museum held happy memories and associations. She hardly believed she was to be admitted into that hallowed band. In addition, although she had loved California until the late tragic events, going back East was going home. With her usual modesty and diffidence, she denied her own abilities and maintained it was all her mother's doing that the job was offered to her. Thus (again from her memoir of her mother):

> Mother persuaded Walter Granger to take me on as a "bone artist." She bought my bus ticket for New York and, characteristically, arranged a stopover in Salt Lake City for a bus tour of the Mormon capital. I was so exhausted that I slept through it and only remember glimpsing gutters running with fresh clean water.
>
> She also gave me a hundred dollars to start me off in New York, and this I repaid at ten dollars a month from my salary of a hundred a month—minus deductions. At our parting, she was nonplussed by my cheerful acceptance of my prospects. She said ruefully, "You raise your children to be independent, and then when they are, it hurts!"

Margaret rode the bus to Providence, Rhode Island, where Betty and Nick were now living, and stayed a couple of nights. Her job was to start on July 1, and she planned to take the overnight ferry from Fall River on the evening of June 30. It would arrive early enough in New York for her to reach the museum on time. She had no place to stay yet in New York but was confident she would be able to find a room in a suitable boarding house at the end of her first workday. If not, there were always hotels for a night or two until she found lodgings.

At the Fall River dockside Margaret, Betty, and Nick went into a small restaurant. Margaret ordered a sandwich but put it down after a couple of mouthfuls. It did not taste good to her.

She said goodbye to Betty and Nick and went to board the boat. As she put her first foot on the gangplank, her stomach gave an ominous lurch. Betty had always been scornful of her sister's tendency to be seasick. She would say impatiently as Margaret clung green-faced to the rail of a bucking vessel, "It's all in your head! Don't think about it." For the first time, · Margaret thought that perhaps Betty was right. How could she possibly feel queasy already, one foot still on *terra firma*? She stepped purposefully up the slope of the gangplank, weaving under the weight of her suitcase. It must be nerves, she decided, over the prospect of the morrow.

⌁ 6 ⌁

New York: Working at the Natch

The boat tied up at the pier in New York harbor next morning, and Margaret disembarked. It was good to tread the pavement of Manhattan again, to hear the familiar roar and clatter, even to smell the garbage and hot tar city smell. But she felt shaky and strange, less convinced by the minute that her alimentary uneasiness could be nerves. She wondered about the sandwich she had nibbled the previous evening. However, she squared her shoulders and hailed a cab to take her and her luggage the short trip to the west side of Central Park, where the American Museum of Natural History is situated.

The unavoidable rites of initiation, registration, and orientation were not very onerous for Margaret; so many of the people she had to talk to were old friends, and the building was her second home. However, because of her queasiness, the morning dragged. Just before noon, Rachel Husband, the museum cataloger, came to see her. Soon to be married to John Nichols, the brother of Betty's husband Nick, Rachel was almost family. She invited Margaret to join her and a group of paleontologists for lunch in the museum restaurant. Margaret was anything but hungry, but she went with them, hoping that food might settle her stomach. One of the group was Edwin Colbert—the young man on the stepladder she had met the year before. She noticed through her discomfort that he still looked anxious. Margaret ordered her usual favorite—oysters. The waitress came with her order and set it in front of her. Margaret looked at it in dismay, gasped, "Excuse me!" and bolted for the bathroom.

Rachel took Margaret home to the apartment she shared with three other young women—all nurses—and they made up a bed for her on the floor. There she stayed for several days, feverish, vomiting. Meanwhile, Rachel talked to another nurse friend, Grace Eves, who she thought might be able to provide a more comfortable and permanent solution. From upstate New York, Grace was a strong and kind person and a great cook. Samuel Eves, her husband, was a musician, a fine cook, and a teacher of English to foreign students. The Eveses lived near Columbia, close to the 125th Street elevated railway station, therefore convenient for access to the museum. Margaret accepted their offer of room and board for thirty-five dollars per month, and moved in.

After that first disastrous week, Margaret started work. Her boss was Barnum Brown, a rather unapproachable scientist with a prodigious reputation for dinosaur collecting, a bald head, and pince nez. She was assigned to work with John and Louise Germann. In their early thirties, the Germanns were a husband-and-wife team of scientific illustrators. They specialized in pen-and-ink drawings of fossil bones for publication in scientific papers and monographs. Their domain was a cubicle, partitioned off from the museum's fourth-floor exhibition room, and in the shadow of a gigantic life-sized model restoration of *Baluchitherium*, an ancient Mongolian rhinoceros.

The Germanns' room had good north light, a long table, and not much else. Margaret said, "We had to keep from jiggling each other as we worked at the long table. John Germann smoked all the time; I smoked too, but John was a chain smoker—and how! Once he wound up with two cigarettes between his fingers and one in his mouth. He was looking distractedly for a way to put down the one in his mouth."

The first thing John Germann said to Margaret was, "Now you have to forget everything you learned in art school." Her work would be strictly science—no room at the Natch for "artiness." Fortunately, the California School of Arts and Crafts had provided her with the practical skills of pen-and-ink technique, drafting, lettering, and the art of precise measurement. She also already understood "orthographic projection."

A conventional drawing uses perspective to suggest the form of an object, but measurements taken from such a drawing are skewed because the lines of projection converge. Measurements from an orthographic projection are taken perpendicular to the plane that represents the drawing plane, and the lines of projection are parallel. Thus, a scientist with a fossil bone in hand can look at a published orthographic-projection drawing and compare measurements of the drawing with those of the specimen with complete accuracy.

For illustrations of objects such as bones, drawings are superior to photographs, even when the most sophisticated camera is used. Parallax problems can be reduced by taking the camera a long way off and using a telephoto lens, but the surface colors and textures of bones tend to disrupt the clarity of the picture, however cleverly lighting and background are arranged. (Nowadays, computer graphics have taken over a lot of the handwork of the technical illustrator.)

The Germanns had acquired a pantograph, an invaluable aid in their work. Pantographs were originally devised for copying maps, designs, and patterns. A pointer at one end of the instrument is linked by a series of jointed arms to a pencil at the other end. When the pointer is moved around the design to be copied, the pencil draws the copy mechanically. Manipulation of the relative lengths of the arms of the instrument allows for the copy to be drawn at a variety of scales.

The museum pantograph was a special type. A German instrument, it consisted of a vertical mast from which was suspended a horizontal arm. At the end of the horizontal arm was the pointer, held in a sleeve to ensure that it moved only vertically. The mast was fixed at one end of a large sandbox in which the scientist arranged the specimen in the way he wanted it shown. The illustrator figured the space available in the text for the finished drawing and manipulated the instrument to provide a suitable scale, taking into account the reduction that would occur in the printing process. Then he or she moved the pointer up and down, touching around the outline of a bone, and picking out salient features such as eye sockets or other openings (fenestrae) in a skull, or grooves (fossae) on a limb bone. Outside the sandbox, the pencil made the corresponding marks on high-quality Bristol board. Margaret said, "This grand pantograph saved endless time. If we drew by sight, although we took measurements with calipers, it was easy to make an error at one point and then chase it around and around—we didn't know where we had made the initial mistake. With the pantograph, we started out with a crude but accurate drawing to use as a basis."

The artist continued the task by hand in pencil. The specimen was removed from the pantograph sandbox and arranged in exactly the same position as it appeared in the pantograph drawing. Vernier calipers were used to measure every detail of the specimen and to check the illustration. By convention, no crosshatching, dotted lines, or stippling were used. Shading was achieved only by weighted parallel lines that tapered or feathered off at the edges, the lines flowing with the surface being represented. Another convention ordered that the source of light came from the upper left. This ensured that a person examining the finished work would be able to "read"

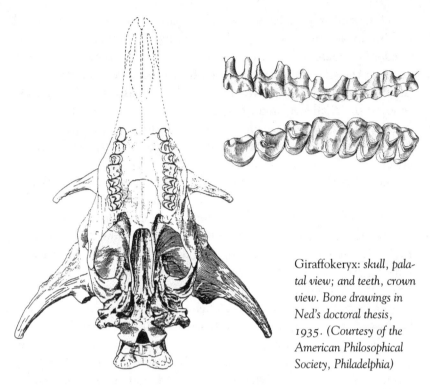

Giraffokeryx: *skull, palatal view; and teeth, crown view. Bone drawings in Ned's doctoral thesis,* 1935. (*Courtesy of the American Philosophical Society, Philadelphia*)

it; otherwise, the drawing could be "turned inside out" by the eye of the observer—a hollow could appear as a bulge, for instance, and vice versa. The reduction that occurred in the printing process tended to flatter the shading, bringing the lines closer together so that they appeared almost as a tone. This, too, had to be taken into account in advance.

After she had completed a pencil drawing, Margaret showed it to John Germann. If he approved it, she conferred with the paleontologist who had ordered the drawing. The scientist checked every measurement with calipers and critically examined the illustration for its overall effect. He might request more emphasis here, or more shading there. When he was certain that everything was absolutely correct and to his liking—"I always got him to say *out loud* that it was absolutely right!"—she inked the drawing.

"It was all too easy to smudge by getting our hands in what we had already done before the ink was dry. We used dip pens with flexible nibs that were good for both fine hairlines and heavier lines. Crow quill we found to be too flexible. A 202 Gillotte, a French pen, was just right. After erasure of extraneous pencil marks, we lettered in the museum specimen number, and the scale it would be in the final printed drawing."

Each new creature added to the museum collections was illustrated and described in *Novitates*, a series published specifically for this purpose by the museum's in-house press. At that time, zinc cuts were used to reproduce drawings. The scientist and the artist both checked the etching proofs, and then the paper went to press. Margaret recalls: "It was very exacting work. I enjoyed the challenge, and I found the forms of bones beautiful. Some were almost too difficult—teeth, for instance. A tooth comes up to a point, and if the projection was from above, it was very hard to express that shape perfectly."

A near disaster occurred quite soon after Margaret started work. Walter Granger wanted her to illustrate a skull of *Dissopsalis*, a Miocene mammal. Margaret took the skull to Granger's fifth-floor laboratory for a consultation. He was a big bluff man with a large sense of humor and a laugh to match. He spent quite a time arranging the skull on a tray; he fixed it with modeling clay and explained to Margaret the projection he wanted.

She started down the long flight of slate steps to the fourth floor, and somehow, the tray tipped. Margaret fought and juggled but, as if with a will of its own, the skull began to slide. It fell, scattering itself in small pieces all down the stairs. Luckily a gate at the bottom prevented the pieces from being trampled by the public. She went back to the laboratory in utter mortification and reported what had happened. Fortunately, Dr. Granger was sensitive and understanding. He sent a couple of his lab men to view the catastrophe. One of them patted her on the back and told her not to fret, the other lent her a large handkerchief. Then they all set to work to pick up the pieces. It took time, but under Granger's direction, they reassembled the skull and propped it back in its original position.

In spare moments from her work, just as she had in her childhood, Margaret would wander over to watch and to learn from such artists as Francis Lee Jaques, W. S. Leigh, and Perry Wilson. She said, "Perry Wilson had done my favorite diorama background at the museum—a painting of Yosemite. Whenever I looked at it, it simply caught my breath, it was so great." Charles Knight was also still working, although he was by now a very old man.

Fossil-bone drawing appealed to the perfectionist in Margaret, and she was very good at it. However, its ultra-discipline was constraining. Her imagination and creative ability were getting little exercise, apart from spare-time painting, and she missed sculpture. When one day a request came down from the editors of *Natural History*—the magazine put out by the

American Museum—for her to do some restorations of extinct animals, she accepted with alacrity.

In illustration and museum circles, the terms "reconstruction" and "restoration" tend to be interchangeable. In this narrative, "reconstruction" denotes a pieced-together skeleton, using original but often fragmented bones of the creature. Plaster or plastic replacement bones or parts of bones are sometimes added when originals are missing. A "restoration" is a depiction—in three dimensions or in two—of the possible or probable appearance of the animal in life.

Dale Russell wrote in *Dinosaurs Past and Present:* "Paleontologists usually do not paint and artists do not usually read paleontological treatises; teamwork can be advantageous. A paleontologist must discipline himself to assemble all of the available data needed and thoughtfully translate it from a technical vocabulary into the vernacular, and the artist must discipline himself to be paleontologically (not compositionally) obedient." Russell was writing specifically of dinosaurs, but his statements hold true for restorations of any prehistoric animal.

Margaret's first *Natural History* restorations were of ancient pigs and hippopotami and were done in wash, worked from drawings of skeletons by other artists. "Skeletons are always drawn from the side with four feet on the ground," she explained, "and early restorations were almost always done in that pose—a creature with four feet on the ground and a tail sticking out behind." By the time Margaret began to work on restorations, it was acceptable—or even desirable—to depict creatures in natural and dynamic poses. The work was challenging: "Unless you are lucky enough to have the actual skeleton reconstruction to look at, you seldom get a view that shows you how 'thick' the animal was. You have to try and judge that from the drawing of the skeleton."

According to Dale Russell: "The construction of scale-model skeletons upon which the myology is directly restored is an essential endeavor. It is often amazing how the 'personality' of an animal emerges as a consequence of working from a skeletal frame." The artist "builds" the musculature onto the drawing of the skeleton. From the bones, or the drawings of bones, the size of a muscle insertion is noted and a suitably heavy or light muscle added —much as a forensic artist builds features onto a human skull to aid in identification. Time constraints, however, frequently preclude the ideal step of model building, and the work is done in two dimensions, while a three-dimensional image of the creature grows in the mind of the artist.

Restoration of Sivatherium giganteum; *illustration for Ned's doctoral thesis, 1935. (Courtesy of the American Philosophical Society)*

Because there is little fossil evidence of integument, artists are free to use imagination as to color and texture of skin, and a few restoration artists go wild. Usually, colors and textures of the coverings of modern beasts living in similar environments are used as a guide to keep artists' fancies under control. Paleontologists supply information about the activity of the animal as far as can be deduced from its form and from indirect evidence such as fossil footprints. Was it fast or sluggish? Fierce predator or gentle vegetarian? Did it run about on four or two feet?

"It is vital to gather together all possible scraps of fact from library sources and from experts before turning the pencil loose," said Margaret. She preferred to make a series of trial sketches, using tracing paper rather than an eraser for corrections or improvements. When the creature lived and breathed three-dimensionally in her mind, she turned to the dynamics of the composition through a series of thumbnail sketches.

Finally, at the composition stage, imagination and artistry could at last come into play. Usually, Margaret left vegetation roughly indicated in her composition and then let it "grow" under her brush. As it grew, however, it still had to be appropriate for the time period and for the area in which the animal was discovered. Similarly, land forms and climate had to be correct. For these details, she collected information from published books and papers and went directly to botanists, paleobotanists, geologists, and climatologists to check the background of her work.

~: 7 :~

Ned

Rachel Husband, John and Louise Germann, and Edwin Harris Colbert became Margaret's closest friends at the American Museum of Natural History. As color crept back into her cheeks, "Ned" Colbert began looking at Margaret with rather more than friendly interest. She returned his gaze and saw an attractive young man whose brown eyes brimmed not only with worry and intelligence, but with unusual gentleness. His dark hair was receding a little, exposing a professorial brow. He was invariably neat, if not fashionable. When one day he told her she was looking so much better that he would like to take her for a walk, she accepted the invitation with pleasure.

She dressed carefully for the occasion. She decided to wear a new outfit that her mother had made for her using materials out of a trunk of old clothes. With her mix of ingenuity and frugality, Kate would make and remake garments out of old fabrics until the material disintegrated. The outfit in question consisted of a simple black skirt and a close-fitting turquoise-blue satin blouse decorated with black fagoting that had taken Kate hours of work. Margaret pulled on new hose and surveyed herself in the mirror. She thought she looked rather good.

When Ned arrived, he asked her preference of a route, then suggested Riverside Park if she had no better idea. They found they could talk easily to each other. But when after a while Ned said something that made her laugh, she felt a strange sensation—a sudden easement around her chest. She looked down and discovered her blouse had split. Ned had obviously noticed—he was keeping his gaze carefully averted. She had been walking with elegant short steps in the straight black skirt. They came to a curb and she had to make a longer stride. With a small but audible tearing sound, a rip appeared in the skirt. Ned glanced down, and his eyes widened. She continued walking for a while, but all of a sudden the sensation as of a spider scampering up her leg told her the new hose had developed a run. That was it for Ned; he turned her around and hustled her home. Ned likes to recount the story: "The first time I took Margaret out," he declares, "I tore the clothes off her."

It was a bad beginning for Margaret. But Ned was undeterred and asked her for another such date quite soon, although he examined her apparel with some concern. Soon, the walks became a regular habit. For the first time in her life, Margaret was enjoying this simple form of exercise. She forgot the pain in her feet. She had lately been subjecting them to alternate hot and cold soaks—Louise Germann had suggested this as a simple remedy for the annoying tic attributed to the Portsmouth chilblains. All the walks certainly contributed to her complete cure.

Both Margaret and Ned were hesitant when it came to talking about themselves, but bit by bit, as they walked, they drew from each other nuggets of information. At his own admission, Ned was unused to female company, but Margaret soon discovered he was a wonderful raconteur; she also realized the depth of his wry and dry sense of humor.

Ned was a Midwesterner, she learned, born in 1905 in Clarinda, Iowa. His mother Mary, née Adamson, the daughter of an unconventional medical doctor, had a tremendous sense of drama–she should have been an actress or a novelist. She was vital, energetic, adventurous—given to practical jokes, although entirely without malice. She was stifled in the role of small-town housewife in the nation's conservative heartland, trapped by her generation and by geography. Apart from occasional amateur dramatics and writing her autobiography, she found no chance to spread her wings.

His father, George Harris Colbert, was a more prosaic character. At the time of Ned's birth, he was superintendent of Page County schools. A year later, the family moved thirty miles south of Clarinda to Maryville, Missouri. There George took a position as professor of mathematics at the Normal School, a new teacher-training institute. Ned remembered him as always scrupulously neat and clean, even when informally dressed. He sang in the local Presbyterian church choir and played the flute well. He was also a serious baseball player. Ned said, "My father was a quiet man, and it was unimaginable that he would do a bad thing. But my mother . . . now she could be naughty."

Ned was the youngest of three boys. The oldest, Herschel, was fourteen years older than he; the middle child, Philip, nine years older. In competition with his peers, Ned, who was rather small for his age, learned early to rely on wits rather than brawn. His brothers were both too far removed in age to be of any assistance in his occasional battles. Herschel was so much older that he became an adored, almost avuncular figure.

Ned explains his perpetual worried expression in his autobiography, *Digging Into the Past:* "For as far back as I can remember, I was, or thought I was, beset by problems—problems that formed a background for every day, making that day, no matter how perfect it otherwise might be, not quite perfect. To a considerable extent, the problems were of my own making, for I was a worrywart, and I still am."

Ned attended the Normal School until his high school years. In high school, he began to develop his love and facility for the English language. From a young age, he was interested in the "great outdoors"—in bird watching and natural history, in archeology, and already, in a small way, in fossil hunting. His room became a museum of found objects.

In 1922, in the summer before his senior year, his father purchased an automobile, and Ned learned to drive. He and his parents drove out to Colorado, where he fell in love with the Rockies—the lakes, the woods, but most of all the peaks. He considered becoming a forester so that he could spend his life in such surroundings, and to this end, he spent four summers during his college years with the Forest Service working on trails in the Colorado Rockies. But after the second summer in the mountains, he began to doubt that forestry was his life's ambition. The work was extremely hard, often lonely, sometimes dangerous. He knew he wanted to spend time outdoors, but he needed books, study, and people too. On his way to and from Colorado he stayed with his brother Philip and his wife in Lincoln, Nebraska, and there he visited the university museum. The geology department fascinated him; in particular, he was intrigued by the fossil skulls and bones in the paleontology section.

The Normal School was now a fully fledged teacher's college, and Ned enrolled there. He took standard liberal arts courses for the first three years of his college education, concentrating on English and chemistry. In 1926, in the spring of his third year, he asked Philip to help him look into the possibilities of a career in vertebrate paleontology. Phil talked to the curator of the university museum, and Ned was invited to come for an interview. He was taken on as a student assistant. Thus, he completed his undergraduate work in Lincoln, and after two summers of work in the field collecting fossils for the museum, he knew he had found his calling.

He applied to Berkeley, Yale, and Columbia for a graduate position. From Berkeley, he received a letter from Dr. William Diller Matthew, regretting that all places were filled. Yale and Columbia both offered him graduate fellowships and, because of vagaries of the mail, he accepted Columbia's offer and came to New York in the fall of 1929. His advisor was William King Gregory, Will Matthew's friend and colleague.

So here was Ned Colbert, a Columbia graduate student attached to the American Museum of Natural History, taking walks with Margaret Mary Matthew. In his autobiography, he reflects on how the course of life is changed by small events. Had the letter from Yale come before that from Columbia, his scientific career might have been quite different. More importantly, "I probably would not have become intimately acquainted with Margaret Matthew, and I shudder to think of it."

The American Museum had a rich hoard of Upper Cenozoic mammals from beds in the Siwalik Hills—a range in northern India fronting the Himalayas. The fossils had been collected by Barnum Brown a decade earlier but had not been described. Margaret's father had studied collections of these fossils in the Indian Museum in Calcutta and the British Museum in London on his 1926–27 trip around the world and had published a paper shortly before his death entitled "Preliminary Observations upon Siwalik Mammals." Clearly, he had intended to study them further and to avail himself of the American Museum's collection. For his thesis project, Ned chose to pick up where Matthew left off. When the museum nominated Margaret to illustrate Ned's thesis, the assignment naturally held special meaning for her, and it also meant she would be spending a great deal of time in Ned's company.

In the fall of 1931, Ned went to England for some months. Since the summer of 1930, he had been research assistant to the same Henry Fairfield Osborn who had held such sway over Will Matthew's life. Osborn was to attend a meeting of the British Association for the Advancement of Science and to study fossil elephants and their teeth in the British Museum. He decreed that his assistant accompany him. After the great man returned, Ned was to stay on to work on the British Museum Siwalik collection and to travel on the continent and visit natural history museums there. It was a wonderful opportunity for Ned.

He left on the *America*. The Germanns, Rachel (now Rachel Nichols), Walter Granger, and Margaret decided to surprise him with a bon voyage party. They waited until he was in his cabin and then thundered at his door. They swarmed in, delighted at his astonishment. They carried a large basket filled with edible delicacies, a bottle of wine, and sundry joke gifts. They shared the bottle and cheered him on as he unwrapped the presents. When the call came for guests to go ashore, Ned looked suddenly forlorn. For Margaret too, the months ahead looked somewhat bleak.

However, she was not lonely. In addition to her museum friends, she had hoards of relatives within reach, including her mother and brother, who were now in West Hartford, Connecticut; as soon as Bill's high-school semester had ended, Kate had let the Berkeley house and moved back East; Bill was to complete his high-school education in Hartford. They were living with Kate's sister Emma. (Aunty Em had married a rather dubious character named Harry Thayer. She still worked as an artist but had also begun writing mystery novels under the name of Lee Thayer. With Harry she ran a small and successful business, designing book covers.) Bess Manning had Margaret over once a week to play piano duets, and Tante Tina's sister Dot Olton and her husband, Percy, extended an open invitation for Sunday dinner at their home. "Uncle" Percy, who came originally from Barbados, was the rector of an Episcopal church in Newark, New Jersey. He had performed the wedding ceremony of Margaret's parents in 1905 and had christened Betty, Margaret, and Bill. "He was an old-time preacher," Margaret said, "but the gentlest and most generous-minded man."

Ned returned to New York in January 1932, bearing an enormous amount of work for Margaret; his thesis was to swell into a thick monograph with many illustrations, including both bone drawings and restorations. Pleased to be together again, Margaret and Ned picked up their habit of walking. As the weather warmed up, Margaret sometimes took her easel. While Ned stretched out on the grass, she would do a lightning watercolor landscape. They were not very finished works, but they helped her through a phase of her artistic life that seemed to be essentially "no-color."

One of Ned's passions was the theater. The first year he was in New York, he went to every play on Broadway. "Then when he started taking me, he went to half the plays on Broadway! For eighty-five cents each we could sit in peanut heaven." In addition, they went to concerts, movies, and of course out to eat.

One morning, Margaret and Ned happened to mention to the Germanns that they had taken a walk the night before along Riverside Park.

"But it was raining!" exclaimed Louise.

"It *was?*" Margaret looked at Ned uncertainly.

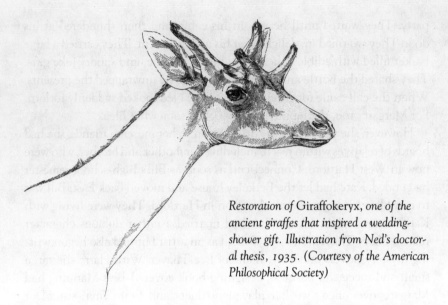

Restoration of Giraffokeryx, *one of the ancient giraffes that inspired a wedding-shower gift. Illustration from Ned's doctoral thesis, 1935. (Courtesy of the American Philosophical Society)*

"Hah!" said John, "You didn't notice! You must be in love!"

Ned and Margaret became engaged in January 1933. For an engagement ring they went to the Madison Avenue shop of Georg Jensen, the Danish silversmith, and chose a moonstone in a silver setting. The Germanns arranged an engagement party for the couple at their home in Valhalla, north of New York City. Most of their museum friends attended, and Margaret basked in the affection and goodwill. She had lately been much occupied drawing giraffes because several giraffe ancestors were among the Siwalik fauna: "John and Louise constructed a most beautiful sewing box. It was a giraffe made of wood. It had four legs, a coffin-shaped body with a hinged lid, a little rope tail, and it was painted appropriately. Engagement gifts were inside, or tied on the outside. We kept that giraffe for many years, until our children finally demolished it—they loved it to death."

They planned a summer wedding. Meanwhile, Margaret introduced Ned to as many of her family as possible. Kate had no trouble accepting Ned as a future son-in-law; she took to him immediately, and he to her. Uncle Ned Manning seemed to be the only one not quite sure; he feared Ned Colbert had no sense of humor, not recognizing the wit, nor perceiving the twinkle in back of the anxious eyes. It is probable that nobody could have been good enough for his nieces; he was very protective of them—perhaps even jealous of any man who dared to steal their affections. He never did warm up to Betty's Nick.

In addition, Margaret had to be approved by Ned's family. His mother expressed some misgivings. Would Margaret—whom she perceived as somewhat racy, ominously artistic, and East Coast to boot—prove too much for her youngest son? Shortly before she died in 1954, Mary Adamson Colbert at last embraced Margaret warmly and told her, "You're a good woman."

Kate Matthew was also entering a new phase of life. For the two years that she lived in Connecticut, she had been receiving letters from Ralph Minor, a professor of physics and later the first dean of the School of Optometry at Berkeley. He was a highly respected member of the university— indeed, one of the buildings at Berkeley has been named after him. Ralph and his wife had become close friends of Will and Kate Matthew in California. In 1930, Mrs. Minor died of cancer; thus Kate and Ralph were widowed at almost the same time.

Kate showed one or two of Ralph's letters to Margaret. They were irresistible—not exactly love letters, but sweet and funny and caring. In addition to the letters, Ralph sent roses, which arrived at Kate's door every Sunday. From Margaret's memoir of her mother: "When Mother finally began to think seriously of marrying Ralph, she consulted Betty, Bill and me, and we were all delighted. The four Minor children were happy, too, to have their father able once more to bask in the blessings of family life—all but the youngest, who was still living at home. She found it hard to adapt to a stepmother. However, time and friendly effort smoothed things over." Kate returned to California, where she and Ralph were married in January 1933. They opted to live in the Cedar Street house, much to the pleasure of the Matthew offspring.

Margaret and Ned fixed the date of their own wedding for July 8, 1933. Margaret had never been to a wedding and was painfully ignorant of protocol. Sometimes she was apprehensive as she planned for their celebration and wished they had decided to go to City Hall and do the deed simply, as Betty and Nick had done. Ned was no help. He said gloomily, "If I see more than twenty-five people when I come into the church, I shall walk out." Most of the time, however, Margaret rather looked forward to the ceremony and pageantry, and she definitely wanted the support of family and friends when she and Ned exchanged their vows.

❧ 8 ❧

Manhattan

Percy Olton was delighted when Margaret and Ned asked him to marry them. His church was on Newark's Broad Street in an area that in 1933 was frayed at the edges but not yet battered into a slum. The church building was small, shingled, plain. The interior had been transformed by a parishioner, Perry Wilson. He was the same American Museum of Natural History artist responsible for Margaret's favorite Yosemite diorama background. Using stencils, Wilson had decorated an arch at the front of the church on the side facing the congregation and on its inner surface. The symbolic designs were executed predominantly in gold and red, and the effect was beautiful. Sadly, the church and its decorations later crumbled out of existence as the neighborhood decayed.

For her wedding gown, Margaret settled on a simple garment of white lace. It cost her seventy-five dollars, a prodigious sum when taken from a monthly salary of a hundred, but it was a lovely dress, and she decided to go for broke. Then came a letter from her mother in California: "I still have my wedding dress," she wrote, "Would you like to wear it?" Sentiment fought with disappointment. She was in love with the lace beauty. Yet, it would feel good to wear a dress that her mother had made for herself and worn to marry her father. Ultimately she did not know how to turn down the offer without hurting her mother.

Kate came from the west coast by bus for the wedding, bearing the dress in a box. Margaret met her at the bus station. To Margaret's consternation, Kate got off the bus moving very gingerly. It transpired that somewhere out on the Great Plains she had been standing in the aisle when the bus driver

60

*Edwin and
Margaret Colbert
on their wedding
day, July 8, 1933.*

braked suddenly, and she had shot the length of the bus. She was battered black and blue all down one side, but otherwise unbowed.

Her dress fit Margaret, except that it was short. To keep the train on the ground, Margaret had to bend her knees. Thus, her progress up the aisle was less stately than she had intended, but the effort to show off the dress to good advantage kept her mind off her nervousness. Ned—who had restrained himself from walking out of the church in spite of the congregation numbering many more than twenty-five—gave no sign of surprise at her suddenly decreased stature when she reached his side.

Uncle Ned Manning had expected to be asked to provide the music, but Margaret wanted him to give her away, so she asked Sam Eves to play the organ for the service. Percy conducted the traditional Episcopal ceremony without a hitch, and now Margaret sported a plain silver wedding band, suitably blessed, beside the moonstone ring. The party of family and close friends trooped over to the Oltons' house, where Aunt Dot laid out simple refreshments. For some reason, it was at this point that Margaret's nerves almost got the better of her. "I nearly ran away," she said. "I didn't know how to behave. I think the Oltons got a good chuckle out of it." She was, of course, persuaded to stay, and in the end the party passed in a cheerful blur. And then it was time for the couple to leave on their honeymoon. Margaret stretched her knees thankfully and changed into traveling clothes.

John and Rachel Nichols loaned their car to the newlyweds. Already several years old, the car was a Franklin with an air-cooled engine; the tires on its enormous wheels were inflated to a very high pressure, which made the ride somewhat hard. Delighted with it nonetheless, the young Colberts set off and followed the valley of the Housatonic River north. After a short stay in Montreal and Quebec City, they drove up the southeast shore of the Saint Lawrence to the Gaspé Peninsula, which was still quite isolated and undiscovered by vacationing hordes. They stayed on the Gaspé for several days, and the sun shone warmly but without the oppressive heat of New York. The sea breezes blew, the ocean sparkled, the small unspoiled fishing towns beckoned. Margaret, of course, had brought her paints. Ned lolled in the sun on the beaches as she worked.

After the Gaspé, they wandered south to New Brunswick. The flint roads of Quebec played havoc with the tires of the Franklin. One after the other, they hissed and died. The car had to be completely reshod—an unexpected expense, but an appropriate way to repay the Nichols' generosity.

Margaret was delighted to share with Ned her childhood summer haunts: the tidal river, the wooded hills and bluffs, the beaches, the Matthew summer homes. They stayed in Tante Tina's cabin at the top of the kitchen garden; at night they listened to the haunting calls of loons echoing across the Kennebecasis.

In Saint John, they paid a visit to the museum founded by Margaret's grandfather. Margaret particularly wanted Ned to see a giant trilobite, *Paradoxides regina*, which her father had found at the age of six in the Cambrian shales of Saint John—his first significant fossil find. The curator was new since Margaret had last been there, so she introduced herself. To her astonishment, the curator's eyes became big and round. He called out his staff to meet her, and showed her off as a major celebrity: "This is the granddaughter of *George Frederic Matthew!*"

Back in New York, the young couple moved into an apartment in Riverdale belonging to George and Bodine Fowler. George taught at the Ethical Culture School. In the summer of 1932, Margaret had left the Eveses' apartment and had moved in with the Fowlers, paying a modest rent in return for babysitting their two small children. The Fowlers were going out of town, and they offered the apartment rent free to Margaret and

Ned for a month. This gave them a comfortable base from which to hunt for a home.

They found at last a three-room, third-floor apartment in a house on Fort Washington Avenue, in Washington Heights. It was next door to a subway station, trains from which ran into the basement of the American Museum. The front of the building faced a small green square—Bennett Park. The back hung over a cliff. Their living room had a fine view to the east and the north over upper Manhattan and the Bronx; on fine days they could see a green haze that was the beginning of Westchester County. At the bottom of their cliff were tennis courts that afforded the Colberts hours of free entertainment from their aerie; neither Margaret nor Ned could have reconciled themselves to the claustrophobic vistas of brick and concrete common from many city dwellings. Margaret wrote a poem, titled "The Last Chuckle," which echoes her feelings about confinement in a city:

Manhattan's little rills
That drain its knobby hills
Must truckle to the city—what a pity!
Once free to find their way
Untrammeled to the bay,
Or, indolent, to slacken in the bracken,
Or hemlock-laced to spill
Through granite, schist or till,
They now are dogged runnels housed in tunnels.
Now oozing from the dark
To bespectacle a park,
Now underground, loquacious and vexatious,
A more than steel-strong net,
Ubiquitous and wet,
Still adds its sullied potion to the ocean.
As long as Gotham stands,
And longer too, slim bands
Will make their music under subways' thunder.
No craft of man subdues
Those old sea-level blues
Nor stays the smallest rill bent on fulfillment.

Of their time in Washington Heights Ned wrote in his autobiography, *Digging Into the Past*:

Living up on the spine of northern Manhattan afforded us many opportunities to get out and away from our building, and even from the city streets. In those days the Cloisters branch of the Metropolitan Museum had not been built, but there was a museum of medieval art on the property of George Grey Barnard, the famous sculptor, just up the street from us. . . . In a matter of ten minutes we could walk up there. . . . And beyond was Inwood Park, a great place to stroll. . . . We liked to walk across the George Washington Bridge, and then hike along the foot of the Palisades on what was then a woodland trail, where we could hear the song of the wood thrush and where we could even get a sense of being out of the great city. . . . Or we would take the subway to Two Hundred Forty-second Street, from there take a streetcar through Yonkers, and then hike along the Aqueduct [the Croton Aqueduct that bounded the Hastings-on-Hudson property of the Matthew family] for as many miles as we wished to go.

In the spring of 1934, Margaret and Ned discussed whether or not she should continue working after the end of her employment year; Ned did not want her to. A factor in the equation was that in 1933 Ned had been given a permanent position at the museum as assistant curator. His salary was anything but munificent, but it was secure, and he believed it was enough to support them both. Margaret knew she would miss the work, the company, and the salary (meager, but her own), but she complied with his wishes. She collected the monies due to her from the pension fund into which she had been paying and resigned from her job on June 30, 1934. She recalls:

I started to learn to keep house and to cook. My mother hated to cook—she always had a cook to do it for her—and she wouldn't or couldn't teach me. (Instead, she taught me to sew, for which I have always been grateful.) I knew how to make a white sauce, and how to boil vegetables until you could bite them, but otherwise I had to start from scratch. I looked everything up in three cookbooks. The first would leave something out that I needed to know, the second filled in that gap, and the third gave me a better overall idea. I experimented—and Ned survived.

Domesticity could not feed her art; Margaret still spent a lot of time at the museum, sketching mounted creatures and skeletons—she had not lost her fascination for the forms of bones. She set up her easel near the living-room window and worked on landscapes and the occasional portrait. Also at this time Storrs Lee, the husband of Margaret's stepsister, Mary Lou,

*Margaret, age approximately
twenty-four, circa 1935.*

commissioned her to furnish scratchboard drawings of small-town scenery
for a book he was writing, a task that she found very satisfying.

The Depression years ground by. At one point the museum was forced to
ask employees to accept a 10 percent cut in pay—the cut was across the
board, so resentment was at a minimum, and most people felt fortunate when
they compared their lot with the misery of the jobless thousands "out there."
One wintry evening, Margaret came home from an errand and found a man
shivering in the meager shelter of the front porch. He was obviously very
hungry, so she invited him in. When Ned returned and found Margaret standing by an unkempt fellow seated at the kitchen table devouring soup and
thickly buttered bread, he was unhappy. After the man had finished his meal
and gone on his way, Ned remonstrated with Margaret, questioning her
judgment in inviting a stranger inside when she was alone. In agitation, he
strode about, and the words "rape," "robbery," even "arson," flew around the
apartment. But Margaret insisted calmly that she knew the man was harm-
less—just cold, hungry, and wretched—or she would not have asked him in.

For her social life, she kept up with her museum friends, and once a
month there was a meeting of an organization for staff wives. Not a joiner
of clubs by nature, she was at first nervous and awkward about associating
herself with this museum organization, but she was soon very glad that she

had done so. "They were such a bright bunch of people—I think museum men tend to marry interesting women."

Once a year the museum threw a trustees' dinner. This was the only occasion the Colberts attended for which evening dress was mandatory. Every year, Margaret put on the white lace dress that had been intended for her wedding, and over it a green velveteen evening coat. Each year she introduced variation in her appearance with something like new gloves, but it was always the same dress.

Because they lived in the city, it made no sense to have a car. They looked at the finances involved and figured they could take taxis everywhere and still come out ahead. "But we never took taxis," said Margaret. "We took the subway—it was so much *quicker*, we told ourselves." And for the first year, Margaret enjoyed people-watching on the subway. Later, she admitted, it became old. "And for the awful trustees' dinners, I would get all gussied up in my long white dress and my long green coat—and ride the subway. I hated that."

At last, Ned finished his dissertation. At that time, Columbia required that a thesis be published before the degree was conferred. After a long wait, it was accepted for publication by the American Philosophical Society in Philadelphia, and he could collect his doctoral degree. Margaret naturally wanted to see him receive his blue and white Columbia hood at the graduation ceremony. But commencement that year, 1935, was so crowded that she had to sit in a room outside the auditorium and listen to a loudspeaker broadcast of the ceremony. As compensation for that disappointment, they learned soon after graduation that Ned's dissertation monograph—with Margaret's illustrations—had been awarded the Daniel Giraud Elliot Medal for 1935 by the National Academy of Sciences.

After the Colberts had been married for about two years, subtle and not so subtle hints and questions began to sprinkle correspondence from Ned's parents and Margaret's mother. Would-be grandparents were becoming anxious. For a while, Ned and Margaret were unconcerned. Then they, too, started to wonder why no child had appeared. But in the summer of 1936, before the advent of real worry, Margaret realized that she was indeed pregnant. She went to see her obstetrician, Dr. Damon. He sat her down in his office to ask the routine questions. Before he began, he snapped open a silver case and offered her a cigarette. She took one. Dr. Damon lit it for her, and one for himself.

"By the way," he asked, "how many do you smoke in a day?"

"Four."

He blew smoke down his nostrils and squinted at her through the cloud, "You should cut down to one while you're pregnant."

Margaret was dismayed. It was costing her considerable self-discipline to hold the line at four. Which of her precious smokes should she retain? The one after lunch? Before dinner? "Yes," Dr. Damon said firmly, "One pack a day is quite enough when you are carrying a child."

On February 9, 1937, she started labor and telephoned Ned at the museum. This time, they did spurn the subway and treated themselves to a taxi to the Columbia-Presbyterian Medical Center, a few blocks south of the Washington Heights apartment. Ned came with her and stayed for most of the ten hours that she took to deliver George. Margaret said, "Unfortunately, my doctor was very modern and believed in wonderful anesthesia, so I was 'out' the whole time."

New mothers were kept in the hospital for a minimum of two weeks. Margaret was bewildered and intimidated by her care-givers. They were more like keepers. Their attitude was that the baby had arrived courtesy of the obstetrics department and belonged to them. Grudgingly, they allowed her to deal with him when he needed to be nursed but hung over her throughout the process to make sure that she treated their baby right. The philosophy at the time was that babies should not be touched except to fill the physical needs of feeding, cleansing, clothing. Otherwise they should be left alone.

When it was time to take George home, Margaret's instructions were to feed the baby every four hours, on the hour. Under no circumstances should she feed him at night—he had been taken off his night feeding in the hospital. He should continue to receive the minimum of touching. Holding or cuddling him would be self-indulgence on her part. Ned arrived with a taxi, and the nurses handed the baby over to his thoroughly demoralized mother. It was snowing hard, and George was bundled in layers of blanket. Only his eyes showed, and he gazed quizzically at his parents for the short ride home.

That first night, George cried continuously. Margaret and Ned tried in vain to ignore the pathetic wails. "It was so hard," she said, "so pitiful." Totally sleepless, Margaret lay with aching breasts. Being at home, however, had restored at least some of her self-confidence and independent spirit. By morning, she had decided to disobey the heartless hospital staff. She would feed her child when he cried; she would try to get some sort of schedule going but would not push it. Ned persuaded her, perhaps for his own peace of mind, to seek her doctor's approval before she took such a drastic step. She called as early as possible and received the doctor's blessing on the course she was determined to take.

Awareness of heavy responsibility and frustration at the sudden curtailment of freedom are feelings common to many new mothers. But the strict instructions, particularly the ban on cuddling and holding, spoiled much of Margaret's joy in her first child. George cried a lot, and Margaret was often anxious and miserable, afraid that she was handling him incorrectly and that she was harming him somehow, physically or mentally. She was very afraid her negative feelings were being transmitted to the baby.

Ned doted on his child. He had not been entirely enthusiastic about being a father; he had been of the opinion that brand-new humans were not attractive—that newborn animals were far more appealing—and that fatherhood was a duty rather than a pleasure. But this had all been in the abstract. Little George converted him in short order, and Ned became the epitome of the proud father.

The lease on the apartment was nearing its end. The Colberts decided not to renew it; it was not the ideal environment for a child. The city was involved in major construction in the valley below them, which generated dirt and noise. When in April they threw open the windows to let in the first warm spring air, the breeze carried in black specks that settled all over George's face and his crib bedding.

A couple of miles into New Jersey across the George Washington Bridge, the small town of Leonia was home to several of the Colberts' friends and acquaintances. Originally settled in the middle of the seventeenth century, Leonia contained Dutch houses from that era and, in spite of its proximity to the megalopolis, still retained its village flavor. Because of easy access to the City and the university, it was—and still is—home to many Columbia faculty members and to an enclave of artists. Ned started to house hunt in Leonia. It took him several visits, but eventually he found a three-bedroom house on High Street for which the landlord was asking a monthly rent of fifty dollars. The house was on a one-hundred-foot lot. Ned was delighted with his find. He bounced back to Manhattan, bursting to tell Margaret the good news.

He heard them before he reached the third floor: a loud cacophony of wails filled the stairwell. He opened the door to the apartment and there was five-month-old George in Margaret's arms. Mother and child were both bawling their heads off. "George started crying," Margaret said, "and I couldn't do anything to make him happy. In the end, I just gave in and cried along with him."

∽ 9 ∽

Leonia and Motherhood

Off to shopping in the City, feeling somewhat less than trig
In a self-inflicted haircut and a home-concocted rig,
When I will have made my purchases and tendered my address
As a number on Park Avenue, the salesgirl will I bless
Who can quell the urge to reappraise my looks from head to toe;
But the crown for tact will go to her who doesn't murmur, "Oh,"
In a satisfied, I-knew-as-much, a *vindicated* way,
When I add the anticlimax of "Leonia, N.J."

Life in Leonia may have inspired Margaret Colbert to self-mocking verse (this she titled "The Sub-Suburbanite"), but the little town was a good place to live. Margaret integrated herself swiftly and happily. The Colberts lived in the High Street house for two years. Then Margaret became pregnant again, and they realized they would need more room than their rental home afforded. When William King Gregory, Ned's erstwhile advisor, went abroad for the 1938 spring semester, he appointed Ned to teach his vertebrate paleontology course at Columbia. The extra income allowed them to consider buying their own home. Once again, they started to house hunt.

The country was still in the last stages of the depression, and the bank owned a lot of Leonia homes. To one of these houses, Margaret and Ned kept coming back. Built in 1926, it was on Park Avenue, in the hilly part of the town, on the wooded back slope of the Palisades. It had a tilted backyard and on clear days a panoramic view west and southwest to the ridge of Watchung Mountain. The house was plain and square, but what it lacked in elegance, it made up for in warm and welcoming atmosphere.

Margaret, David, and George, 1940.

They moved to Park Avenue in the summer of 1939, just before the arrival of the new baby. Margaret was quite overwhelmed at the amount of room she suddenly had at her disposal. She told Louise Germann about all the space, and Louise laughed and said, "I can see you crouching in corners."

David was born on July 19. "I thought that Dave would be a girl," said Margaret, "because that's how it's supposed to be. You have a boy and then you have a girl!" She did not mind, however, "as long as the child was healthy." She was much more relaxed with this second child. George had convinced her of the toughness of small children. After two years of experience and courage, the hospital staff could not intimidate her as they had with George.

Lucky it was that she did not feel deprived at the lack of a daughter; on the steamy, hot afternoon of July 16, 1940 (before a year was up), she gave birth to Philip, another son. "Phil was a happy accident, and we were so tickled with the little boys we already had that it was no shock that he was a boy!"

George examined the new baby and shook his head solemnly: "Davey is one year old, but Phil isn't *any* old," he pronounced. Margaret was charmed by George's way with language, and she collected "Georgisms." They included "biggetty-controlion," for the Victrola and "hipinapondamus," for hippopotamus. When he had an unsettled tummy, he had the "upsetica." He stumped Kate Minor with: "Grammy, what do I don't know about whales?" One of Margaret's favorites was a puzzled query: "Mommy, what is a 'tate' and how do you 'hez it?'" This mystified Margaret, until he started to sing a kindergarten jingle: "Green means 'Go!' Don't hes-i-tate."

Ned and (l to r) Philip, David, and George

Ned rolled up his sleeves and made improvements to the house; his Forest Service summers had equipped him with carpentry and masonry skills. He built brick terraces at the front and back of the house, constructed a play gym for the children, put in storm windows, made bunk beds with built-in drawers for the boys—and fixed up a screen to separate the bunks of David and Philip. "Perhaps because they were three days less than a year apart in age, those two boys would giggle endlessly at bedtime. If they couldn't see each other, they would settle down." Margaret and Ned together used Aunty Em's stencils of the *Through the Looking Glass* characters to decorate the boys' quarters.

In 1940 Ned registered for the draft as was required for men in his age bracket. When the United States entered the second world war in 1941, his age (thirty-six) and status as a father with three young children made it unlikely that he would be called up for active duty. He was, however, summoned first by the army and then by the navy and interviewed for specialized tasks in faraway places. In the end, others were chosen for the jobs—much to Margaret's relief. And indeed, Ned himself did not feel deprived. He became an air-raid warden for their block in Leonia and patrolled the streets at night, telling people to turn out lights. Ned supposed the appearance of an enemy bomber in the night sky was not *totally* beyond the bounds of possibility, and the exercise in futility served to remind people that the country was at war, if nothing else. He also rented a strip of land for a "victory garden" and planted and tended it diligently.

A fleet of military blimps intended for spotting enemy submarines was based nearby. The almost silent airships would loom sudden and enormous over the horizon, and they took some getting used to. From the perspective of the children, the blimps were probably the only visible sign of the conflict. Nonetheless, the three little boys and many of their small friends were really fearful of the war. One Fourth of July Margaret decided something had to be done to give the children a sense of control over the situation; in any case, something had to be done to celebrate the day. Fireworks were forbidden, no programs had been arranged for children, and no playgrounds were nearby. Margaret blew a bunch of eggs, filled them with flour, and drew upon them faces of all the bad guys with whom the children were familiar—Hitler, Goebbels, Mussolini, Hirohito, and the rest. She collected several neighbors and their youngsters and they all gathered on the slate steps behind the house. The children took the egg villains and whammed them down onto the steps. They burst in satisfying explosions of white. A party with lemonade and cookies followed, and everybody felt much better.

Margaret's philosophy about the war was mixed. She perceived the evil of Hitler and the necessity of stopping him but nonetheless believed war to be a somewhat ridiculous way out of any international dispute. She saw nothing glorious or noble about mowing down human beings—nor about being mowed down. Wars might close one can of worms, but they inevitably opened others. When the atomic bombs were dropped on Japan on August 6 and 9, 1945, she could not unreservedly join in the rejoicing at the end of hostilities. That her country had used weapons capable of wiping out seventy thousand people in an instant filled her with horror. She said at the time to a close friend and neighbor, Hope Bogert, "Two bombs have been dropped. If they drop another, I just don't want to be here any more."

That August Ned was in California, having been invited to teach a summer course in paleontology at Berkeley. There he met Charles Camp, who had preceded him as a student of Dr. Gregory at Columbia and who had been Will Matthew's colleague and friend at Berkeley. Margaret had earned pin money baby-sitting his children when she lived in California. The university museum contained skeletons of phytosaurs—giant crocodile-like thecodont reptiles from the Triassic—collected by Camp from the Petrified Forest region of Arizona, and from Ghost Ranch in northern New Mexico. Thus was Ned's interest in Ghost Ranch first piqued; the Ranch was to loom large in his future and in Margaret's.

Ned lived that summer in the Cedar Street house with Margaret's mother and stepfather. Kate's prodigious energy had not diminished; she wrote in a letter to Margaret: "I've been working . . . on the publicity for the Day Nursery—10 articles printed, so far. Still teaching sewing at the Day Nursery, sewing on Thursdays for the Red Cross & finishing up the unfinished work during the week beside making pajamas, 6 suits every two weeks for the British Relief. Thank God I don't have to be idle, just finished my 110th sweater, not counting the few I have made for our families."

Kate's sister Em was now living with the Minors. The advent of dust covers had bankrupted the Thayer book-cover business. Her marriage had also come to grief; after a peccadillo or two, the redoubtable Harry had actually brought another woman home to live with them. Em stayed with him until they had paid off all their debts—a slow and painful process—then she sued Uncle Harry for desertion and went out to Berkeley to live with her sister. She was still writing her Lee Thayer mystery novels. (By the end of her life she had published sixty-five. She wrote the last one at the age of ninety.)

Ralph Minor had retired from the university but was involved in several enterprises. Some years before his retirement he started a small press, the Oquaga Press, from which he produced greeting cards, visiting cards, and a small number of beautifully made books. He was also part-owner of an olive orchard. When he first started teaching at Berkeley, the university had no pension plan; so as a means of providing funds in lieu of a pension, he and four fellow professors each bought forty acres in the upper part of the Sacramento Valley—where volcanic soil provided ideal growing conditions—and planted mission olive trees. After the trees began to bear, a crate of olives from the "Wyandotte Cooperative" arrived at the door of each member of Ralph's and Kate's families every Christmas. During the war, imports of olive oil from Italy dried up, and the cooperative made a killing.

Ralph was a generous man, and delightfully impulsive. The summer after the war ended, he and Kate drove east, as they did every year without fail. Margaret was cooking dinner for them in Leonia. She swung her old oven door open. With a loud complaint from worn-out hinges, it fell to the floor. Ralph came to the kitchen when he heard the crash, and stood there surveying his red-faced, flustered hostess.

"Now if you could have exactly the stove you've only dreamed about, what kind would it be?" he asked.

"Oh, a Chambers," Margaret answered without hesitation.

"Do they sell them around here?"

Margaret nodded.

He said, "Hop in the car!" There and then he bought her a Chambers range with a griddle and three burners, and a well with a burner at the bottom like a fireless cooker. It was a range that she swore saved her sanity.

The necessity of saving time and effort—even if sanity was never in question—was to become more important in 1944. On the evening of March 27, neighbors Tom and Grace Ierardi drove Margaret and Ned to Columbia-Presbyterian Medical Center. Grace wrapped around Margaret's knees a blanket on which she had pinned a big pink bow. It did no good at all. The next day, March 28, Daniel Colbert—as male as he could be—came into the world. As a new baby, Danny enchanted his mother by "cooing." Margaret would lay him in her lap and support his head, and he would begin a little soft sound, like a pigeon in the rafters early in the morning.

Pregnant with her fifth child in 1946, Margaret went into labor early. This time, she beat the doctor to the event. The hospital staff did not even have time to wheel her into the delivery room. Charles was born on a trolley outside the delivery room on February 26, without anesthesia, and without Dr. Damon.

"It wasn't until Charles was born that I *experienced* bearing a child. It was quite wonderful—a tremendous upper. I didn't want to sleep all that night, I was too happy. Not," she interjected hurriedly, "that I wasn't happy to see the other boys, but with them I was denied that experience. Under anesthesia, I was aware that I screamed during the birth of the first four—Ned confirms that I did. But with the fifth—without even an aspirin—I started to scream because it was expected of me, and then I thought: I don't have to do this!— and I simply stopped. Of course the nurses told me how *brave* I was!

"With anesthesia, you scream because you are out of control. With natural childbirth, there is pain—and it really is big pain—but you know it's going to end and it's for a happy reason, something you've been looking forward to for a long time."

By mistake, the hospital assigned Margaret to the Harkness Pavilion, a very upscale part of the establishment, usually reserved for rich and famous folk. For the births of the other babies she had been in the Sloane Wing with her fellow lesser mortals. In the Harkness she had a private room and was allowed to choose her meals from a menu brought around every morning. Physically she was very comfortable, but she was still not allowed to hold her child when she wanted. Meanwhile, Ned became steadily more panicked about the bills that would certainly roll in for Margaret's fancy accommodation. He went to see Dr. Damon to plead for mercy and to suggest Margaret be moved back to the Sloane Wing. The obstetrician said he thought Margaret deserved a break and that she should stay where she was. To Ned's astonishment, he offered to subtract the difference in cost from

Sketch of the boys and the play gym Ned built. Drawn from memory. Circa 1988.

his own bill. Ned thought the doctor was assuaging his guilt because he had failed to be present at Charles's birth.

From the very beginning, Charles was an agreeable, happy child. He was so easy to get along with that Margaret thought at times he received less than his fair share of attention.

Five boys—all duly baptized by Percy Olton in the little Newark church—were enough. The house on Park Avenue, which had seemed so spacious at first, now bulged at the seams with the pressure of boys. Like every mother in charge of young children, Margaret was busy with what often seemed endless, mindless, fruitless tasks—tasks that had to be done all over again all too soon. She tried to keep her sense of humor and proportion, and wrote:

> Already it is getting light
> And much is waiting to be done.
> Much sits leering at me in a lump
> Or peering slyly out of bureau drawers.
> Much, I'll hack away at you today
> Perhaps I'll merely split you into many.
> Perhaps, with luck, there'll be some few
> To put aside as done at sundown.

The task of raising the children fell almost entirely on her shoulders. The nature of Ned's work afforded him very little time to be with his children. His daily workload mounted as his responsibilities expanded. The American Museum made him curator of fossil amphibians and reptiles in 1942, replacing Margaret's old boss, Barnum Brown. The reptile exhibits, including the splendid dinosaurs, were now his domain. Then William King Gregory retired from Columbia University; Ned was invited to take his place; thus, in the fall of 1945, Ned joined the Columbia faculty to teach vertebrate paleontology. He was also writing books and editing journals, and he spent months away almost every year, collecting fossils.

As Ned's national and international reputation grew steadily, a certain amount of formal entertaining was mandatory, on top of the daily feeding of six males. Margaret invested in cookware from a restaurant supply house; regular pots and pans were never big enough. She bought meat in bulk and stocked a basement freezer.

She was not entirely without help; she hired someone to clean the house. "House-cleaning was something I never learned to do properly," she said, "and I never wanted to!" In addition, Leonia women were an enterprising bunch. Before the Colberts left the High Street house, Margaret had become part of a cooperative play group with four other mothers. Each woman took one day a week to have all the children in her home, at least for part of the day. This organized group fizzled soon after the move to Park Avenue, but similar arrangements continued in a haphazard, but effective fashion among friends and acquaintances. They used each other constantly—swapping children back and forth—to gain those precious hours of freedom from keeping track of lively young bodies.

One role Margaret was largely spared was that of chauffeur. Leonia occupied only one square mile, and the children could, from a very young age, walk or bike to their destinations in safety. Only when the weather was truly outrageous did Margaret have to drive her young around.

She did not sew the boys' everyday clothes—they were cheap enough to buy and posed no interesting challenges. But she sewed imaginative Halloween costumes—five per year, until the children became too big to indulge in trick-or-treating. When George was five, he wanted to be a skeleton. Margaret put much effort into the creation of a very nice skull of papier-mâché. To hold it on his head, she found an old pair of underdrawers that still had elastic and used the seat to go down the back of his head. George threw a fit. How could he possibly be seen walking around with underwear on his head?

A formal family picture, 1953.
Back: David, George, Philip.
Front: Charles, Ned, Margaret,
Daniel.

Following the example set by her own parents, Margaret listened to her children with respect, and when they asked her questions, she answered thoughtfully and seriously. Philip wrote in 1993:

> When I was 7 or 8—we had a 1937 Dodge sedan in those days—I remember driving somewhere with Mom and suddenly wondering what made the car go. I knew, of course, it was the motor, but how did *that* work? It appeared lifeless, mysterious. When I confronted her with the question, instead of bypassing the matter as she could have with some nonsense about the burning gas making the motor go "round and round," or some such fop, she treated me to a wonderful verbal picture of the interior of an internal combustion engine, tailored to my level of understanding, with appropriate pauses for my mental ruminations to run their course. At the end of 20 minutes or so, and starting from ground zero, I had a truly accurate—in essentials—picture in my head of the internal combustion engine, with rapidly expanding gases in a cylinder forcing down pistons, which by means of connecting rods caused an eccentrically configured crankshaft to rotate; of a carburetor metering the fuel as demanded; of a camshaft with lobes pushing on rods which would open and close valves in the cylinder to let in fresh fuel and allow burnt gases to escape, all in timed sequence; of a distributor rotor delivering a hot spark to the fuel at exactly the right moment when the valves were closed. . . . I wonder how many mechanics could deliver a discourse like that.

Although she never believed she lived up to her mother's example, Margaret became involved in what she thought of as her "civic" activities. She helped in the organization and running of a little museum for children in Leonia, and with the local Cub Scouts. She joined a food cooperative that proved onerously time-consuming, although the food was fresh and good.

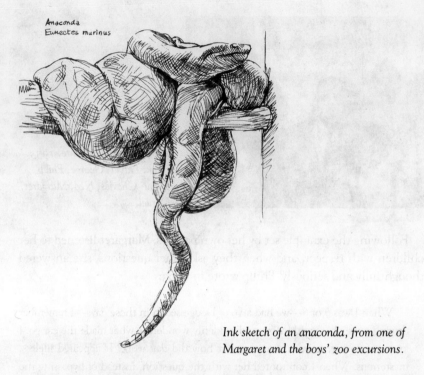

Anaconda
Eunectes murinus

Ink sketch of an anaconda, from one of
Margaret and the boys' zoo excursions.

Once a week, when Dan and Charles were little, she taught art at the nursery school; it paid for their fees there. She said, "I experimented and I learned a lot. I would make a piece of a drawing and ask the children to name it and finish it. And when I had the kids painting with colors, it was my function to pull the painting away before they spoiled it. To start with, their ideas were exciting and interesting, but after a while they would turn into mud as they got carried away."

Occasionally she took the boys to the Bronx zoo. She brought along her sketch book, and, between counting heads of her offspring to make sure nobody had jumped in among the lions or the bears, she sketched the animals, recording the way the living creatures moved and arranged their bodies and limbs.

She took the children to visit the American Museum on frequent occasions. She wanted her boys to love it as she had as a child, and it was a joy to introduce them to those of her own pet exhibits that were still there.

The usual childhood ailments—chicken pox, measles, mumps, whooping cough—went through the posse of boys with varying degrees of virulence. Before the advent of vaccines, families almost welcomed these more or less inevitable infections, because after they were over, they were over for good. Other diseases were treated with less equanimity. Both George and David contracted scarlet fever, which modern antibiotics deal with swiftly. Margaret nursed them through it, thankfully without any of its dreaded lingering complications. But a more difficult trial loomed. "The hardest thing for a mother to bear," said Margaret, "is when you can't cope with some hurt in a child. There are some things that are bigger than your capabilities."

Since babyhood George had a volatile temper. As he grew into his teens, his spells of rage grew worse. Margaret was confused and frightened, and Ned had no more idea than she of how to understand him or of what was the best course to pursue to deal with him. Help for emotional problems was not easy to come by. The counselors and therapists to whom one can turn nowadays were barely invented. At last, in desperation, and amidst agonizing doubts over their decision, Margaret and Ned had their son admitted to the hospital.

"It still makes me weep to remember." Margaret felt she had abandoned her son, given up on him, but perhaps separation from the family was essential for George's healing. The hospital gave him no medication, and he ultimately straightened himself out by his own courage and strength. Margaret finally allowed herself to accept that she and Ned did the right thing— or at least that they did their best, given the times and the circumstances.

Looking back on all her acquaintances in the Leonia years, Margaret said, "Everyone was just great." There were particularly good friends, of course. Hope and architect Neil Bogert and their two boys lived down-slope and "catty-corner" across the backyard of the Colberts' house. Among many other joint activities, Margaret and Hope sewed their "home-concocted rigs" together. Very early on in their friendship the Colberts and Bogerts made a pact to protect each other from New Year's Eve parties. If either couple was invited to one of these anathemas, they always had a previous engagement—with the other couple.

Next to the Neil Bogerts and a little further downhill lived Tom and Grace Ierardi, who also had two boys. The Colbert plot met the Ierardi yard at one corner and Ned and Tom extended existing slate steps to facilitate access between their homes. The Colbert and Ierardi children shared toys and pets—the Colbert cat (named "Smocko" because he always chose to lie on Margaret's painting smock), an Ierardi rabbit, an assortment of rats and mice—and trotted freely back and forth between the two homes.

And then, the Coles: Charles and Grace Cole were silversmiths who made beautiful hand-wrought jewelry and taught classes in silver-work to about a dozen students at a time in their Leonia home. These classes were run in a highly professional manner. In the wintertime, Margaret sometimes attended; she made some original and interesting jewelry but gave almost all of it away. Charles created Margaret's second moonstone engagement ring, whereby hangs a tale.

One fall day, Margaret took Dan and Charles to the museum. Drifting around the exhibits, she looked down at her hand, and saw that her moonstone engagement ring was not on her finger. At first, she hoped she had simply not put it on that day. But when she got home, she turned the house upside down and inside out to no avail. She notified the Natch "Lost and Found" but weeks passed and nobody turned in the ring. She resigned herself sadly to the loss. In April it was time to put her winter purse away in the attic. She hauled down her summer purse and looked inside. Behold—a silvery glint. The ring was caught in the lining. She slipped it on her finger, ran downstairs, and sat herself next to Ned on the couch. She thrust her hand under his nose and waited for a gleeful response. It did not come. Puzzled, she looked at his face. His expression was, as she put it, "going around and around." She understood when on her birthday, Ned presented her with another moonstone ring—a new stone, in a different but equally lovely setting, designed and executed by Charles Cole.

Phil Colbert made a particular friend of Charles Cole Jr. (Jay); the two went from kindergarten through college together. Phil was an inveterate collector and rescuer of wild creatures and over the years kept a succession of rodents and reptiles. When they were teenagers, he and Jay combined their resources and purchased an enormous snake—some sort of a boa constrictor. They kept it, with the other creatures, in the Colbert basement. The boa had to be fed live food and the two boys caught pigeons to sustain their pet. (Appropriately enough, Jay became a herpetologist and eventually curator of reptiles at the American Museum.)

The McKennas were not strictly Leonians. They lived in the next town, Englewood. Malcolm McKenna was a colleague of Ned's, a paleontologist at the American Museum. His wife, Priscilla, played the harpsichord professionally in New York and some years later became mayor of Englewood. She accompanied Malcolm on his field expeditions and, at least in the early days, was the camp cook. For some years before the late 1920s, the American Museum had been involved in a series of paleontological studies in central Asia. In the mid-1960s, a move was afoot to continue the investigations, and Malcolm and Priscilla planned to start the ball rolling in Outer Mongolia. It seemed a wise idea to have at least a smattering of

Russian under their belts before venturing into those particular wilds. At about this time, as relations between the United States and the Soviet Union began to thaw, Ned Colbert had been receiving publications from Russian paleontologists. He thought it would be nice to have some idea of what they were about, and Margaret was interested in learning Russian for her own edification. Thus, the McKennas and Colberts together arranged for a Russian-born teacher, Jhenya Lux, to give them weekly lessons in the McKenna home. Margaret did not learn enough Russian to converse, but she enjoyed the language. She was able to help Ned, who did not share her flair for languages, with the Russian publications. And, she gave herself much pleasure translating Russian poetry. The following is her translation of "The Cliff," by Mikhail Lermontov (1813–1841):

A golden cloud one night was pleased to lie
On the seamed bosom of a cliff. At day
She, rising early, through the azure sky
Insouciantly pursued her merry way.

Yet in the old cliff's crevices of stone
Some traces of her moist embrace remain.
He ponders deeply, standing all alone
And softly weeps into the desert plain.

As a preview to the proposed field trip, the McKennas took a tourist bus trip to Mongolia and other parts of the Soviet Union in 1964. On the bus they encountered a small red-haired woman whose name was Jenny Pingrey. When she found out the McKennas were from the American Museum of Natural History, she asked them eagerly if they happened to know Margaret Matthew and told them she had been Margaret's high school history and civics teacher. After the McKennas returned from their trip, Priscilla and Margaret visited Miss Pingrey in Hastings-on-Hudson. Margaret thought she looked even smaller than she remembered and that her red hair was a trifle faded, but otherwise she was unchanged. Miss Pingrey rummaged in a cupboard and produced two little figures—sculptures of Elizabeth I and Henry VIII, carved from Ivory soap, yellowed now with age. Margaret remembered them then—her offering to a favorite teacher. She was astonished and touched that Miss Pingrey still had them. She remembered also a poem that she had written to share with classmates; she sincerely hoped Miss Pingrey had never seen it:

> Why we should study history
> Has always been a mystery
> To simple eggs like me.
> The more dates you learn, the less
> Of room you have for happiness—
> To hell with history!

Margaret had considered herself to be like her father—an apolitical animal. (Will had been impatient with politics and politicians. Government had to be respected, he allowed, but he never expected much of it.) But Ned was an avid reader of history—he loved paleontology because it was part of the grand historical picture—and he followed all aspects of the news and the political scene because that was history in the making. Marriage to Ned inevitably worked on Margaret's attitude toward politics. Philip wrote:

> In the early fifties, during the McCarthy Era, half of America and most of our neighbors held a heartfelt belief that we were locked in a life-or-death struggle with Communism, particularly the Russian variety, and that extraordinary measures, even extra-legal or unconstitutional ones, had to be taken to confront the mortal threat. . . . Mom found the hysteria plainly absurd, and I recall her patiently & kindly suggesting as much to a neighbor friend with words to the effect that perverting our own democratic process might make us all the more vulnerable to the supposed threat from abroad. Later the same friend admitted to me in all candor that Margaret had caused her to "see things in a different light." By this time McCarthy had departed in disgrace, and I suppose that helped.

In the late 1960s, Margaret marched with busloads of other demonstrators, on Trenton and on Washington, to protest racial injustice. The protest was held in front of an apartment block situated on the Englewood municipal line. The landlord of the apartments had refused to rent an apartment to a black family, on the grounds that his "good" tenants would move out if blacks moved in. The organizer asked Margaret to join in, and to dress in smart clothes for the occasion. It was a cold October day. About twenty women with placards gathered outside the apartments. They radiated respectability in their high heels and dresses or skirts. Curious, the tenants looked out of their windows and one by one came out to ask what was going on. The demonstrators explained. The tenants were surprised and appalled at the landlord's prejudice. In short order, the apartment block was integrated.

The Vietnam war engendered activism on a different scale. There was less hope of effecting change, more anger, more despair. One Fourth of July, Margaret was one of a group of men and women that wanted to have a peace contingent in the Leonia parade. They simply wanted to march with signs that said "Peace." Nothing else. The parade committee denied them permission. The group (which included the actor Alan Alda and his wife) went to the town council. They applied formally through all the proper channels and could not, under the Constitution, be denied permission to hold their own parade. The police assigned them half a block of sidewalk near the main crossroads in Leonia, and they marched in a narrow oval up and down this limited space. The police arrived and stood around watching. At one end of the oval a group of men gathered. They swore and cursed at the protesters but could do nothing else because of the police presence. Nonetheless, their concentrated hatred and fury were disconcerting.

Margaret was bitter about the war and the atrocities she perceived Americans were being led to commit for the purpose of propping up a corrupt, if anticommunist, regime. Try as she might, she could see nothing intrinsically evil in communism. It was not particularly attractive to her, but theoretically it made sense. She saw little to choose between extremist leaders on the left and those on the right; power-hungry fanatics were always dangerous and malevolent. Several times she fasted for days at a time, in a personal but, she realized, useless protest.

Dan was the only Colbert son to be drafted into the armed forces. Margaret did not know how to say goodbye to him. Dismally, she thought it might have been easier had she believed the Vietnam War to be a just cause. Perhaps then she could have felt stirred at the sight of him in uniform, even some pride that he would risk his life for good reason. As it was, the thought that she might lose her son to such a war choked her with fear and desolation. She hugged him and he hugged her back. "I said to him, 'Danny, you are a person who can do hard things.' That was all I could offer."

Dan was lucky; he spent his whole tour of duty in Saigon working on psychological warfare scripts that were printed on leaflets and dropped from aircraft to the ground. It was hoped their messages would affect the hearts and minds of the Vietnamese people. Dan said later that he was sure the projects were futile, but at least they did no harm.

~ 10 ~

Hurricanes, Farms, and Forays

Margaret's mother always stoutly maintained that the regular separations from Will were partly responsible for the happiness of her marriage, that being apart allowed each partner to grow out of the other's shadow and taught self-reliance, that she and Will appreciated each other all the more when they were together because of the times they were not. In the summer of 1938, Margaret had her first opportunity to test these brave beliefs. The Philadelphia Academy of Natural Sciences offered Ned the opportunity to work in Agate, Nebraska; he accepted eagerly because he had done no fieldwork since 1929 and had become, as he put it in *Digging Into the Past,* a "kind of closet naturalist . . . studying the fossils collected by other people." After the initial lonesomeness and strangeness of his absence, Margaret and one-year-old George settled into a routine and the hot and humid summer rolled by without major incident.

Apart from the summers of the summers of 1939 and 1940, when he stayed at home because of the impending births of David and Philip, Ned was absent for at least part of almost every subsequent summer. Margaret was resourceful, unafraid of coping alone, but emergencies seemed to crop up with regularity when Ned was away. "One summer," she recalled, "all five boys came down with measles and took them very hard. At the same time we had painters. You just long for a little support under those conditions."

In 1941, Ned had been in the field in South Dakota since early summer. He came back to civilization temporarily for a Society of Vertebrate Paleontology field conference in Lincoln, Nebraska. Kate and Ralph were about to return to California after their annual visit back East, and Margaret decided to farm the children out among friends and drive west with the Minors. Kate

84

and Ralph would drop her off with Ned in Lincoln. It seemed such a good idea: after extra time with her mother, she could be with Ned for a while—alone without children for the first time in four years. The plan was that she and Ned would ride the train together from Lincoln part of the way across Nebraska. She would then take a train back to Omaha and fly home, while Ned continued on to Lusk, Wyoming, where he was to meet Walter Granger and Bill Thompson for the next phase of fieldwork.

Margaret recalls: "That train trip was one of the miseries of my life. We'd been apart for so long, and I had so much to say to Ned. I wanted to hold his hand some. But he would have none of it. Because of flooding, some of the railroad bridges were in doubt so the train crept along very slowly. Ned's whole attention was taken up with getting there. He was so agitated and angry at going slowly that he couldn't sit still. I kept telling him, 'We're not going to get there any faster by fussing. Couldn't we have this little time to talk?'" He could not do it. He was totally in his work mode, unable to give Margaret the attention she craved. Margaret was very hurt. Afterward, Ned was shamefaced and apologetic and of course she forgave him, but she could not forget. The terrible haste had been because Ned could not bear to be late to meet Walter Granger; when he finally did reach Lusk, he learned that Granger had died suddenly of a heart attack the previous night.

In 1936 Betty and Nick acquired an early–nineteenth-century farmhouse on eighty acres of wooded land about twenty-five miles south of Providence. It was in the township of Exeter, which consisted at that time of a firehouse, a police station, a dairy farm, and a couple of houses strung along two or three miles of roadway. The frame Rhode Island–style house was built into a slope—the site scooped out of the hill. A former owner had removed the original central fireplace and put in a wood-burning stove. The Nichols added a bathroom and installed running water, and a generator for electricity. Some of the property was cleared, and Nick arranged for local people to harvest hay grown on these acres.

Nick was a resident psychiatrist in a Providence hospital when they bought the property, intending to use it as a summer retreat. However, after he joined the navy in 1940, they had to move every two or three years at the behest of the military. They kept the farm as their real home, their roots, although they were not often able to return to it. They lent it to Margaret and the boys for the summer months, and for years it was the Colbert family's escape from torrid heat. The few times Betty, Nick, and their three children (Tom, a couple of years older than George; Lee, born in 1938; and Jane, Dan's age) were in residence, the Colberts used a little cottage on the property. Each summer, Ned tried to return from the field in time to spend at least some days at the farm. In 1942, the year he became curator of fossil amphibians and reptiles, he had too much to do at the museum to take time for fieldwork; he joined his family at the farm for the whole summer and commuted to New York.

The farm was a boon because, as they grew beyond babyhood, the children were so easily and happily occupied that Margaret had reasonable time for painting and drawing—either fulfilling commissions or working for herself. One year she and Ned once again copied onto the walls of one of the farm bedrooms the stencils that had adorned her childhood room— Aunty Em's celebration of *Alice*. She always took along a big box labeled "Things to Do on Rainy Days." The boys found so much to do outdoors, even when it rained, that she never opened it. She did impose some limits—it was too easy to get seriously lost in the woods. Most of the land comprised second-growth woods with tall trees, and dense undergrowth full of brambles, cat briar, poison ivy, and sumac. Old stone fences ran through the woods, indicating it had once been cleared. The woods were full of birds and bird song, the whippoorwills loud at night. For the following poem, written at the farm and titled "Vireos by Day and Whippoorwills by Night," Margaret won a national poetry contest award.

> At dawn or dusk, in modulated phrase
> A thrush speaks for the static woods: Relax.
> Touch our serenity. No pillar we
> Of cloud or fire, but enigmatic dust
> Grown tall with acquiescence. Still the thrust
> Of aspiration counters apathy
> As whippoorwills' insistence fills the nights
> And brassy din of vireos the days.

Margaret sometimes longed for adult company: "When I was up at the farm alone with the children, it was fine all day, but then evening would come around. The kids would go off to bed, and I hadn't talked to a grown-up all day. At times I felt I hadn't talked to an adult for weeks." By good fortune, it was only twelve miles through the woods to her brother's home. Bill and his family frequently joined Margaret and her brood at the farm, and Margaret and Bill's wife Gladys became very good friends.

Bill Matthew was not scholarly like his sisters, and he believed he must have been a disappointment to his parents. He carried around this weight of inferiority for many years and strove for qualities he considered tough and masculine to compensate. When he went away to college after graduating from high school in Hartford, he purchased factory-worker shirts; he wanted to wear nothing remotely fancy.

Bill attended Antioch College in Ohio, an innovative and creative liberal-arts school. As part of the college curriculum, Antioch sent him to work during summer vacations at the Gorham factory in Providence, making silver and plated-silver flatware and other items. One year he made friends with Gladys, a young secretary at Gorham's; the friendship deepened, and by the end of the summer, Bill proposed marriage. When Gladys accepted, Bill decided he could not do without her through an academic year and elected not to return to Antioch to finish college; instead, he stayed with Gorham's and got married. Except for a period during the war, when he worked for the Whiting Company making gold-plated medical instruments, he continued with Gorham's for all his working life. He finished with the title of director of research, which meant he was the factory troubleshooter —if a problem arose on the production line, Bill sorted it out.

Bill's great hobby was sailing, a legacy of Tante Tina in New Brunswick. He first built himself a twelve-foot boat, then, when he and Gladys started a family, he built a bigger craft and then traded up until, by the time all four children—Billy, John, Betsy, and Mike—were big enough, they had a yacht that would sleep six, in which they could all go cruising. He began to study celestial navigation and, after retiring from Gorham's in the mid-1970s, taught the subject at the University of Rhode Island for several years.

In the late summer of 1954 the Colberts were preparing to leave the farm. Hope and Neil Bogert had invited them all to have breakfast at their summer cottage near Guilford, Connecticut, on their way home. It was raining very hard, the wind was freshening, and the sky was ominously dark, but they were too busy packing to listen to the radio and weather reports. When they finally set off and left the shelter of the trees, however, they realized the weather was out of the ordinary. The heavy car—laden with luggage, the aging Smocko, Ned, Margaret, and five boys—was blown around as if it were a flimsy buggy. Water was already deep on the road in some places, but they made it to Guilford. They staggered against the wind to the cottage door and knocked. Hope appeared, wild-eyed, beckoning them inside, her arms full of towels. The cottage was awash, rain coming through the walls as if they were not there, Hope and Neil were mopping up with towels. Ned made some comment about unusual weather, and Neil informed them dryly that the storm was indeed out of the ordinary: Hurricane Carol was coming ashore.

The electricity had not yet gone out, and Hope managed to serve breakfast. Through the window they watched the moored boats on Long Island Sound leaping and lunging in the wind. Even as they watched, one filled with water and sank. Soon the Colberts piled back into the car and started to drive along the road that would connect them with Highway 95. The boys were unnaturally quiet and still, but the cat—who hated riding in the car—moaned in the back. They had not gone far before they met an impassable barrier; uprooted trees were blocking the road, and downed electric wires whipped and lashed like dangerous snakes. Smocko threw up. The family retreated to the Bogerts and "watched more boats being swamped."

The inaction was impossible for Ned. He paced and fretted, and finally he convinced Margaret that they should set out again and try to get through to the highway by another route. They stopped in a hamlet and asked directions from a local man. He directed them to a dirt road that skirted an inlet of the Sound and had no electric wires. They joined a short line of cars attempting the same escape route. Every time a downed tree or other obstruction blocked the road, the men from the little cavalcade—including George, who was now seventeen—got out of their vehicles, trousers rolled up to their knees, and waded out to move it. One time they had to move a rowboat.

This time they made it to the highway. They got as far as New Haven, and there the storm stopped. Suddenly it was bright. The gutters were full of umbrellas, turned inside out, rushing along like strange little sailboats. They drove out onto the bridge over the Quinnipiac River, whose water was up to road level. And then the light at the far end of the bridge turned red. They had to sit there on the bridge, along with a lot of other cars, and wait. They watched the raging brown torrent and wondered how the bridge could withstand that weight of water. "But," said Margaret, "the bridge held! We made it. And because we were all together, it was an adventure. Nobody got *too* scared."

Hurricane Carol had followed almost the same path as the infamous Long Island Express, which had devastated the East Coast in 1938. At that time, no weather warnings had been issued north of New York City, so Rhode Island was unprepared. A tidal surge had flooded Providence, and hundreds of people in the city and up the coast had lost their lives. Carol's winds of 120 miles per hour had pushed storm waves over the islands and beaches of New England, with flood marks almost up to those of 1938. Property damage was dreadful, but this time the death toll was much lower because advance warnings had been issued.

In 1952, the whole Colbert family drove up to New Brunswick for the summer. Ned was writing a book and brought his work with him so that he would not suffer from idleness.

Ned Manning had died suddenly a few years earlier. (Margaret had been to his funeral, and it had been a bad experience. She said, "The minister droned on about 'miserable sinners,' and it grated on me. Surely of all people, Uncle Ned had been one of the most innocent and upright.") Bess had moved back to Canada. She was in a house that overlooked Sugarloaf Mountain and the Kennebecasis River. She found a cottage nearby for the Colberts; it was primitive accommodation, but not impossibly so, and the boys had a wonderful summer building rafts and putting sails on them, and generally enjoying the water.

The New Brunswick poverty was striking and, for the first time, Margaret became aware of how backward the province was. Bess's only source of water was an open cistern in a corner of her grassy plot, from which she dipped up water as she needed it. Neither her house nor the Colberts' cottage was electrified. (Light was from oil lamps.) No laundromat existed in Saint John. A Chinese laundry was available, but after Margaret collected her first load from that establishment, the family refused to wear the clothes because they smelled so unpleasant.

Margaret wanted the boys to see their great-grandfather's museum in Saint John. She loaded them into the car and took them into the city. The New Brunswick Museum was still there, but the paleontology section had vanished. The museum had been taken over by the Saint John's Historical Society. It held exhibits such as yellowed documents, collections of domestic items, wagon wheels. Some pieces of charred wood from the Great Fire of 1877 were of interest—Margaret remembered her father telling how, at the age of six, he had watched his own home burn to the ground in that conflagration. She tried to find somebody who knew what had happened to the fossil collections. Nobody there had even heard of George Frederic Matthew.

∼ 11 ∼

Artist in Leonia

Few artists in any discipline are able to earn a living from their creativity. The vast majority must find other work to support their art. Many shunt their skills into practical applications—writers become editors, visual artists take up drafting. Much can be learned from such applications, and on a certain level, they can be satisfying and enjoyable; however, they use the same energies—the same neurons—as original art, and imagination and creativity are lost to overstimulation and exhaustion. Drawing fossil bones at the American Museum of Natural History had intrigued the part of Margaret's nature that was controlled, ordered, and enjoyed minute detail. But after a day at work, she had rarely had much creative energy left. Motherhood and homemaking were physically exhausting, but they left Margaret's creative batteries relatively undrained.

However, anyone who has brought up a child, let alone five children, understands the problem of time. Days are fragmented, uninterrupted hours a luxury; ten minutes are snatched here, twenty—with luck—there. And so, through cluttered and sometimes frustrating years, Margaret squeezed her art into the little spaces left over from motherhood. And she was productive. A more difficult hurdle was the attitude held by almost everyone—perhaps including herself—that art was an outlet, rather than a raison d'être. Commissions made it easier. Working for someone other than oneself, and for pay, validates tasks that otherwise feel too much like fun to be work.

In 1942, Ned drafted Margaret to design a logo for the Society of Vertebrate Paleontology (SVP). After rejecting several preliminary ideas, she produced a design of a Marsh pick—the special hammer used by vertebrate paleontologists—head uppermost, with part of a vertebral column crossing

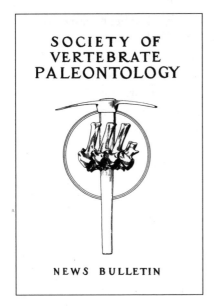

SOCIETY OF
VERTEBRATE
PALEONTOLOGY

NEWS BULLETIN

Society of Vertebrate Paleontology logo;
Margaret's design and lettering.

its shaft. A friend, Bob Salkin, modeled the logo in copper and white metal. Another acquaintance, George Frost, cast it in silver and gold for pins and tie tacs. The society paid her nothing, but she received ample gratification because the logo is still in use. At the SVP annual meeting, on October 16, 1993, before a loudly applauding seven-hundred-strong audience, she was presented with an award recognizing "Her Artistic Gifts and Her Design of the Emblem of the Society of Vertebrate Paleontology."

Most of the jobs Margaret obtained as a freelance illustrator were restorations, honing the skills she had developed while still working at the Natch. Over the Leonia years, she illustrated many magazine and journal articles and several books. *Natural History,* the American Museum publication, continued to throw occasional jobs her way. Ned quite frequently wrote articles for the magazine, and these she illustrated on a regular basis. She illustrated his *Natural History* articles on ancient giraffes and on pandas in 1938; on dogs, including the cover design, in 1939; on mammoths and on cats, in 1940; one titled "Animals that Went to Sea" in 1941; and "Circus without Spectators" and the "Triumph of the Mammals" in 1942. Also in 1942 she drew a restoration of *Xenocranium,* a small extinct mammal, for an article Ned published in *Frontiers,* the magazine of the Philadelphia Academy of Sciences. In 1947 Ned wrote a *Natural History* article on the little dinosaurs of Ghost Ranch; thus, for the first of many times, Margaret drew a restoration of *Coelophysis.*

Sometime in the mid-1940s, *Natural History* asked her to design a cover for the magazine. Margaret painted in full color the head of *Pachycephalo-saurus*, a bony-headed and warty dinosaur, gazing in benign surprise at a tiny shrew-like mammal that happened to be on an eye-level branch. At the last minute, the magazine decided against using it. They decided it was better and cheaper to use photographs for covers. It was difficult to see how they could send a cameraman out into the bush to obtain a photograph of *Pachycephalosaurus*; however, the powers-that-be knew best. They turned Margaret's painting into a giant-sized postcard to sell in the museum shop.

In order that Margaret could have her work materials ready to use, and to avoid having to stow everything out of reach of the small boys, Ned mounted a regular foam-centered door on four brass pipes for a table. He fastened this table to the wall under a small window in the basement of the Park Avenue house and set up a good light over it. He constructed a box hinged onto the door; this would shut like a deep lid and fasten with a hook. Margaret could safely leave work-in-progress, bottles of ink, paints, and brushes, and whatever else she was using on the table, with its lid fastened down. A final inspired touch was that the lid was lined with soft board into which she could stick push pins; thus, she could post preliminary drawings, zoo sketches, or simply shopping lists and messages to herself.

Margaret relied heavily on books, on Ned, and on other experts to ensure the credibility and accuracy of her illustrations. As granddaughter, daughter, and wife of paleontologists, she had been absorbing fossil science since childhood. Thus, in spite of her lack of formal scientific education, she had a keen understanding of the discipline. And she brought to her work an expert observer's eye.

Margaret's "eye" is, in fact, a special attribute that extends beyond her work. She *sees* shapes, patterns, forms missed by most people—until she gently points them out. In 1993, her son Philip wrote:

> To Margaret there seems to be a beauty in everything she looks at in the natural world, however commonplace and unworthy of comment it might seem to others. You could take a stroll with her down a woodland path . . . and lo, within a hundred yards or so of that lane she could bring you face to face with the exquisite beauty of a clump of ferns; you would find yourself for the first time enjoying the bizarre contours of a bracken fungus, the strange colorations of a slime mold in a small rivulet, the patterns of sunlight on a mossy forest floor. . . . And she would do this without really *saying anything!* It was an uncanny, almost zen-like experience, and so many of [us] delighted in the restorative quality of a

Preparing fossils for transport from the field; scratchboard illustration from Millions of Years Ago, *1958. (Courtesy of Edwin Colbert)*

walk with Margaret. . . . For some years the family maintained membership in the Greenbrook Sanctuary, a natural woodland atop the Hudson River Palisades on the New Jersey side of the river. I suspect this was done to meet the burgeoning demands of family and friends alike to go strolling with Margaret!

The time she had spent sketching at the Natch was very useful. The hours at the zoo were also invaluable; watching and drawing modern creatures helped her deduce how extinct relatives would have moved and interacted, which made her illustrations plausible.

Sometimes a job required color, in which case Margaret's preference was for gouache (opaque water color) or acrylic paint. However, most of the work for publications was in pen-and-ink, or on scratchboard; crisp contrast and allowance for reduction were required, and it was cheaper to print than color.

The medium of scratchboard was one of Margaret's favorites. A scratchboard illustration looks, and feels in spirit, similar to a wood engraving. Scratchboard is heavy card, coated with a white clay substance covered with a layer of black ink. The artist cuts through the black layer to the white base, leaving white lines. Several preliminary drawings and a high level of skill are necessary because lines cannot be erased.

In 1955 and 1956, Ned was at work on a book for children, titled *Millions of Years Ago*. The book is an overview of evolution, and the illustrations, all of them Margaret's scratchboards, depict many different creatures. The last picture shows Leonardo da Vinci hunting fossils.

Scratchboard illustrations, including Leonardo da Vinci fossil-hunting, 1958. From Millions of Years Ago. (Courtesy of Edwin Colbert)

Jurassic scene, gouache painting, 16 x 12 in., from The Age of Reptiles. *(Courtesy of Weidenfeld and Nicolson, London, England)*

For the frontispiece of *Millions of Years Ago*, Margaret had presented the editors with a drawing on stipple board, which requires a different technique. The editors turned it down because they wanted all scratchboards. However, the drawing is an example of the unusual way her mind works: a hand riffles the pages of a book; as they open, the pages become stratigraphic layers beneath a hilly landscape. Margaret named it "Turning the Pages of Geology." One of her favorite projects, the book was published in 1958.

Ned's book *The Age of Reptiles*, published in 1965, was a much larger project. Margaret used pen-and-ink and gouache for the illustrations for this volume.

Over the years, different types of freelance "plums" fell into Margaret's lap. As they were growing up, she occasionally distributed the boys among her friends for brief periods and flew out to Berkeley to spend time with her mother. On one of these Californian sorties, Margaret renewed her acquaintance with Charles Camp, a recognized historian as well as a paleontologist. Margaret drove out to visit him, his wife Jessie, and their children, whom she used to baby-sit. She found them at the site of a house they were having built on a hillside in Orinda, east of Berkeley. They were cooking on a wood-stove in the open and sleeping on beds under the stars. The naked frame of the new house was equipped only with a bathroom and a telephone. The unconventional family was quite unfazed by the light drizzle that was soaking their bedding. It would dry out—the weather was warm.

Subsequently she kept in touch with the Camps and the connection paid dividends in the shape of an interesting commission in the late 1960s. Charles Camp was working on a history of southern California since the beginning of time, and he asked Margaret to illustrate it for him. The book, *Earth Song*, published in 1970, is a slim volume that intersperses well-researched history and prehistory with passages that can only be described as purple prose. Among the dozen or so scratchboard illustrations by Margaret are representations of prehistoric fish, amphibians, reptiles, and long-horned buffaloes; early mammals and birds trapped in a tar pit; and life in a Chumash Indian village.

In 1960, the National Science Foundation initiated a major textbook project. At that time school biology textbooks were very poor, and none mentioned evolution. It was important that this be redressed. The NSF convened a large group of scientists from all over the country at the University of Colorado in Boulder to write the new books under a crash program called Biological Science Curriculum Studies. Ned was one of the scientists, and Margaret was hired as an illustrator. They spent the whole summer in Boulder. They slept in a university dormitory, ate in the student cafeteria, and worked in another building. Three groups of books were planned, each with a different emphasis; one group focused on ecology, one on genetics, and the third on molecular biology. The writers wrote all morning. After lunch, they circulated their morning's production, then gathered to agree on modifications and to select pictures from the artists' work. Ned had a roving assignment to check that evolution was treated accurately and appropriately in all three groups.

Four artists worked together in one room. Among their resources were some of Margaret's drawings to be used as reference material—referred to as "scrap"—for guidance. Margaret was a little worried by this. "I told them *not* to count on them," she said. She was assigned to do scratchboards of glyptodonts—an extinct mammal that was similar to an armadillo but had a high shell like a turtle instead of jointed armor—and several other creatures. But mainly she drew fruit flies, *Drosophila*—those ubiquitous insects that are always turning up in genetics research. She enjoyed it—it was something quite new and different. She was given normal flies to draw, and then

Bust of Will Matthew, 1945.

instructed to give some of them curled wings in the diagrams that illustrated inherited characteristics.

Technical illustration brought in a little money and kept Margaret closely in touch with the paleontological world. It satisfied her paternal genes, but the genes from her mother's side of the family also clamored for release. She needed to be involved in freer work that would allow her spirit to fly. She lived in the right town; Leonia was home to several artists of considerable ability who were willing to share their expertise and facilities.

Alice Sharp was an amateur potter. Her basement was fully equipped to serve her craft with ample work surfaces, clay, potter's wheels, a kiln, and tools for sculpting clay. She allowed people to come and use her equipment, and Margaret went to Alice's basement once a week for several years in the 1940s. Among many other works, she modeled there a small ceramic head of her infant son Danny.

In 1945, pregnant with Charles, she sculpted the bust of William Diller Matthew, her father, fifteen years after his death. She modeled from memory with the help of numerous photographs. It was a difficult task but one that gave her enormous pleasure as her father's features emerged slowly beneath her fingers. Otto Falkenbach, one of the preparators at the American Museum whom she used to visit as a child, cast the bust in plaster from her water-clay original. Casts of this sculpture are today found at the American Museum,

Watercolor self-portrait and watercolor sketch of Ned, 1947.

at the University of California at Berkeley, and in the Colbert Library at the Museum of Northern Arizona, Flagstaff.

Charles Chapman was an interesting and inventive painter and a member of the National Academy. Margaret found much of his work quite stunning. For a lot of his paintings he used automobile lacquers, which, Margaret commented, "behave in peculiar and difficult ways, which was why he liked to use them!" The backgrounds of his compositions were very loose, and he used his brush to add touches that made the whole make sense. He created meaning out of obscure beginnings. Margaret said, "It was like looking at a cloud, thinking it looked like something, but not quite; and imagining a shadow here, a highlight there, which would allow that 'something' to emerge." He also experimented with oils, using tricky techniques that were difficult to handle, but inspiring. Margaret worked with Mr. Chapman for several years. She painted quite a few portraits with him. Even after she had stopped doing portraits, he would summon her to come over when he had an especially interesting model.

In 1947 she set herself the challenge of painting all the members of her family, including herself, in watercolor. She did them life-size, without any preliminary drawing. "It was quite a trick, but I was into trying hard in those days." She had Ned and the five children sit, and the portraits had to be very quick. "Watercolor is wonderful for that." When Dan and Charles grew up and moved away, they requested their portraits. Margaret still has the others.

‿∴ 12 ∵‿

A Year of Misery

When I come shyly knocking
at your lovely pearly gate,
I know not when the time may be,
but be it soon or late,
These favors I would humbly ask
(I never was a shirk)
Please make me young and strong again
and give me lots of work.
    —*Kate Matthew Minor, 1952*

The Berkeley doctor said the cancer in Kate Minor's bladder had probably lurked for as long as fifteen years. She had complained for some time, especially on automobile trips, of what she called coyly the "curse of old age." She dosed herself for years with a concoction of mineral jelly and honey, which she believed helped her "plumbing." In the early spring of 1955 her symptoms dramatically worsened, and examination revealed a tumor that had already spread beyond help.

For Ralph it was especially hard because he had also lost his first wife to cancer. He was frank about the situation when he wrote to the family, but he said, "We don't mention *that word*—we don't tell her that's what it is." Margaret said, "I'm sure Mother knew, but she played along." With kindness and love, everybody tiptoed carefully around the topic that must have been overwhelming Kate's consciousness. Kate, too, avoided the issue, no doubt believing that it would make it easier for everybody else. One day, however, she asked Margaret to bring her an anatomy book; she simply wanted to know what was happening to her body. Margaret wondered then if Kate were not longing for someone to tell her the unvarnished truth and give her permission to talk about it.

Betty and Margaret flew out to California by turns to be with their mother. In May, on Margaret's last visit, Ralph's older daughter, Mary Lou Lee, was also in the house. All day, Margaret and Mary Lou worked staunchly at keeping Kate's spirits up, even as she was visibly weakening and slipping away from them. At night, in the twin beds of the guest room, they both sobbed, exhausted by grief and what they felt was obligatory good cheer.

Kate died in June 1955, on Betty's watch. She did not have to go into the hospital, and she died peacefully, without much pain. She had lived a full and interesting life, with two exceptionally happy marriages. Margaret knew she had wanted very much to be a "remarkable old lady." She thought briefly, "Oh, what a pity she won't make that!" and then realized that her mother had been seventy-nine. She had not done so badly. "And she *was* remarkable. She always had such indomitable energy that I had never noticed she was getting old."

Margaret flew out for the funeral. She was asked if she wanted to see her mother's body, but she declined, knowing she would rather remember her alive. Together, Betty and she performed the sad but cathartic rite of sorting out their mother's belongings—the clothes still heavy with Kate's fragrance; well-worn shoes, with their particular pathos; the few items of jewelry. Margaret searched high and low for one pin. Evocative of a sunflower and designed specifically for Kate, it was one of the pieces she had made at the Coles' house. It seemed extremely important that it be found; it never was.

A year later, Ralph, Betty, Margaret, Bill, and Gladys took Kate's ashes to New Brunswick, and placed them in the Matthew crypt at Gondola Point, next to Will Matthew and baby Christine.

Kate Minor's verse at the head of this chapter serves as a suitable epitaph. She titled it "My Prayer, at Seventy-five." It appeared in *Christmas Greetings and Other Verses*, a book of her poems that she and Ralph printed in 1952 at the Oquaga Press. The poems are simple, rhyming, and gently humorous; they are about home, family, Christmas, with an underlying horror of the violence and strife "outside." Each poem is accompanied by a tiny linoleum-cut print of a rose, for example, or a sprig of mistletoe, or a fir cone; mainly executed in black and white, a few have a light color wash. Some of these prints are by Margaret; the rest are signed Lee Thayer (Aunty Em).

Troubles rarely come singly, and 1955 turned into the year Margaret would prefer to forget. Soon after Kate died, George's emotional health required another spell of professional help. Margaret believed that her distraction and her frequent absences from home through the months of Kate's illness were contributing factors.

Ned was firmly of the opinion that small liberal-arts establishments were the ideal college education. Accordingly, in 1953, he and George had spent a lot of time on the back terrace of the Park Avenue house perusing brochures from the smaller colleges, and they finally picked Carleton College in Northfield, Minnesota. George had breezed through high school, and Carleton accepted him eagerly and gave him a scholarship. He entered college in the fall of 1954 at the age of seventeen.

Margaret said, "George came home that first Christmas and didn't want to go back to school. Foolishly we persuaded him to do so, talking about his future and so on." He was, however, obviously miserable, and not doing well at his studies. Later Margaret blamed herself bitterly for not listening to what he was really saying, for not recognizing that he was perhaps not yet ready for college. In any event, he had only been back at Carleton for a few weeks when the authorities sent him home after an episode when he had been unable to control his temper. It was the wrong time. He was at home with an over-extended father and a mother preoccupied with events in California. Both parents were again at a loss as to what George needed.

However, a spell in the hospital once more gave George the strength to pull himself around. After his recovery, he began to look for new and positive directions in life.

But the fates had not yet finished with Margaret. She had for some months been suffering from increasingly heavy menstrual bleeding, which lasted more than two weeks at a time; possibly the tension and anxiety of the preceding months exacerbated the trouble. In any case, by the fall of 1955 her periods were lasting thirty days, and it was time for action. Her doctor advised a hysterectomy.

The night before she was to be admitted to Englewood Hospital for the surgery, Ned took her to a drive-in movie at Palisades Park. She sat, his arm around her, and tried to get involved in the movie. It was not enough; she was afraid of what the medicos might find, depressed at the abrupt end of her "womanhood," as she could not help but see it, and desolated by what the year had already dealt her.

In spite of her apprehensions, the operation went well; her convalescence was long but uneventful. And it was at this time that Ned was working on his children's book, *Millions of Years Ago*. Margaret hired some extra help to look after the boys and the house, and went in with Ned to the Natch and worked on the illustrations there. She had the time she needed without interruption, and as the work began to engage her, she started to enjoy herself. It was the best antidote for her sadness.

13

Ghost Ranch

Back in the spring of 1947, Ned had struggled long and hard with bureaucracy to obtain a government permit to collect fossils from the Petrified Forest National Monument. (It did not achieve national park status until December 8, 1962.) He didn't head for Arizona until well into that summer, the precious document at last in his pocket. With him were George Whitaker, a paleontology technician from the American Museum of Natural History, and Tom Ierardi from Leonia, who came along as a volunteer. After seeing Charles Camp's phytosaurs in the Berkeley museum in 1945, Ned was curious to see the Triassic beds from which the fossils had been excavated. Ghost Ranch, fifteen miles north of the tiny town of Abiquiu in north-central New Mexico, was barely out of the way. They obtained permission from the owner of the ranch, Arthur Pack, and set up camp for—as they thought—a couple of days.

Their adventures are related in detail in Ned's autobiography, *Digging Into the Past,* but a sketch of what happened is appropriate here. George Whitaker came upon a small claw and a few bone fragments on a talus slope. Ned examined them and recognized them as possibly belonging to the very early dinosaur, *Coelophysis.* A few vertebrae and pieces of pelvis and limb bones from this creature had been found in Triassic rocks of northern New Mexico more than seventy years earlier; they were now in the American Museum of Natural History as part of the Cope Collection. (Edward Drinker Cope of Philadelphia was one of the early giants of paleontology. His enormous collection of fossils was purchased by the American Museum in 1895, and one of William Diller Matthew's first tasks when he joined the museum had been to catalog this collection.) Because Ned's

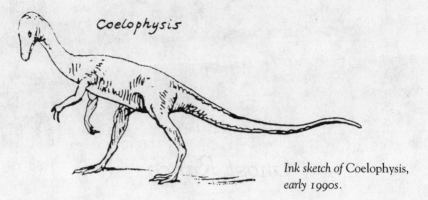

Ink sketch of Coelophysis, *early 1990s.*

specialty was Triassic fauna, he was familiar with the museum fragments of *Coelophysis*.

The trio worked up the talus slope toward the red rocks of the Triassic Chinle Formation from which it derived, and as they went, they found more bone fragments. When they reached the rocks, they found what Ned described in *Digging into the Past* as "a paleontological treasure beyond one's wildest dreams." As they dug, they found not only the skulls, jaws, and teeth essential for a definitive description of a beast, but many articulated and partially articulated skeletons. Almost all the bones were of *Coelophysis*. An occasional phytosaur and a few other creatures turned up, but the vast majority were of the little dinosaur from two hundred million years ago.

Suffice to say that at the risk of annoying Washington bureaucrats, Ned scrubbed his Petrified Forest plans and opted to spend that summer at Ghost Ranch. The American Museum dispatched more help, and they quarried out many blocks of stone containing hundreds of fossils and shipped them back to the Natch to be studied.

It is estimated that the remains of as many as ten thousand *Coelophysis* are present in this one locality. *Coelophysis* was a carnivore—a small one by dinosaur standards. The biggest *Coelophysis* excavated so far is only about eleven feet from nose to end of long tail, its body the size of a large turkey; most are much smaller. The puzzle is how they ended up there, and why; carnivores—at least modern carnivores—tend not to congregate in large herds. So how and why did so many die at once? One theory suggests a catastrophic flood; this satisfies some of the questions, but not why other species are practically absent from the quarry. It is a conundrum that keeps paleontologists and geologists arguing happily.

Before leaving *Coelophysis* to the scientists, it should be mentioned that in 1977, on the strength of Ned's quarry, the U.S. Department of the Interior made Ghost Ranch a National Natural Landmark. Later, *Coelophysis* became New Mexico's state fossil, and a restoration of the reptile is the logo of the recently built New Mexico Museum of Natural History in Albuquerque.

Margaret visited Ghost Ranch for the first time in 1949. She and Ned flew out to Albuquerque, rented a bright red Volkswagen Karmann Ghia, and drove the 120 miles north to the ranch. Ned had, of course, described to Margaret the Ghost Ranch landscape and told her it was lovely—told her to imagine Zion National Park on a smaller, more comprehensible scale. She was nonetheless unprepared. Cliffs and mesas formed the backdrop to the ranch, stratified in shades of white and lavender-gray, in yellows from lemon through mustard, in reds from rust to plum, the whole set off by a deep blue sky. Even in the hard light of high noon, the colors glowed. At sunrise or sunset, they were glorious. Coming from the muted gray-green hues of the east, Margaret found it almost too much—her breathlessness had little to do with the 6,500-foot altitude.

The ranch itself consisted of a small group of adobe buildings in a green oasis. Loud with robins, flycatchers, grosbeaks, orioles, and chickadees, the tall cottonwood trees cast deep pools of shade. Arthur Pack and his wife, Phoebe, welcomed them and entertained them. George Whitaker was there again and he undertook to drive Margaret up the rough track to the quarry to see the dig in process. "I'd never ridden in a jeep before. He scared me half out of my wits!"

Ghost Ranch is a piece of heaven on earth—except for its bugs. A special breed of "no-see-um" haunts the ranch. They are not really fussy where they chew, but seem to have a special liking for the hairline, where they raise itching welts and weals, well out of proportion to their own size. Some people become allergic to the tiny horrors: Tom Ierardi returned to Ghost Ranch in 1948 and was so blitzed by the bugs that he had to be taken—eyes swollen shut, gasping for air—to the hospital. Margaret developed allergic symptoms during later visits and learned to arm herself with copious amounts of insect repellent and to go indoors when the bugs were biting.

The summer of 1953 saw the entire Colbert family traveling west. They were driving two cars: the family car (a Chevrolet Carryall) and a similar museum vehicle. Thirteen-year-old Philip was so ashamed of the Chevy that when he was in it, he scrunched down out of sight. That year the Packs had donated the ranch to the Presbyterian Church; they had taken up temporary residence in a trailer near the entrance to the ranch. The Colberts were assigned the Ghost House for the two or three days of their stay. It was the original homestead of the ranch, built around 1830, and rife with legends and ghosts. They climbed out of the cars and explored the tiny building. Three of the boys went to investigate the bathroom. Margaret noted a strange taut silence and she peered over someone's shoulder. In the bathtub sat a scorpion, tail arched over its back, awaiting a victim.

After Ghost Ranch, the Colberts drove on to Flagstaff, Arizona. There they met up with Charles and Grace Cole, who were, as usual, out west for the summer, buying Native American silver and other artwork for their annual fall show.

Ned worked for several weeks that summer with the Museum of Northern Arizona in Flagstaff. The Colberts stayed for the duration in a cottage at Lake Mary, a dozen miles southwest of the city. Ned took the three older boys out into the desert with him to collect fossils. Margaret, Danny, Charles, and Grace and her two children, Kay and Jay—occasionally joined by Charles Cole—explored the pueblo villages and other special places in the area. In Zuni one afternoon they learned there was to be a native dance. They climbed onto a suitable viewing point, a low flat roof, and sat down and waited. Suddenly, directly beneath them, a drum began to beat. To their consternation they realized they were sitting on top of a ceremonial kiva; this was most inappropriate, and they scurried down to ground level and sat among a group of Zuni Indians. Some Zuni women had big woolen blankets, which they were holding up to make shade against the cruel sun, and they invited the children to join them in the welcome shadow. It was Margaret's first Native American dance and her first experience of the brilliant and strange kachina costumes, of the insistent and eerily moving chants and drum beats. Etiquette did not permit sketching or photography while the dance was in progress, but when she got back to Lake Mary, she did some quick drawings from memory.

It was twelve years before Margaret returned to Ghost Ranch. In 1965 Ned organized a trip to show off the Triassic of the Southwest to eminent colleagues A. W. (Fuzz) Crompton, director of the Peabody Museum at Yale and originally from South Africa; George Haas of Hebrew University in Israel; and Mario Barbarena of the University of Rio Grande do Sul in Brazil. Together with Margaret, and Fuzz's son Peter and a young friend, the "Four Continents Trip" set off from Leonia, again in two vehicles. On the itinerary were the canyon country of southern Utah and northern Arizona, Petrified Forest, and Flagstaff; Ghost Ranch, of course, was on the way.

Their route led through some very barren terrain. Margaret made some remark about the desert, and George Haas said, "You call *this* desert?" (Later that year, she and Ned went to Israel and George showed them the Negev

Desert. Then she understood.) As they approached Ghost Ranch and George Haas saw the colored cliffs, Margaret noted, "He was speechless for once. He just waggled his head in his broad hat."

Ghost Ranch was then into its fourth year as an adult study center of the Presbyterian Church. In addition to seminars on religious themes, James W. Hall, director since 1961, included in his vision for the center a variety of courses normally considered secular. He believed that in such a place of peace and beauty, getting in touch with the environment, the earth, and the stars was as spiritual as any devotional activity. Under his direction, Ghost Ranch was to become vitally concerned with ecology and with nurture of the environment—this at a very early stage in a national movement. From the handbook issued to all visitors and seminar participants, *Welcome to Ghost Ranch:*

> Ghost Ranch is committed to a program of soil conservation and restoration in the hope that over the years the 21,000 acres will become an example of what can be achieved in this region.
>
> This commitment is not alone economical, but ethical and theological as well. Its roots are found in the 'ecology' of the ranch. . . . Christian education, in our understandings at Ghost Ranch, includes an appreciation of the natural processes by which the land and the living things upon it have achieved their characteristic forms.

This dynamic director was not one to miss an opportunity when it presented itself. In the couple of days the Four Continents stayed at the ranch, Jim Hall press-ganged Ned and Fuzz into agreeing to run a paleontology seminar the following year. He soon became a keen amateur paleontologist himself.

After that first seminar in 1966, Fuzz Crompton and Ned took turns running the courses—Fuzz one year, Ned the next—and Margaret went with Ned almost every time. Jim Hall's wife, Ruth, became one of her close friends: "Ruth Hall was remarkable. She remembered everyone that ever came to the ranch and greeted them by name. She truly enjoyed people. She was also crazy about fossils." She became a competent amateur paleontologist and a member of the Society of Vertebrate Paleontology. Early on in her years at Ghost Ranch, she found a phytosaur. She was determined to prepare it herself and worked for years to extract the bones from the matrix. One year she spent two months at Yale with Fuzz Crompton working in the preparation laboratories of the Peabody Museum to polish her skills.

Oil portrait of Ruth Hall, late 1970s.

She took many of the children who came to the ranch with their parents on fossil-finding expeditions that the youngsters found unforgettable. A fine little paleontology museum at Ghost Ranch was founded in 1989 and named for her.

In addition to her abilities as a paleontologist Ruth was an amateur artist. One summer she and Margaret decided to go out into the desert to do some oil painting. They set up their easels, and Ruth started a landscape. While she worked, Margaret painted her portrait. When they returned to the ranch, Margaret asked her to hold in her hand a fossil—a piece of her phytosaur. She rapidly sketched the hand and then worked it into the portrait. This portrait now hangs in the Ruth Hall Paleontology Museum at Ghost Ranch. But, Margaret said, "It was all done in one morning and was never really finished."

Tragically, Ruth developed Alzheimer's disease. For the last years of Jim's directorship, she was a ghost of herself. She retained her gracious manner for a long time, but little else. Her husband was always there at her elbow, helping her through impossible situations. Eventually she deteriorated to a point where she had to go into a rest home. Ned and Margaret visited her in a Santa Fe nursing home in 1991 after Jim had died. "We tried to get some response from her, but there was nothing left."

Another name inextricably connected with Ghost Ranch is Georgia O'Keefe. She lived in a small adobe house just outside the boundaries of the ranch. She had first come to Ghost Ranch in 1934, at the age of forty-seven and had bought her house in 1940. She was sixty years old when Ned first met her, in 1947—a difficult time for her, because her husband, photographer Arthur Stieglitz, had died the previous year. She was struggling to settle his estate—commuting back and forth from New York—and to settle herself after a strange and stormy relationship.

Georgia O'Keeffe had been curious when she heard of the discovery of the fossil quarry, and she decided to investigate. Ned was working at the quarry when she appeared over a rise with—incongruously—four nuns in habits. O'Keeffe and Ned became quite good friends. Ned identified for her the rocks, minerals, and bones that she had found beautiful and picked up in the desert. She invited him to dinner at her house several times, and once or twice they went on picnics together. Ned knew well her reputation for prickliness and for being a recluse, but he said, "I had no problem with her because I never broached the subject of art." Actually, Ned's gentle and unobtrusive attitude was probably a primary factor in the friendship.

One year in the early 1970s, Jim Hall arranged for both Margaret and Ned to visit O'Keeffe. Ned had not seen her for many years. She was by then in her eighties, and her eyesight was failing. They met under the portal of her house at eight o'clock in the morning. The house was a classic small western house, built of genuine adobe, with real wooden vigas. Under the portal, which went around the three sides of the courtyard, were tables laden with stones and bones. Margaret said, "We had a short but very pleasant conversation. She was a beautiful old lady."

It is tantalizing to wonder what relationship might have developed between the two women had they met earlier, alone, and informally. A quote attributed to O'Keeffe is displayed in the Ghost Ranch headquarters building: "Because there were no flowers, I began picking up bones. . . . It never occurred to me that they had anything to do with death. They were very lovely."

Did O'Keeffe know of Margaret's talents? Probably not. In awe of her, Margaret was too shy to mention that she too was an artist, or even to discuss her own particular fascination with the forms of bones; because Ned was so careful not to mention art to Georgia, he would not have talked of Margaret's abilities. Although their art took very different directions, Margaret and Georgia would surely have had much to talk about.

~ 14 ~

A Taste for Travel

It seemed to Margaret at times that Ned was more often away from home than not. Either he was in distant parts of the United States doing field-work or he was abroad for meetings, conferences, congresses. While the five boys were young, Margaret accepted being left behind; her fare to far-away places was beyond their financial means, and the logistics of organiz-ing five youngsters for extended periods were daunting. Ned's letters home from his peregrinations were full of complaints of the hardships of travel, and Margaret was amused. "Everything was always horrible and awful," she said. "He did it, I knew, to make me feel better about having to stay at home."

But the boys grew up, and the cash-flow situation eased. Accompanying Ned became a possibility, and in 1958, Margaret left the shores of North America for the first time. Ned needed an objective for every excursion or activity. The celebration in England of the centennial of Charles Darwin's *On the Origin of the Species by Means of Natural Selection* was a reasonable excuse for a journey across the Atlantic.

Against her better judgment, Margaret agreed to go by sea. She thought that if the ship were big enough she might escape seasickness, and it might even be fun. Accordingly, they boarded a large ocean liner, the *Atlantic*, in New York. No sooner had they left the harbor than the sky thickened and darkened, spume flew from the mounting crests of the waves. The storm followed the ship the entire way across the Atlantic. Huge as the vessel was, it pitched and rolled with what seemed studied malevolence. In spite of the storm, it was impossibly hot. The ship had just been overhauled and fitted with air conditioning, but this broke down within a few nautical miles of New York. The Colberts were fortunate to have an outside cabin with reasonable ventilation. Inside cabins were uninhabitable; their miserable occupants slept in the corridors, in which the super-heated air at least moved a little.

Margaret and Ned had not known they should sign up for deck chairs and they had nowhere to sit except on the beds in their cabin. Sometimes they appropriated other people's deck chairs, but they had to keep their eyes open for the approach of the legitimate owners. Passengers were not allowed on the open decks because of the weather, and the only way to get exercise was to stumble around the enclosed decks, tripping over the feet of people occupying the redoubtable chairs. Dramamine made Margaret dry-mouthed and dazed—and barely touched her nausea. "It simply prevented me from getting rid of what was troubling me," she said, and made a solemn vow never ever to set foot on another ship.

In spite of Margaret's fears to the contrary, the voyage did come to an end. The ship steamed into Zeebrugge in Belgium. The Colberts reeled gratefully ashore and were met by a Dutch couple named Hooijer, who had spent some time in New York at the American Museum of Natural History.

The Hooijers had a car and a driver, and had planned an itinerary to show the Colberts all over Belgium and Holland. The first destination was Brugge; Margaret was surprised and delighted at every turn. The town was more or less exactly as it had been in its heyday before about 1600, when the estuary on which it was located silted up so that ships could no longer use it as a seaport. Unlike ghost towns in the United States, it was full of people who lived in the old houses. The late-fourteenth-century town hall was a veritable palace. On an upper floor was a tiny chapel; the view from its windows revealed that it was actually inside the big town church, just above the chancel.

"A costume parade took place in the town square, I suppose mainly for tourists, but so snappily done. There was so much to digest that I wanted to go back home—*not* by ship—think about it for a month, and then come back and go on with the trip!"

They visited polders—areas reclaimed from the ocean by means of dikes. "Each polder had been built at a different time and the original houses were still there. In the oldest ones, the cattle lived in the same house as the people. They were strong roomy buildings and the animals lived downstairs so that their warmth rose and kept the living areas toasty."

At the border on their way into France, Margaret received a different kind of surprise. "The sanitary facilities there were unisex. I went into a booth and a whole family followed me in and made themselves comfortable too." She recovered quickly from this culture shock and they drove into Paris. There, on July 8, she and Ned celebrated their twenty-fifth wedding anniversary, in honor of which the Hooijers presented them with a tiny silver spoon. Then it was time for Darwin and his centennial and the Colberts flew across the Channel to London.

Several trips were organized for participants of the celebration, and one of the organizers turned out to be a particularly excellent guide. He knew his geography, paleontology, and history and made the trips extremely interesting. One such excursion took them along the south coast. On the bus was a Dane, Dr. Christensen. The tour guide would say, "We're coming to such and such a place, where King Alfred defeated the Danes." Christensen maintained a dignified silence. At last they arrived at a location where the Danes had defeated King Alfred, and Dr. Christensen stood up and took a bow. Everyone applauded him with enthusiasm. He said solemnly, "We Danes are not so fearsome as we used to be."

Another bus took the celebrants to Darwin's home, Down House, in Kent; Darwin and his wife had moved from London's Gower Street to this abode in 1842 to escape the stresses of city life. Down House is a mere sixteen miles from London, but the driver managed to lose his way. After a circuitous journey, the bus at last pulled up in front of the rambling country house. On the back porch of the house was a wicker chair—Darwin's "thinking chair." Everyone took turns sitting in it and gazing over the flower beds, shrubberies, and green lawns. It was essentially exactly as it had been one hundred years ago and, for this group of people for whom Darwin was held in such veneration, it was almost a religious experience.

Once the celebration was over, the Colberts rented a car and motored up to Scotland. Margaret wanted to see the region from which her forebears had come. The Matthew family had been farmers from the Carse of Gowrie, between Dundee and Perth, on the Firth of Tay. In the middle of the eighteenth century, Margaret's great-great-grandfather, George Matthew, left home and went to sea, later marrying Jane Hamlin, a young woman from County Cork, Ireland. The couple crossed the Atlantic and settled in Philadelphia, which suited them well until the American Revolution. The Matthews were loyal to the British Crown; after the Rebellion—as it was perceived by those of their political persuasion—they were unwelcome in Pennsylvania, so they fled—along with many other Tory Loyalists—to Canada. George Matthew, by then master of his own ship, transported many of these refugees. In 1783 he shipped Jane and their seven children to wild and undeveloped New Brunswick. In some respects it resembled the Carse of Gowrie, and this may have influenced the decision to settle there. But Jane Matthew surveyed her surroundings and announced in deep discouragement, "They should have left this to the wolves and the bears."

Margaret roamed the churchyard in which ancestral Matthews were buried. The shape of the hills and the feel of the Carse of Gowrie area was familiar and comfortable. It was indeed a little like New Brunswick; it made her wonder if there was such a thing as genetic memory.

In one of the little towns of the region was a manor house that had belonged to a Patrick Matthew in the early and middle nineteenth century. Whether or not he was a relative was unclear, although it would seem likely that a connection existed: his name was spelled the same, and he hailed from the Carse of Gowrie. His specialty was trees—he was an arborist. Twenty years before Charles Darwin published *Origin of Species*, Patrick Matthew had published a paper on his trees that included a succinct summary of the theory of evolution just as Darwin presented it. He never elaborated on it and never became part of the furor that surrounded Darwin.

When she read Patrick Matthew's paper, it occurred to Margaret that his thought processes resembled those of her grandfather George Frederic Matthew. She saw also a sample of Patrick's handwriting and noted its similarity to that of George Frederic. It would have been interesting to study and pursue the genealogy, but there was no time; they had to head south and catch an airplane from London's Heathrow for the flight home.

The excursion to Europe whetted Margaret's appetite for travel. It was the first of many journeys with Ned; she would never again be content to stay at home while her husband roamed. Neither Ned nor Margaret was acquisitive of material objects, and they never returned from trips with trunks full of souvenirs or artifacts. With her acute observational ability, however, Margaret was a glutton for new sights. She was also intensely interested in what made different peoples tick. Viewing her home country from the outside proved valuable; Margaret was both humbled and liberated by the realization that the hub of the universe is not, after all, the United States of America—that much of the world functions without interference from Americans or indeed Europeans.

Margaret took a camera on her journeys. Sometimes she took photographs to assist Ned, when he was otherwise engaged with fossils and fossil hunters. She also photographed plants as an aid to her own work: "I had been cool to the plant world until I had to paint backgrounds—until I had to have something authentic for my restored animals to walk through. At first I was baffled by botany—there are so very many plants! But then I began to study the subject, and soon found it fascinating. I've been in so many different climes. I can now draw on my knowledge and experience, and I have a feeling for which types of plant would have grown in what types of environment."

However, the camera often got in her way. Not only was it a burden around her neck, but it intruded into her observation. Instead of really looking at her surroundings, she was taking pictures and counting on them to revive a memory, especially on occasions when their hosts in a foreign land hustled them along too quickly. When in the mid-1980s she gave all the camera equipment to her grandson Matthew, it was a relief to be free of it.

On all her journeys, Margaret took a sketch book. She worked either with a roller-ballpoint pen or a carbon pencil. She made rapid on-the-spot sketches if it was possible, but she was also very good at sketching from memory and made a lot of such drawings in the evenings to remind her of what she had seen in the day. "I used the sketches as scrap. I never copied them to make a finished painting. I was strictly trained as a child not to copy, and I simply won't do it now—I *can't* do it."

Ned and Margaret traveled the well-trodden paths and saw many of the great sights of the world, including natural wonders, monuments, buildings, museums, art galleries. Those experiences were grand, but on several trips she also followed Ned into his field areas, finding herself in places to which tourists rarely, if ever, gain access.

Ned's stature in paleontological circles continued to grow. In 1957 he was elected to the National Academy of Sciences, the supreme accolade for a scientist in the United States. (At the time of his election, Ned was away on a few days' spring jaunt with the youngest sons, Dan and Charles. When, upon his return, Margaret greeted him with the news, he was sure she was teasing him.) His fame afforded them both VIP status all over the world. Margaret was able to tell her guides what interested her, and they indulged her whims. "That kind of privilege may have belonged to the wealthy years ago, but it is almost unknown nowadays," she observed. She treasured those journeys to out-of-the-way places, where she had time enough to become familiar with local flora and fauna, and the opportunity to interact with local peoples and to observe their lifestyles and their art and cultural artifacts.

~: 15 :~

South America

In southern Brazil are red rocks—sandstones and siltstones—that contain Triassic fossil reptiles, including rhynchosaurs and dicynodonts. These creatures, which predated all but the earliest dinosaurs, are typical fossils of Gondwanaland, the giant mass of land that existed in the southern hemisphere until about 180 million years ago, when the present southern continents began to float apart on the backs of tectonic plates. The same fossils are found in all the southern continents, but in the late 1950s Ned had not yet encountered Gondwana creatures "in the wild." Indeed, he was still not sure that he believed in Gondwanaland and the theory of continental drift, but it surely interested him. When a letter arrived from the Conselho Nacional de Pesquisas do Brasil, the approximate Brazilian counterpart of the U.S. National Research Council, inviting him to spend some time working in the region with Brazilian colleagues, he was delighted—particularly as the invitation included Margaret. The three older boys were now independent; and Dan and Charles, aged fifteen and thirteen, could stay with trusty Leonia friends.

The fall of 1958 saw Margaret and Ned at the Berlitz Academy in New York, taking a crash course in Portuguese. Margaret found the language relatively easy to learn, and, once she had learned the rules, pronunciation was consistent.

The Colberts flew by Varig, the Brazilian national airline, and left New York on the morning of January 2, 1959. Varig had not yet graduated to jet aircraft, so the flight in a Constellation was long—close to twenty-four hours with fuel stops—but very comfortable. Leg room was generous, and the service and food were superb; in those days, everyone who flew was treated as a first-class passenger.

As morning broke on January 3, Margaret gazed down on the Amazon basin; they were approaching Rio de Janeiro. The trees looked like massed heads of blue-green broccoli. Margaret said, "We came in over the escarpment and the captain asked us to fasten our seat belts. I strapped myself in. This wonderful, marvelous city appeared below us, and I started to cry. Of course, I had no handkerchief."

They were met by Llewellyn Price and Carlos de Paula Couto, two of the geologists who would be working with Ned, and driven to a small hotel right on the beach at Copacabana. Margaret walked through the room and went out onto the balcony. She looked down and marveled: "All these people just getting on famously—speaking Portuguese without any problem at all—without any attention from us!" Copacabana was built up solid, one hotel after another, interspersed with tall apartment houses. The number of people thronging the colorful, tessellated sidewalk below was astonishing.

At the hotel, breakfast each day—served on the balcony, which overlooked the sea—consisted of half a fresh papaya (which Ned did not care for), dry, crusty rolls, and good, strong coffee. The surf was dramatic, and every time one of the enormous waves thunked on the beach, the building shuddered. On the beach lay colorful kites, waiting for a breeze to bring them to life. A kite is a *papagaio* (parrot) in Portuguese, and indeed they looked like so many bright birds, wings resting on the sand.

The third geologist host was Fausto Luiz da Souza Cunha. For the first ten days of the trip Llew, Carlos, and Fausto took turns showing off the sights of Rio de Janeiro—one of the most densely populated cities in the world—and its immediate surroundings. Rio buzzed with a festive vitality absent from most American cities. It was an odd mixture of the primitive and the sophisticated; some of the *cariocas*, as the inhabitants of Rio are called, were extremely elegantly and stylishly dressed, and some were in rags. They were of many different ethnic groups: Indians, Europeans of all types, and a large proportion of Africans (Brazil had been a slave state until the end of the nineteenth century). The *cariocas* thronged streets named for prominent Brazilians. Elegant dwellings rubbed shoulders with squalid *favelas* (slums or shanty towns); the gap between rich and poor was very evident, but even in the slums, despite the abject poverty, there seemed to be a general air of cheerfulness.

Now choice residences, some of the houses in the old part of the city dated back to the end of the eighteenth century, when Brazil was still a colony of Portugal. The streets there were cobbled with big round stones or paved with bricks. The Brazilian geological survey was housed in a gracious old building right under Paõ de Acúcar (Sugar Loaf), one of the sudden conical hills of granite that thrust up all over the city. A *favela* straggled up the side of Sugar Loaf.

The Colberts were taken to street markets, where country people sold fruits and vegetables, herbs in bunches, live birds. Men carrying *sestas* (big, shallow baskets) waited to be hired by women shoppers who filled them with their purchases; the men then hoisted the *sestas* onto their heads and carried them to the women's homes. On one corner a street entertainer sang and Margaret slowed to listen, but the geologists hustled her quickly past, explaining that he was singing dirty songs. "But I didn't know enough Portuguese to tell!" They visited the Museo in the sumptuous old imperial palace, lunched at a yacht club, and visited Rio's botanical gardens.

From almost everywhere in the city they could see the modern sculpture of Christ with outstretched arms on the top of Corcovado, another of the granite hills. They were urged by their hosts to visit it, and a little streetcar took them most of the way, toiling upward through dense exotic vegetation. From up close, the figure was gigantic, overwhelming, almost as big as the Statue of Liberty.

One day they went to Ipanema, a beach south of Copacabana. To reach it they went over a hill, and at the top of the rise was a park in a tropical jungle, Alta da Boa Vista. There they drank tea in the shade of tree ferns and watched a waterfall slide about seventy-five feet over polished rocks. Through its spray and in and out of the dark vegetation fluttered brilliant blue butterflies, iridescent wings flashing in the hot sun.

One evening Carlos invited them to a game in Rio's stadium. It was an important football (soccer) match between Botafogo and Vasco da Gama, and Carlos had jumped through many hoops to obtain the tickets; he was excited and proud to give his American friends this treat. The game began after dinner. Unfortunately, it was not customary to serve coffee at the end of a meal. Margaret was exhausted from the frenetic activity of the Rio days, and she was full of good food; she needed coffee.

Carlos shouldered his way through the throng and got them to their seats. Much as a rock star will have a lesser band open his or her show to whet the appetite of the crowd, the big match was preceded by a short game played between teams of oldtimers. On the cement bleachers, Margaret managed to concentrate through this brief melée and even quite enjoyed it once she grasped the essentials of the game. But as the Vasco da Gama and Botafogo teams loped onto the field to the roar of the two hundred thousand spectators (Rio's stadium is the biggest in the world), her eyelids drooped inexorably. She put her elbows on her knees, propped her head between her hands—"I hoped Carlos would think I was totally absorbed in the game . . . "—and gave in. Ned said, "It was a very exciting game. The fans roared and yelled, and every time someone scored, the crowd leapt up and let off Roman candles. Margaret slept through it all."

Vasco da Gama won, four goals to two. Ned surreptitiously shook Margaret awake. Groggy still, she followed the backs of Carlos and her husband as they battled their way to the street. Carlos hailed a taxi for them, and Ned and Margaret climbed in and waved goodnight. The vehicle started off with a jerk and, horn blaring, headed straight for a throng of people. Miraculously, the crowd parted like the Red Sea, and the taxi hurtled through at more than thirty-five miles per hour. Margaret woke up. Through the city they careened— without lights, except at intersections. Apparently it was customary for drivers to switch on their lights only to claim right of way. By the time they reached Copacabana, Margaret wondered if she would ever sleep again.

Junket time over, the Colberts and their geologist hosts flew south to Pôrto Alegre (happy port) in the province of Rio Grande do Sul. The southernmost province of Brazil, Rio Grande do Sul shares its western border with Argentina, and its southern border with Uruguay. Pôrto Alegre sits at the head of Lagoa dos Patos, the almost landlocked estuary of the Jacuí River. It is a huge expanse of water—about 150 miles long and perhaps 45 miles across at its widest—that eventually flows through a narrow channel into the South Atlantic.

Neither Margaret nor Ned had heard of Pôrto Alegre before, and they expected an inconspicuous coastal town, with a small harbor, perhaps serving a few tramp steamers and a fishing fleet. To their astonishment, they found a modern city, with skyscrapers and avant-garde architecture, parks, monuments, government buildings, and a population of over a million. Parts of the city resembled old European towns, but at the edge of most of these areas wrecking balls were busy, sending clouds of dust into the air, reducing fine old buildings to rubble, making room for stark, up-to-date structures. To Margaret's satisfaction, the Brazilians scoffed at many of the new designs and gave the buildings unflattering nicknames.

Llewellyn Price had grown up in the city. He left for about ten years to be educated in the United States, and he admitted that when he returned to Pôrto Alegre, he could not find his way around after all the construction.

It was days before he found a little park that he recognized and could get his bearings.

Llew was born in 1905, the same year as Ned. His parents were missionaries—Americans of Welsh descent. He had been a student of Alfred Romer, a close friend and colleague of Ned's, and had worked with him in Chicago. When he returned to Brazil, he married and became a Brazilian citizen. Llew held a government job and his wife was a librarian. Llew was, of course, completely bilingual, which frustrated Margaret's attempts to speak Portuguese—he could not spare the time to wait out her efforts. She was particularly delighted to discover that Llew was also an illustrator. At his office in Pôrto Alegre, the drawers of a map chest held life-sized colored drawings of every fossil specimen he had ever collected. He was an excellent artist, and Margaret spent hours poring over his work.

The education department of the American Museum of Natural History in New York had instituted a program to introduce children to different ways of life in foreign lands. This involved displays of costumes, utensils, and tools in current use from various parts of the world, which Museum staff members presented and demonstrated at local schools. To add to their collection, the Natch had requested that Margaret acquire a traditional Brazilian gaucho outfit—a costume worn at that time from southern Brazil to Tierra del Fuego at the tip of South America, crossing national boundaries.

While he took Ned off to look for fossils outside the city, Llew left Margaret in the care of a woman who spoke some English. This most distinguished-looking lady was to take her to different stores, instruct her in the various items of gaucho clothing and equipment, and coach her in the correct Portuguese terms. Margaret was then to return alone to make the purchases. The preliminary tour of the stores took a long time; her guide kept meeting people she knew. She would kiss them on both cheeks, and the acquaintance would kiss her back on both cheeks. Margaret would then be introduced and some polite conversation would ensue. At last the two Brazilians would kiss each other on both cheeks again, and Margaret and her guide would get back to business—until the next friend approached.

Let loose at last, Margaret was eager to exercise her fledgling Portuguese. She said, "It wasn't too difficult because of course the people in the shops were already primed as to what I wanted!" She pointed and gestured when her vocabulary failed her. She bought everything to complete the gaucho outfit: a black felt hat (some of them were red), broad-brimmed and flat-crowned, with a *barbacasha* to snug under the chin; a loose-fitting shirt the color of young rhubarb; *bombashas*, baggy pants with an inset on both sides of pleated material and buttons for decoration; leather chaps; a heavy full-length cape of dark felted material ("Those were gorgeous, and I bought one for Ned when we returned to Brazil in 1967."); wonderful boots ("I'd never seen boots like them. They were high and straight-legged down to the ankles, and there they were wrinkled like an accordion, creased on four sides with three or four horizontal creases. I put them on the counter, and with one finger I could push them in any direction. They gave the wearer wonderful mobility."). In addition she purchased a leather saddle, with a sheepskin to tie over it; brass stirrups; a *faca* (long knife); *bolos* (three metal balls on leather thongs used to hurl at an animal to entangle it); and a *laço* (lasso). "I figured I had everything except the horse!" At the time, these were garments and equipment for a regular working man, found in ordinary stores at outrageously low prices. Perhaps the outfits are still to be seen in deep country areas of South America, but already in 1959 a craze for American cowboys' clothing as seen in western movies was beginning to encroach upon the traditional styles.

The field area—the major destination of the Brazilian jaunt—was a little way out of the city of Santa Maria, in the province of Rio Grande do Sul. Ned, Margaret, Llew, Carlos, and Fausto drove the two hundred–odd miles from Pôrto Alegre to Santa Maria in a van loaned by the geology department of the University of Rio Grande do Sul in Pôrto Alegre. Their route took them over the Jacuí river on a ferry run on a cable—like one that Margaret remembered crossing the Kennebecasis in New Brunswick. To her glee, onto this ferry strolled a gaucho. He was fully equipped except that on his feet were *chinelas*, scuff-like slippers, with his heels hanging out. The fancy boots were reserved for horseback riding, the geologists informed her. Later, as they bumped over the red dirt roads that crossed the pampas, they passed several ranches and saw gauchos mounted on compact and strong little horses with Roman noses.

After settling themselves in their Santa Maria hotel, the men drove out to their field area. It was right beside the road at a little settlement called rather unimaginatively Quilometre Tres (Three Kilometers), which marked its distance from the center of town. The van had been returned to Pôrto Alegre, so they drove out every morning in a taxi. They slept and ate evening meals and breakfasts at the hotel, and Llew arranged for the team to eat lunch each day with the family of a hospitable local farmer named Huebner. All this was almost unheard-of luxury for fossil hunters. However, the red rock *sangas* (gullies) from which they were collecting their fossils were not so comfortable; it was hot, humid, and atrociously muddy—mud of an awesome stickiness. And it rained. The scientists worried when the frequent violent storms broke, because with a fossil half exposed, all or part of it could be washed out and away by the rushing water. Such rapid erosion is a mixed blessing in the trade; it exposes more treasure but sometimes destroys it in the process.

Margaret opted to stay in town most of the time. Santa Maria was a small country city. Its sidewalks were pleasant with flowers and trees, and the air was redolent with burning eucalyptus wood, used for cooking fires. The view from the hotel room was over a courtyard with stacks of eucalyptus logs, and then the red-tiled roofs of the town and the green, green grass and vegetation. She spent relaxed enjoyable days, with sketch book and camera. She wandered the main street, window-shopping the little stores. She admired metal wood-burning stoves, hand-painted in exuberant patterns and colors. Everywhere she saw sets of stacked dinner pails. The main hot meal of the day was always served in the middle of the day. If the man of the house worked in the fields, the woman took the meal out to him, carried in these stacked white enamel dishes, each one containing a different food item.

In the center of the city was a square with a gazebo over which grew a luxurious vine with purplish flowers. Every evening, the townspeople gathered there for a band concert. The children turned up dressed in their best clothes and rather solemnly played formal games until it grew completely dark.

After some days Margaret came down with a nasty attack of traveler's complaint. The diarrhea took its time to clear up, and Llew Price thought it advisable that she see a doctor. But because the doctor was a man, she could not go unchaperoned. At the end of Santa Maria's main street was an educational facility conducted by North Americans. Llew persuaded a woman teacher from this establishment to accompany Margaret. The doctor's appointment book was crammed and he could not see her for three days, by which time she had recovered. Etiquette demanded that she keep the appointment, however, so she visited the doctor's office, trailing the dutiful teacher, and feeling foolish. The doctor was evidently very knowledgeable; that is to say, he displayed a lot of Greek diplomas from impressive-sounding institutions on his walls. In addition to the diplomas, his office was decorated with two copies of what must have been a famous painting: a physician in a white coat stood to attention; slung over his left arm, a nude woman was fainting away while a skeleton tugged at one of her dangling arms. It was not very encouraging. "I was glad I already felt better!" She had to do nothing as drastic as undress. "His method of examining me," she said, "was to lift my skirt just a little bit and peek here and then peek there."

Margaret decided to try out the local hairdresser. She was curious to see what a Santa Maria hairdo would be like—it would in any case be preferable to a struggle with a hotel washbasin. Three other women sat around the salon in various stages of shampoo or curlers. The girl who took care of Margaret spoke no English, but lacing her Portuguese with gestures, Margaret established more or less what she wanted. "The girl brought out a lovely brass basin on a stand, high enough to reach the back of my neck, and then she poured warm water onto my head from a beautiful brass and copper pitcher and shampooed me. She wound me up in rollers while the other ladies got a big kick out of watching and listening to my struggle with Portuguese. It was all very good-natured—and I was pleased with my hairdo."

As she left, Margaret noticed a few items displayed for sale in the salon window. Among them was an unusual necklace. She thought about it overnight and returned next day. "I went into the shop at the front of the salon and pointed to the necklace, indicating I would like to buy it. Meanwhile the salon emptied itself. All the women came out with rollers in their hair, and towels around their necks. Eyes as big as saucers they leaned on the counter to hear me try and buy this necklace." News of the foreigner must have blazed around the town. Santa Maria was inland and isolated and visitors from the outside world were rare indeed, and of great interest.

Two or three times, Margaret went out to the paleontologists' dig area and stayed for part of the day. She remained on the rim of the sanga, out of the mud, and watched the team carefully dig around blocks of the red rock containing the gray fossil bones. It was hot, hard work. The local traffic rumbled by continuously: pedestrians carrying meat and produce to market in the city, two-wheeled horse-drawn carts, covered buggies hauled by mules, ox-carts with loudly squeaking wheels. The farmers deliberately kept one wheel squeaking—they claimed the oxen liked it and it kept them moving; Margaret noted, however, that they also poked at the animals with long wooden goads that the oxen doubtless found equally encouraging. Not infrequently the procession ground to a halt when a passerby stopped to watch what was going on in the sangas.

Next door to the Huebners lived the Pereira family. They were also small farmers. Two or three times a day, the weary and muddy team hauled out of the sanga and went over to the Pereira home. Senhora Pereira appeared barefoot at the door with cool liquid refreshment. Senhor Pereira was middle-aged, relaxed, and retired. He was dressed *de pajama*—wearing loose cotton trousers such as those worn in India—and chinelas. The Brazilian definition of bliss is *sombre, e agua fresca, e chinelas largas* (shade, fresh water, and loose sandals); Senhor Pereira was evidently a happy man.

The Pereira daughter approached Margaret one morning and shyly invited her into their home. (Margaret had been sketching Fausto with his shovel; he was interrupting a procession of small leaf-carrying ants—the insects milled about, confused by the monster destroying their established course.) The Pereiras' house was a typical country home, tiny and hip-roofed, with one room and no glass in the windows. After a cool drink and a little conversation, the young woman wanted to show Margaret the main attraction in Quilometre Tres—the local cemetery. For some reason—and Margaret's Portuguese did not rise to discovering it—she did not want Margaret to wear a hat. It was apparently more appropriate for her to carry an umbrella. "So I took my shade hat off and left it on her bureau. And then she offered me her comb . . . " The comb was black and clotted between the tines; Margaret hesitated one embarrassed moment, but knew she had no choice. She used it, then followed the woman to the cemetery under the borrowed umbrella. Picturesque in a very Latin and ornate way, the graveyard contained a large number of elaborate mausoleums. Many graves were decorated with photographs of the deceased.

In mid-February, Margaret was to return to the States. Ned had further work to do in South America and would stay another month or so, but Margaret was uncomfortable leaving the boys with her friends any longer. Ned, Llew, Carlos, and Fausto all took time off to escort her to the Santa Maria airport. She was to board a small aircraft for the hop to Rio, where she would pick up her connection for the States.

The paleontologists had unearthed a satisfying haul of fossils. Their prize was a large rhynchosaur—a brute about the size of a large pig. To protect the skeletons during transportation, the fossil hunters jacketed the blocks of rock in a thick layer of plaster of Paris. The rhynchosaur was half encased but still in its sanga, ready to be turned over and plastered on the other side. As the little party stood around at the airport waiting for the aircraft to arrive, a huge purple-black cloud heaved over the horizon, mounted rapidly heavenward, and spread ominously sideways at its base. The paleontologists' brows creased; they clutched their *cafezinhos* (small cups of coffee), and muttered. Margaret thought they were anxious for her safety, setting off as she was into such a sky. Then she realized: "Nobody was giving a hoot for me! They were worried about their rhynchosaur." Half amused, but also a little hurt, she resolved not to look at the sky until she had to.

The plane arrived. It was very small, and it looked fragile and less than airworthy in the forbidding light. An airport employee in a snow-white suit escorted Margaret across the tarmac. As they started out, the rain began, then the man opened a vast black umbrella, and together they galloped through the downpour. Crouched in the low doorway of the aircraft, Margaret turned to wave to the party. All she could see was a rapidly dwindling view of their backs as they scampered to the taxi that would take them back to the sanga.

In spite of all indications to the contrary, Margaret made it without incident. But New York was ice-cold, bare, and gray, hard to take after the lush green warmth of Brazil. To keep the language in her head, and to preserve the aura of the country, she set herself the task of translating a humorous and colorful Brazilian short story from the Portuguese.

Eight years later, in 1967, the Colberts returned to South America when the International Union of Geological Scientists conference was held in Mar del Plata, Argentina. This meeting became the first of a continuing series of international Gondwana symposia.

The trip was made particularly enjoyable because they traveled with Al Romer and his wife, Ruth. Al Romer of Harvard (Llew Price's mentor) was a legend among paleontologists. "He was," Ned said, "for many years the doyen of our profession in the United States." Aside from his professional eminence, Romer was possessed of a joyful sense of humor. He was a natural entertainer and raconteur, and "It was simply fun to be with him." Romer and Ned had first worked together in Texas in 1943, and Ned always said that was the jolliest field trip he ever had. Margaret enjoyed Ruth Romer's enthusiastic good nature. "Ruth was always very brave and confident." She added—ingenuous and admiring—"She did so much for Al. She kept all the tiresome details away from him."

In Mar del Plata, the accompanying spouses were shown around the town. They were on a street called "October 12th" in Spanish. Ruth remarked to their guides, "All these streets are named for dates, and we in our ignorance don't know what they commemorate." "Oh, this is Columbus Day—the day Columbus discovered America!" she was told. Ruth blushed, but she had to laugh.

The conference members and spouses flew to Mendoza and then took a bus to the foothills of the Andes to see Triassic sediments and fossils. The glistening white spire of Aconcagua, at 23,035 feet the highest peak in the Andes, pierced the distant sky.

The Ischigualasto region was so like the Painted Desert that Margaret felt quite at home. In Valle Fertil, they were housed in a building the original purpose of which was unknown. They were fed in one long room, and after dinner all the tables were carried out to make room for cots. The men were to be housed in one room, the women in another. While the furniture removal progressed, everybody sat around the walls, rather weary and lacking direction. Ruth spoke a little Spanish. "She was sport enough to try it out," said Margaret, "and she started to make conversation with a local man, and she was doing her very best. The Spanish style is to speak right into your face, right up close. Americans like a good yard of distance. Ruth and the man started talking in one corner of this great long room. Ruth kept backing up and the man kept following, and they went the whole way down the room and stopped only when Ruth reversed into the opposite corner!"

When the sleeping quarters were ready for occupancy, the men and women moved into their respective rooms. Ruth remarked, "The men will be kept awake all night! Al snores abominably." Pamela Robinson, a British paleontologist from London University, said, "I don't think I snore, but I sometimes scream in my sleep." Nobody found this very reassuring. They settled onto their cots, and almost immediately thunderous snores began to shake the air. Heads popped off pillows to locate the perpetrator. It was Ruth.

To Margaret's delight, another field excursion was planned that would take them into Rio Grande do Sul, and Pôrto Alegre and Santa Maria. But before they flew north into Brazil, everyone returned to Buenos Aires for more presentations. Ruth and Margaret went on a shopping expedition for gifts to take home. Ruth had been in Argentina before and advised Margaret on suitable purchases. (Margaret was to return the favor in Pôrto Alegre, as she knew Brazil.) Ruth had friends in Buenos Aires, Rosendo and Nellie Pascual. She took her shopping bag of gifts to their home and asked if they would keep them for her while she went to Brazil. "Oh, the perils of language barriers! Nellie misunderstood and thought all the presents were for her. Straightening that one out was very embarrassing for both Ruth and Nellie."

Santa Maria had changed quite a lot. It had grown in the last eight years and was less a small country town than a young city. The evening band concerts at the gazebo no longer took place. But the town dignitaries put on a concert for the visitors. Ned and most of the scientists declared they were too tired to attend. Margaret went. "Someone had to go." She was embarrassed by the general lack of enthusiasm. Her virtue was rewarded. "It was a lovely concert—particularly one Telemann flute solo, just beautifully played."

The last phase of the scientific meeting involved a drive to Montevideo, Uruguay, with stops on the way to examine yet more rocks and fossils. A bus came to fetch the party of scientists and their spouses. They reached the border quite early in the morning. The Uruguayan border guards turned everybody off the bus, and had the bus driver unload all the luggage. The bus driver shrugged an apology and drove off, back the way they had come.

The guards took everybody's passport to a mud hut, and with maddening officiousness and slowness copied everything from each passport into some sort of ledger. The party was there all day. They had no food or drink, no bathrooms—no facilities of any kind. Ned was agitated because the field schedule was disrupted. The bus did not reappear until after sunset, after which it was too dark to see anything at all. To pass the time meanwhile, somebody produced a ball and suggested a game of soccer. They divided themselves into two motley teams—the Drifters and the Non-Drifters, depending upon whether they subscribed to the theory of continental drift or not. Ned and Al Romer watched. "They sat on the fence!" said Margaret.

~: 16 :~

South Africa

George Colbert's wife, Jenny, said, "If you don't go, I'll not speak to you again!"

In 1962 Ned was awarded a National Science Foundation grant to study Gondwana fossils in South Africa. He suggested Margaret join him. It seemed to Margaret self-indulgence to consider the trip. Ned's airfare was dealt with, but they would have to find many hundreds of dollars to pay for her ticket. Although the boys were now young men—even Charles, the youngest, was sixteen and largely able to look after himself—college expenses were heavy and looming heavier. Should she use precious funds to enjoy herself? On the other hand, such an opportunity might never come her way again.

George had married his Irish Jenny in 1960. George and Jenny's genial, happy-go-lucky brother Buddy had been chums in Leonia. When Jenny came as an *au pair* to the house of a Leonia doctor, Buddy introduced her to George. She had left Ireland in her mid-teens with the equivalent of only a fifth-grade education, but, in spite of her youth, she was determined to use this chance in a new country to continue her education and to make a success of life. Margaret and Ned admired her courage and strength, but if George had asked them if he should marry her, they would have advised against it; she seemed foreign to them, and headstrong. But two weeks before Margaret and Ned returned home from Boulder and the National Science Foundation text-book project, George and Jeanette O'Regan married in Leonia with a minimum of fuss and fanfare. George called his parents to tell them the marriage was a fait accompli. They were disappointed not to have been consulted or invited, but they swallowed hard and resolved to welcome their daughter-in-law.

Still wrestling with her conscience over the South African trip, Margaret visited George and Jenny in their Fort Lee, New Jersey, apartment. When Jenny uttered her dire threat, Margaret laughed: "Well then! I have no choice!"

Ned went on ahead. He spent time in Israel and before Margaret joined him he worked for a week or two in the Karoo desert of South Africa, collecting Lower Triassic fauna—in particular, *Lystrosaurus* specimens. *Lystrosaurus* is a dicynodont (two-tusked or dog-toothed) mammal-like reptile that is a marker fossil for certain Gondwana strata.

Margaret left the States in the last week of June and flew via Copenhagen so that she could spend a few days with son David. As an undergraduate at Wesleyan University in Middleton, Connecticut, David had taken part in a Scandinavian seminar program and fallen in love with Denmark and a Danish weaver, Edith Thomassen. He had returned to Denmark before graduating from Wesleyan and was now at the University of Copenhagen, studying Danish literature and folklore. Two weeks before Margaret arrived in Copenhagen, David married. Edith was considerably older than he, and Margaret found it uncomfortable to have a daughter-in-law who was closer to her own age than that of her son. But again she accepted the situation; David was obviously happy. It seemed she might have to become accustomed to her sons marrying without her presence or her approval.

On the evening of July 2, Ned was there to greet Margaret as she landed in Capetown after the long flight from Copenhagen. While Ned attended a conference of the South African Association for the Advancement of Science, they were to stay in a dormitory of the University of Capetown. Margaret sank gratefully into bed and fell asleep to a melodious chorus of frogs on the campus lawns. In the middle of the night she awoke to hear lions roaring—appropriate enough for a first visit to Africa, even though the lions were in a nearby zoo.

Paleontologist and museum director A. W. (Fuzz) Crompton was the Colberts' guide and host. (He was to be a participant in the 1965 "Four Continents" trip to Arizona and Ghost Ranch. He and his family emigrated to the United States not long after the Colberts' visit to South Africa.) He was a big, not quite burly man with blue eyes and sun-bleached blond hair. The nickname Fuzz had been with him since childhood. Christened Albert, he had always hated the name.

Fuzz showed Ned and Margaret Capetown and its environs. The city's setting was indeed spectacular: the coastline was glorious, with mountains coming right down to the water. Rainfall was sufficient and the air damp enough for lush green grass and luxuriant vegetation. He whirled them through grand areas of the city, past elegant homes and spotless Afrikaner neighborhoods with traditional Dutch-gabled houses; and through older areas occupied by Cape Malays and Indians, with color-washed houses, a general air of decrepitude, and piles of trash.

In the Kirstenbosch National Botanical Garden out on the tip of the cape, Fuzz introduced Margaret to Gondwana flora. She got busy with her camera and sketchbook. Many of the plants were quite new to her; it was the first time, for instance, that she had seen cycads growing.

When the scientific meeting ended, it was time for field work, with the objective being the Upper Triassic beds in and around what was then Basutoland. At the time, the country was still a British protectorate; this status had saved it from being swallowed up by the Union of South Africa, which completely encircles it geographically. Now, although still four years in the future, independence was in the air and happily anticipated. On October 3, 1966, Basutoland became independent and changed its name to Lesotho.

The total area of Basutoland/Lesotho is hardly bigger than Maryland. It is a high country; its lowest point is five thousand feet above sea level. The land slopes upward to the east and becomes mountainous and rugged, rising toward the eleven-thousand-foot snow-capped Drakensberg Mountains, which form the boundaries with the Natal and Cape Provinces.

Erosion is so swift in the foothills and "lowlands" of Basutoland that it can be seen happening. The summer months of October through April are supposed to be the wet season, but the rains fail all too often. When rain does fall it is usually in violent, short-lived storms that wash out the soil. The land is severely overgrazed, and the lack of vegetation spells dust storms in the dry months; the resultant badlands-type erosion, however, is good news for paleontologists. Fuzz remarked that a plan was afoot for irrigation projects to control erosion. "I'm against it," he said, tongue in cheek.

They set off from Capetown with two vehicles: the Crompton family car and a museum Land Rover. It was a long drive with two overnight stops: one in Beaufort West, one in Bloemfontein. Fuzz feared difficulties and obduracy at the Basutoland border. When in 1961 South Africa broke away from the British Commonwealth because of Britain's opposition to apartheid, refugees fled in large numbers to Basutoland. This irritated South Africa, and the government reduced already limited rail and air services in and out of the country and significantly increased border surveillance. However, the Crompton-Colbert party crossed into Basutoland without incident.

Ned and Fuzz were to work in the foothills of the high Drakensbergs. They were after large mammal-like reptiles of the Upper Triassic period. Fuzz had arranged for everyone to sleep in local houses—very basic accommodation, but superior to tenting. Cooking over a camp stove, they prepared most of their own meals from supplies brought with them. After they had finished their lunches, Fuzz would leave their emptied tin cans beside the road; within seconds, a mob of children would appear from nowhere to lick them spotless.

They were away from the more populous areas, among truly rural communities. Margaret was struck by the easy friendliness of the people. They looked her right in the eye with a natural equality, self-respect, and dignity that took her by surprise. She was shocked and somewhat shamed that this should be unusual, and she remembered that the Basutos had no history of subservience to whites. Interaction with the people was delightfully relaxed and pleasant, although language was a problem.

It was cold at that altitude and at that time of year. The local people draped themselves in large, rather stiff and heavy, South African–made cotton blankets woven and dyed in intricate individual patterns. Popular headgear for men was a two-eared woollen cap, but at the same time, some men seemed to be unaware of the cool wind and low temperatures and strode after plows in nothing but loincloths.

It was poor country for agriculture because it was so dry. At the time of Margaret and Ned's visit, the ground was being prepared for the planting of millet. Oxen were used for contour plowing of the ground, and teams of six oxen dragged crude sleds or harrows, some of wood and some of metal, raising clouds of dust. Women winnowed rather pitiful piles of grain and swept the winnowing area carefully to be sure that every last kernel was picked up. They ground the grain using stone pestles, and mortars that appeared to be natural hollows in the limestone.

Aloes were everywhere; they seemed to have been deliberately planted. A kind of cactus resembling prickly pear with "warts" rather than thorns formed dense hedges around individual homesteads. Cattle grazed the cactus as high as they could reach. Above cow-head height, it branched out, healthy and thick. Around some other homes were beautifully and evenly made hedges of what were probably millet stalks—millet grows tall, a little like a skinny cattail; the vertical stalks were bound together in an intriguing way with horizontal coils of some other vegetable material. Within the hedged areas, tiny kitchen gardens struggled for survival, and in some places, small groves of apricot trees did reasonably well. Fences were not evident away from the homesteads. In addition to the cattle, goats and sheep—kept for their meat and low-grade wool and mohair—roamed the countryside freely and climbed on the mesa-like hills, subsisting on occasional dry grass stalks. In the few places where the livestock had not eaten it down to nothing, a pink grass grew head high.

The vehicles bumped and creaked over the dirt roads of the high country, moving from one field area to the next. The Land Rover was in perpetual danger of losing a wheel, and Margaret found this a little too exciting at times; she saw nothing resembling a service station. They occasionally came across groups of men riding stocky, shaggy little horses. At the time of this visit, among South African native peoples, horses and horse-back riding were peculiar to the Basutos. Riders used thin rope for reins and carried knobkerries (short wooden clubs with knobs at one end). Once they passed a man riding a cow or an ox with very long horns.

Farming was not even subsistence level for most people, and at least half the Basuto men were employed in the South African gold and diamond mines, where wages were pitiful but better than no money at all. They would sign up for two or three months at a time, then return with gifts and cash. When all was spent, they signed new contracts and did another stint in the mines.

"We watched a group set off for Johannesburg," said Margaret. "It was festive. The men climbed into a big truck sent to fetch them and the women and a dog of questionable ancestry followed the truck quite a way down the road." The women sang and clapped. They wore light-colored—mostly yellow—cords wrapped around their feet and ankles. The effect was like dancers' or gymnasts' leg warmers. Some wore men's black leather oxfords, which looked many sizes too big for them and must have represented several weeks' wages at the mines. Some women had tattoos on their faces: a round spot on each cheek, and thin blue-black lines across their foreheads and down their noses.

Most dwellings were *rondavels*—"round hovels"—a basic design found in many areas of southern Africa. They were constructed of crude, dry stone, with added mud or plaster daub, and often the plaster was painted, or decorated with patterns scratched into it. Other homes were long, rectangular structures, some of which were built of brick. The reed thatch of the roofs was very thick and dense, smoothly finished off. The effect was almost sculpted, and it was impossible to see what held the thatch down. Interior walls were plastered and tidily finished. Most homes looked cared for—their owners obviously concerned about appearances—and the general impression was that the people were poor but certainly not sunk under poverty. Margaret was delighted to be shown around a compound inhabited by a man and his three wives. Members of the family lined up smiling for a snapshot while others of the community—men and women both—sat on the ground smoking foul-smelling pipes.

Fires for heating and cooking were fueled with dried dung; firewood in that terrain was almost nonexistent. A local laundromat consisted of a pool between rocks, into which a small stream sometimes flowed; the washed clothes were spread on surrounding rocks to dry.

Driving in tandem along a road one day, the occupants of the two vehicles noticed groups of people standing or sitting by the roadside. By and by a battered Volkswagen bus appeared; it was the mobile health clinic, which was run by white doctors and came by once a week, stopping to aid the sick and injured gathered in knots on its route. The clinic staff treated the sufferers as best they could, then rattled on to the next groups.

Music was apparently an individual matter. Margaret photographed several musicians playing crude homemade instruments for their own entertainment: a man with a small concertina; another with a simple instrument with a single string that he plucked as he walked, holding it close to his ear because the sound was so soft; a woman with a stick in her mouth—perhaps to make a resonator on the general principle of a Jew's harp—that she bowed with a crude bow.

Celebrations seemed to crop up with little prearrangement or excuse. Leading the way to a party one afternoon came a line of women, each balancing a keg of beer on her head. Both men and women began to dance to the music of drums alone. People arrived for the party more elaborately dressed than the everyday wear: a woman came in a leather cape, with an apron over it, and an ostrich plume in her hair; another wore a woven skirt possibly fashioned from one of the cotton blankets; a man sported a skirt made of dassie (hyrax) skins, with long sheep's wool wrapped around his feet.

One morning, Ned and Fuzz climbed a short way up a hill to an outcrop. Margaret remained in the settlement in the valley to converse with a woman who spoke a little English. This woman was turning a hand-cranked sewing machine on the ground. Children were running around and playing. One small boy in a billed cap many sizes too large for him came over to gaze at Margaret. Another woman with a baby on her back was weaving a mat without a loom; she had the warp laid out on the ground and simply wove the weft in and out by hand without even a shuttle. It was an industrious, domestic scene, but its peace was suddenly shattered by shouts. Startled, Margaret looked up to see a small army of men running up the hill toward Ned and Fuzz, brandishing sticks, clubs, knobkerries. She froze. What could two simple fossil hunters have done to provoke such an attack? In the distance she could see the pair had stopped work and were watching the men approach in obvious apprehension. The mob rushed on, reached Ned and Fuzz—and ran right by them. They were after a rabbit.

Just before the party left Basutoland, Fuzz took the Colberts to visit a mission quite close to Maseru, the capital city. It had been founded by a protestant missionary from France called Ellenberger; he had built himself a house like an Arizona Anasazi cliff dwelling, between two ledges of sandstone. Across the ceiling marched small dinosaur footprints of a familiar aspect. Ned believed they had been left by a relative of *Coelophysis*. The local people had revered the priest and kept the site as a memorial. It was fenced in to preserve it from the sheep and goats, and a profusion of the tall pink grass grew inside the fence. One of the priest's sons still lived there, running a combination store and museum on the place.

(Unfortunately, Margaret and Ned came into contact with another son of the Reverend Ellenberger when they were in Argentina in 1967. The man was a professor at the Paris Sorbonne and was attending the Gondwana symposium. On the bus on the way to the Ischigualasto region Professor Ellenberger took it upon himself to stand up and deliver a harangue, in English, about the iniquities of the United States. Most of his captive audience were American. The passengers became very quiet. Margaret said, "Although I agreed with some of Ellenberger's sentiments, I thought he was very rude.")

The party left Basutoland and drove the short distance to Fort Hook in the Herschel District of Cape Province. There they lodged with Malcolm and Lorraine Hepburn, Seventh Day Adventists who ran the Fort Hook trading post. Mr. Hepburn had hired for Margaret a jeep and a native driver named George. While Fuzz and Ned disappeared to hunt fossils each day, Margaret set off into the countryside with this driver. Attired in a European suit with a snappy fedora on his head, George was a boon. He was adept at the local Xhosa and Thembu languages, good at talking to people, and a fine interpreter. He asked Margaret if she would care to see inside some native homes. She told him she would like it very much, if it could be done without offence. He was very formal in his approach. He talked to the lady of each house, and then turned to Margaret with a flourish: "Kindly entuh!" he said.

At her request, George taught Margaret some elements of Xhosa. These languages are "click" languages, very difficult for a western tongue to master. Margaret said, "I'm sure my click was never quite in key!" (It was good enough, however, to impress an American Museum of Natural History anthropologist. He was among a group that assembled on her return to view her slides and the artifacts she had collected for the museum.)

She also asked George to take her to see local artists at work, and he took her to watch a potter in a nearby settlement. The woman's method fascinated her, and she had him take her back there three or four times so she could watch the entire process. The potter added finely ground feldspar to a pile of earth that she had dug up, wet the mixture from a bucket of water, and dumped it all in a burlap sack to keep it damp. And then she wedged it (kneaded it like dough, to get its consistency uniform and to work out air bubbles) on a special stone. She worked it with a pestle and mortar, her muscular arms gleaming in the bright sun as she labored. Initially she made the pot without a bottom. It was a slab technique, and the potter built up the vessel bit by bit, pulling at it gently and using soft clay to heal the cracks she made; at the end she added the bottom, and smoothed the whole outside with a knife. Margaret had never seen a pot made this way and wondered if it would not be weak where the bottom met the sides, but after firing, the pots seemed to be fine.

The potter made little animals with the remains of her clay. She rolled small lumps of clay, then swiftly pulled out legs, ears, and tails, creating animals such as bulls and horses. Although crude and stylized, they were smooth and pleasing, and instantly identifiable. They were sun dried, not fired like the pots. She also made peculiar humanoid figures, armless, with elephantine legs, and to these she added color—blue hair, red eyes, blue nostrils, and dots of yellow for mouths. George the interpreter established that the animals and the figures were toys for children.

George drove Margaret out to a waterfall behind which were prehistoric rock paintings. She had to crouch on a rock and peer around the waterfall to see them in the cave behind. Done by Bushmen ancestors, the drawings were rust colored—some sort of iron clay must have been used. The rock was pink and yellow, with streaked stains that looked like the desert varnish seen on sandstone in the American Southwest.

"When I got home, I made a painting for over our fireplace in Leonia. I painted the rock cliff with ferns growing out of the cracks, and I did restorations of the mammal-like–reptile fossils the men were finding near there.

Terra-cotta figures of Thembu
man and woman sculpted in the
early 1970s.

I painted them in a reddish-brown color in the style of the ancient cave drawings. When Malcolm McKenna first saw the picture he flopped down on the couch and laughed and laughed. He at least thought it as funny as I did. Unfortunately, I used latex paint for a base—I didn't know any better. It was all wrong, especially over the fireplace by the hot chimney. I tried to move it one day, and it shelled right off the latex base."

Most of the local people who frequented the Hepburn trading post were of the Thembu tribe. They were friendly, cheerful, and relatively light-skinned—in some lights their skin had a bluish cast. Men wore dark felt hats like soft helmets, blankets similar to those of the Basutos, and large boots. They carried knobkerries. (Margaret tried to purchase one to add to the collection she was making for the American Museum education department. She discovered they were very personal items and not for sale.) Women wore big, soft turbans, and Margaret had Mr. Hepburn ask one of the women to show how she draped her turban. Smiling shyly, the woman removed the headgear and demonstrated. She turned her head upside down and loosely wrapped the broad strip of fabric around her head. Then she started to roll it up like a cuff. When she was about halfway, she took the cloth left over, and tucked it in on one side. Margaret said, "It was quite simple, and really stunning to look at." (On a cabinet in the Colbert dining room in Flagstaff stand two charming terra-cotta sculptures of a Thembu man and a woman, about eight inches high, modeled by Margaret after she returned home. The man wears his hat and boots and blanket, the woman a skirt and blanket, and the turban.)

One evening the Thembu tribesmen held a mock battle or stick dance. They whacked at each other with their knobkerries. It looked dangerous, but they had wrapped their arms in thick layers of fabric for protection and nobody got hurt. Many barrels of beer were laid on for the party, and people arrived in their finery; turbans, for example, were more festive than the everyday ones, with contrasting fabrics added. As in Basutoland, large lace-up men's shoes seemed to be the preferred footwear for women. One woman had an aluminum bucket on her head; she wore it as if it were a stylish hat. A man who was some sort of functionary at the festivities wore bells and rattles on his legs and a towering headdress; the effect was somewhat compromised by large safety pins holding his vest closed.

Again at the request of the Natch education department, Margaret spent time researching local cookware. She collected pots, pans, and Dutch ovens in various shapes and sizes, made of iron, tin, and ceramic. She purchased a few samples and photographed the rest, suitably arranged.

Work in the field completed, the party made its way to the southeast coast of Cape Province and stopped in East London to visit Miss M. Courtenay-Latimer. In 1938, she had been curator of the local museum in East London when a trawler captain who had been fishing in the Indian Ocean brought her a five-foot fish. She realized it was extraordinary and notified Professor J. L. B. Smith, a fish expert of Rhodes University, Grahamstown, who described and identified it. It was a coelacanth—a "living fossil"—related to fossil bony fish from late Devonian and Cretaceous times. He named it *Latimeria chalumnae*, after Miss Courtenay-Latimer. Margaret was feeling unwell and queasy as they approached Port Elizabeth. She did manage to be polite to Miss Courtenay-Latimer, but soon became quite ill and could remember little of the visit or of the coelacanth exhibit in the museum there.

Back in Capetown, Fuzz and his wife took the Colberts to visit their parents. Anne's mother and father lived in Stellenbosch, in the wine country, about a thirty-minute drive to the east of the city. Established in 1679 by Dutch settlers, Stellenbosch is the second oldest town in South Africa, after Capetown. The mountains rising four or five thousand feet reminded Margaret of Yosemite, although they were softer and not so vertical. In the old thatched house with its high, stepped gable, Margaret sat on a settle within the inglenook fireplace and peered upward. Darkness had fallen. The chimney rose straight and wide and framed the stars of Africa, surely hanging closer to the earth than those of the northern hemisphere.

The next day, they drove on to Ceres, further inland and at a higher elevation, where lived Fuzz's parents. The older Cromptons owned an almond grove. Many of the trees were still bare and lifeless in the austral winter, but some were already covered with tiny, sweet-smelling blossoms and swarming with coley birds—little gray creatures sometimes called mice birds because of the way they creep and scurry about.

Once more in the city, Fuzz turned Margaret and Ned over to the Singer family, who treated them to a traditional *brai vleis*—a South African barbecue. Ronald Singer taught anatomy at Capetown's medical school, but his research interests centered on fossil mammals. His wife Shirley was an anti-apartheid activist, and the Singers were also to emigrate to the United States when they could no longer live with South African government policies; Dr. Singer would obtain a position at the University of Chicago. The present picnic took place in the evening at Hopefield, northwest of Capetown, close to the ocean. Tremendous sand dunes swelled there like frozen waves. They contained fairly recent (Pleistocene) fossils. Margaret said, "By a fascinating suction effect, the dunes sucked up iron-laden water and iron was deposited in their interiors. The tops of the dunes were constantly wet. If we simply kicked the sand as we walked about, up came beautiful mahogany-colored bones, colored that way by the iron."

The Colberts left Capetown with some regret and flew to Johannesburg. During the flight, Margaret fussed at Ned; stowed in the overhead bin was a box wrapped in newspaper and tied with string. It contained Ned's field shoes. "Ned, we're supposed to be VIPs—with proper luggage!" Ned pointed out that it was too late to worry now. He could not leave the shoes behind.

They were met by Ian Brink, an Afrikaner paleontologist at Witwatersrand University. He gave them a tour of the city, and as he drove, he lectured them on the merits of apartheid and why it was necessary and good. "He showed us white residential areas, and then with pride took us to see the homelands. He wanted us to understand that this was an example of what big-hearted whites were doing for the blacks."

The overall impression of the homelands was of an enormous featureless development of two-roomed brick houses, spreading back over the hills. This was Soweto. One or two homes had little flower gardens, struggling to introduce brightness into an otherwise dreary sprawl. The Colberts were silent and noncommittal. Ian was their host; what could be said in the face of his enthusiasm and conviction without giving offence?

Discomfiture over apartheid and political differences aside, Ian Brink, his musician wife Anna, and their two girls, Olga and Ammalie, were warm and generous hosts. Margaret and Ned stayed with them at their home in Emmerentia, a suburb of Johannesburg.

Ian took the Colberts to Makopan, the Witwatersrand University field station. Cut into a steep hillside on which grew tall euphorbia trees was a large cave containing all manner of fossil treasures. In an area fenced to deter marauding goats, a collection of native plants had been planted and fostered. Ian and the Colberts stayed overnight in a small building that held sleeping quarters for visitors and station workers. Bathroom facilities were primitive; early one morning, Margaret visited the outhouse, and, as she emerged, tiny animals—long-legged, huge-eyed—shot upward into the euphorbia branches. She stopped in astonishment and delight at the creatures that seemed to float aloft on the rising morning mist. They were galagos—bush babies—feather-light, nocturnal primates. "They made me believe in fairies!"

For a very different experience, Ian arranged for Ned and Margaret to visit a gold mine. They had already seen the slag heaps—Johannesburg was full of them; areas as big as two or three city blocks were covered by mountains of dross. Margaret was asked if she would like to go down into the mine. She was not sure that she wanted to, but thought she should. She and Ned donned hard hats and heavy waterproof coats. The mine was unimaginably deep—it was difficult to grasp the fact that men had dug down through those thousands of feet of rock. Inside the coat Margaret sweated uncomfortably; proximity to the earth's molten core kept the mine extremely hot. The idea of working day-in–day-out in such an environment appalled her, and she breathed fresh air with huge relief when the elevator bore them up again.

The miners came from all over southern Africa, from many different tribes, and they spoke a multitude of different languages. Coming from distant villages and settlements, they were out of their own cultures. Before they went below ground, new miners had to be instructed. A guide at the mine took Margaret and Ned to observe a classroom where rookies spent many hours before they began work. Tools and equipment and the use thereof were demonstrated in concrete fashion, because many could not read even if they understood the language.

On Sundays, team-dancing competitions pitted the different tribes against each other in cheerful tension-releasing rivalry. The Colberts were spectators at one of these events, where music was played on marimba-like instruments and some of the dances were performed on enormously tall stilts—attached to the men's shins so they did not have to hold onto them.

The area around the head of the mine was almost like a small town. Various trades were plied. Barbers shaved rows of heads. A tailor worked with a sewing machine. He specialized in patching pants; the miners bought new pants and he patched them so that they would not look new and their owners would not appear to be neophytes. Margaret tried to purchase a patched pair for the American Museum, but as with the Thembu knob-kerries, she was unsuccessful—they were too precious.

Before they left, the Colberts watched a gold brick being poured. The mined rock was crushed and heated, and the molten gold poured into a mold. Ned was told if he could lift a cooled brick with one hand, he could take it. "He tried, but of course he couldn't do it. We consoled ourselves by thinking what it would have cost us in excess baggage to take it on the plane!"

As a final kindness, Ian Brink and daughter Olga took the Colberts to Kruger National Park, where a satisfying number and variety of wild animals presented themselves to view: impala, elephant, eland, kudu, lions, hyenas, jackals; and a baboon that jumped onto the hood of their vehicle and rode with them—every time they stopped, it knocked on the windshield as much as to say, "Get going!"

The road to Kruger ran beside the railroad. As the train rattled along, Margaret caught a glimpse of two women gathering coals and sticks for fuel beside the tracks. The train was moving too fast for her to sketch them on the spot, but the scene imprinted itself on her mind's eye and was the inspiration for another work from memory after she returned home: a dark watercolor of the two figures bending to wrest a little warmth and comfort from the leavings of the trains.

~ 17 ~

India

January 4, 1964, and an Air India jet: cabin-wall coverings, chartreuse damask; food, spicy and unfamiliar; flight attendants in saris and with vermilion *tikka* marks on their foreheads; accents, lilting . . . Through the cabin windows, views of the western Ghats, then rolling country, innumerable villages, mosaics of small fields, terraces, rivers that were pale ribbons of sand—until the thick vein of the Ganges. The aircraft circled in the misty air over the Hooghly River and Calcutta, and landed.

Margaret and Ned were met and seen through customs by Pamela Robinson—the same London University paleontologist who would, in 1967, in the Ischigualasto region of Argentina, admit she sometimes screamed in her sleep. Pamela was a protégée of Professor Prashanta Mahalanobis, the director of the Indian Statistical Institute. A prominent mathematician and scientist, Professor Mahalanobis had founded the institute in Calcutta many years earlier to forge links between statistics and the natural sciences. Pamela swung between London and West Bengal; several of her London students were associates of the institute. (These included Sohan Lal Jain and Tapan Roy Chowdhury, who had obtained doctorates under her tutelage, and Bimalendu Roychoudhuri.) Her task in Calcutta was to arrange paleontology programs in conjunction with the institute museum, and it was she who had initiated the invitation to Ned.

The official communication invited both Ned and Margaret to be guests of the institute for almost three months. Field excursions were planned to collect *Lystrosaurus* and other Gondwana fossils in the Damodar River valley and in other areas of India. In addition, Prashanta Mahalanobis and his wife, Rani, were to personally organize sightseeing excursions for the Colberts all over the subcontinent.

The institute car, driven by Bimalendu, wound its way through an astonishing mass of pedestrians, bicycles, carts, buses, and goats on the Barrackpore trunk road. Everybody and every vehicle moved politely aside for thin, humped cattle with long, drooping ears. The road was lined for much of the journey with squatter shacks of tar paper, and corrugated iron. The crowds on the road hardly thinned, but as they neared the institute about ten miles out of the city, the surroundings became more rural, with palm trees and open country, bungalows with squash vines growing over their roofs, and houses with wooden shakes.

The institute campus was enclosed within high walls, with gates and watchmen at intervals. Several science departments, including biology and geology, were housed on the campus. The buildings were not old, but since the Indian climate causes masonry to age swiftly, they had acquired an air of dignified antiquity, offsetting a shabbiness evident on closer inspection. They were surrounded by formal terraced gardens, lush and green, shaded by towering trees. The driveways were lined with tubs of brilliant flowering plants, as were broad flights of steps leading down to several pools.

The professor and his wife lived in a building known as Amrapali, which doubled as the administrative headquarters; the top two floors were spacious and opulent guest apartments. Unfortunately, Rani Mahalanobis was sick, and Margaret and Ned saw very little of her. The professor was formal, but very welcoming, and he had lots to say, on many subjects. The Colberts and Pamela dined with him almost every day of their Calcutta stay in the Amrapali dining room, and the professor spun the meals out with long discussions and discourses.

On the sultry evening of their arrival, they sat in the living room, which was open on three sides, providing a welcome flow of air. Its roof was supported by pillars, its marble floor inlaid in a geometric pattern. As dusk began to fall, a servant wandered around the living room with a squirt gun, waging a futile war against mosquitoes. Bahadur, Professor Mahalanobis explained, had been with them for some years. He came from a northern Indian tribe: "Until recently, this tribe lived in the trees," said the professor, conjuring some unlikely images. Bahadur had been rescued from a drunken existence, he continued, and rehabilitated. He was a sad-looking little man, thin and dark; perhaps, Margaret thought, he was homesick for his trees. When it was dark, small bats flew in and out in pursuit of mosquitoes Bahadur had missed.

The day after the Colberts arrived, a major riot broke out between Hindus and Muslims in Calcutta. The government slapped a rigid curfew on the city; nobody was allowed on the streets, and armored vehicles ranged the city, carrying soldiers with orders to shoot loiterers. Official numbers were never released, but rumors flew that over a thousand were killed in the riots. For the Colberts and their hosts, the institute walls and the guards on the gates were a source of comfort and security, the grounds an island of calm while mayhem raged outside.

After five days, the curfew was modified; people were allowed out until 5 P.M. Margaret and Ned ventured into the city, visiting the New Market, which had been in existence at least since Victorian times. Apparently anything in the world could be purchased there: "Anything, from ivory and gold to cabbages," wrote Jon and Rumer Godden in 1972. Fruits, vegetables, seeds, beans, were arranged for a visual feast. Vendors squatted on their haunches and sorted split peas and lentils into colored piles on the ground, then sat cross-legged and waited for customers. Meat hung in hunks, studded with flies. Using a cut-throat razor, a barber shaved a customer in the street while the crowds swayed and jostled by. The humid air was heavy with the odors of cattle and massed humanity, of flowers and ripe fruit, all overlain with spices—turmeric, coriander, cumin, ginger. The color and activity were irresistible to Margaret: "But everywhere in India, as soon as I prepared to use my camera, children appeared from nowhere. They swarmed like bees around me, then settled themselves in stiff and solemn poses. After I had snapped them, they would buzz away, and I could take the picture I had planned."

The Colberts watched the time lest they be out in the street after 5 P.M. Nonetheless, they found themselves enveloped in "great white waves of people largely consisting of men in white pajamas and punjabis . . . hurrying toward their homes," as Ned put it in Digging into the Past.

January was in Calcutta's dry season. Nonetheless, the water table was just below the surface, and ponds, streams, wetlands were everywhere. Outside the institute walls, a street followed a small stream, where tiny kingfishers flashed above the water, like animated blue-green jewels. In a backwater, strange little fishes (Periopthalmus) swam with their big raised eyes above the surface and, using front fins as limbs, climbed up semi-drowned logs and flopped around on the land, rolling in mud to keep their skins wet.

Everywhere uncontrolled cattle roamed the streets, subsisting on garbage; in spite of their sanctity to Hindus, most of the beasts looked abject and thin; Professor Mahalanobis explained that they had owners, and although their flesh was never eaten by Hindus, they could be milked, and after they died, their skins could be cured for leather. Oxen and water buffalo could be used as draft animals. Their excrement was a precious gift, a valued resource. "A woman in a white sari walked toward me," said Margaret. She was lovely, erect and stately. She held one hand out before her. Piled upon it was the cow dung she had gathered—her treasure." To dry it for fuel, manure was slapped onto the walls of houses in gobbets, as close together as possible to make room for more. Dung was used to waterproof pots and baskets. Mixed with water to make a kind of slurry, it was spread on dirt floors to make a smooth surface. Cattle dung was in no sense unclean; on the contrary, it was considered a cleansing, even hallowing commodity.

As usual, Margaret was interested in artists and artisans and enjoyed watching them at work. Just outside the institute walls, a maker of musical instruments worked in a one-room establishment, which could not have been more than ten feet square. It was his store, his workshop, and his home. Squatting on the dusty floor, his wife and small child watched him work. He made sitars and tambouras, and stringed instruments of various shapes and sizes, similar to dulcimers; several of his finished pieces hung on the back wall of the shop, their polished woods gleaming in the dim light. While Margaret watched, he sat cross-legged and carved a block of wood into a gourd-like shape. The wood was crimson, and crimson curls flew from his chisel.

"I am constantly amazed and humbled," Margaret remarked, "by the marvels that people create without sophisticated tools or modern equipment. Their tools are skill, artistry, and endless patience. But they have few clocks. Folk whom we are pleased to call 'primitive' have so much more time than we 'developed' people. The idea of 'wasting time' is foreign to them." *Kal* is the Hindi word for both yesterday and tomorrow—an interesting philosophical point.

Festivals were numerous. The Colberts watched a group of men preparing figures of goddesses for a celebration. Forms of straw-bound sticks and wire were covered with some sort of clay or flour-and-water paste. "We saw some of the headless forms before the paste was added. The artistry and movement in those skeletons were beautiful." The white paste was molded on and allowed to dry. The heads were made by potters and added to the figures before they were intricately painted and decorated. The finished effect was rather garish to western eyes, but it was appropriate in the surroundings. At the end of the festivals, the images were carried in procession through the streets in juggernauts—large wooden carts—hauled by oxen, or on decorated trucks like carnival floats. The sculptures were destined to be ceremoniously dumped into the Ganges River, which seemed a waste after so much time and effort. But life is cyclical, especially in India; the year would revolve toward the next festivals, the next images.

Rani Mahalanobis must have had control of the family affairs, or perhaps independent money, for not far from the institute, she had built a new house without telling her husband. The Colberts were present when the secret was revealed; the professor took the news very calmly. When the house was complete, down to the detail of potted plants, and the footprints of Lakshmi—the Hindu goddess of good fortune—painted onto the front doorsteps, she organized a dinner party. She invited her husband and several friends and included Pamela, Margaret, and Ned; but she herself was too sick to attend.

Toward the end of their stay in Calcutta, Professor Mahalanobis announced that he had arranged for the Colberts and Pamela to visit and take tea with the prime minister of India, Jawaharlal Nehru, in New Delhi—an immense honor, which both Margaret and Ned viewed with considerable trepidation, but there was no way out.

In the Indian hierarchy, the professor was a man of some stature, and on the day of their flight to Delhi, Margaret and Ned observed what this meant in practical terms. He had booked seats for them all on a commercial flight in the evening of the day before the tea party. Everybody was packed and ready to leave, and they sat around in the Amrapali living room. The professor was talking. And talking. Ned, who liked to be at an airport in plenty of time, risked a glance at his watch, and still Mahalanobis talked. Ned began to fidget, unable to conceal his growing agitation as the hands of his watch crept inexorably forward. Finally, the professor noticed his nervousness: "Don't worry. We'll make it," he insisted airily and continued his discourse. At last, he decided it was time, so they piled into an institute car and were driven at a mad dash, horn blaring, down the trunk road to the airport, where they arrived twenty minutes late. On the tarmac, the engines of their aircraft were already turning. Airport officials opened the gates, and the car drove right up to the plane. The professor strode aboard, completely unabashed that an entire cabin-full of people had been kept waiting. His guests followed, trying to be invisible, but apparently none of the Indian passengers found the professor's behavior unusual. (Pamela told the Colberts later that he had once tried the same trick at London's Heathrow Airport, and was quite nonplused when his flight took off without him.)

Tea at the prime minister's residence was at five o'clock. For this, the professor was on time. A majordomo led the party through long corridors and took them into a sitting room, and after a short wait, Nehru entered the room, accompanied by his daughter, Indira Ghandi. Their discussion revolved around Triassic fossils and Gondwanaland, and the desirability of natural history museums. Nehru seemed interested and well-informed, but he looked exhausted; the recent invasion of Tibet by China was evidently much on his mind. The Chinese army was sitting uncomfortably close to India's northern borders, and, for security reasons, India had clamped down on the sale of ordnance survey maps of the area. The professor and Ned complained mildly that it was difficult to work without detailed field maps; Nehru smiled politely and suggested that war changes things. Pamela pointed out that the embargo was close to futile, as maps were still readily available from England. Nehru's daughter scowled and shook her head—obviously a signal that their audience was at an end.

They flew back to Calcutta for a few more days, then it was January 17 and time for a scheduled West Bengal field trip. Margaret was loath to leave Amrapali: "Amrapali was magical. I became very attached to its bats; also to the little geckoes that appeared at dusk and dawn, clinging to the walls and ceilings."

At the railroad station, the platforms were dotted with sleeping blankets, and the air was blue with smoke from brazier cooking fires. Skinny dogs, goats, and chickens searched for scraps. The station offered a modicum of shelter and room to lie down and many of the people there were squatters rather than travelers. When trains pulled in, people got in—or on; passengers were draped all over the outside of the rail cars, clinging to whatever projections they could find.

First-class tickets assured Pamela Robinson and the Colberts of seats when their own train at last arrived. After several rather warm hours, they pulled into Asansol, about 125 miles northwest of Calcutta. Two institute men had driven from Calcutta in a Land Rover and were there to meet them. As Margaret, Ned, and Pamela walked toward the vehicle, a crowd of children surrounded them, and one little boy gave a surprised cry. All the children fell at Margaret's sandaled and nyloned feet, chattering and gesticulating. Pamela translated their astonished exclamations: "She has no toes!"

The Land Rover left the station and headed for the camp, jouncing through people on foot, who were ankle-deep in pale dust; people on bicycles; trucks and carts pulled by oxen; the inevitable cattle and goats. The camp was a few miles north of Tiluri, a town of about 5,500 inhabitants.

The travelers were housed in a rural health center, which was still under construction, although a clinic staffed by a doctor and two nursing sisters had recently opened. The scientific party occupied two rooms, each with its own bathroom, in a building destined to be a residence for nurses. The beds were *charpoys*, surprisingly comfortable wooden frames with rawhide strings stretched over them. From the roof was a fine view over fallow rice fields and scanty pasture dotted with sal trees. The Damodar River was to the north, with its large earth dam and a steel plant beyond. To the south was Tiluri, dominated by the tower of one of its temples. To the east and west, the conical jungle-covered Panchet hills jutted abruptly out of a perfectly flat plain.

The party ate in a schoolhouse, also under construction. A resident cook prepared spicy chicken, lamb, and fish, various types of lentils and beans, and rice and chapatis—served on a table spread with a spotless white cloth. The setup for washing dishes after meals consisted of sinks and counters in a wall-less structure with a tiled roof. The floor was bare earth; in the monsoon season, it would surely be liquid mud.

The morning after their arrival (on Saturday, January 18) Ned and the rest of the scientific contingent congregated around the Land Rover and jeeps. Local men hired to do menial tasks were to be paid a princely sum: the equivalent of forty U.S. cents per day. They lined up, cheerful and grinning, for Margaret to take a picture, and then the little convoy departed in a cloud of dust for their fossil localities in the Damodar river valley and the Panchets.

Margaret was dispatched to do serious sight-seeing. She had been assigned a jeep and two guides: Sri Khirod Roy, who worked at the Statistical Institute and whose wife's home was in Tiluri; and his brother-in-law Shyam Pada Choudhury, who also lived in Tiluri. They ushered Margaret into the vehicle and immediately began calling her "Mother." She was a little taken aback at first and they apologized and sought to improve matters by explaining that it was their custom with "older women."

Margaret indicated her special interest in arts and crafts but told them she was happy for them to be responsible for the itinerary. The guides listened to her request and conferred briefly, then they started the engine and drove to Tiluri. It was still early, and the lines of the little town were softened by the smoke of innumerable dung fires as the inhabitants cooked breakfast.

Perhaps Sri Khirod and Shyam thought that because Margaret was "Mother," she must surely be interested in schools. That morning they visited three: the senior basic girls' school, the primary girls' school, and the high secondary boys' school. It was a cool day, but shutters in the schools were closed over barred windows. As her eyes adjusted to the gloom, Margaret saw children on benches with copy books and the small children of the primary school on the floor with slates. As Margaret was conducted into different classrooms, the children thundered to their feet and saluted with the Indian greeting, bowing deeply, hands joined together palm to palm, finger-tips to foreheads. At each school, all the children were herded out to have their pictures taken with Margaret and the teachers. Herself five-foot, four inches, and quite slender, Margaret was by no means a large woman among her western sisters, but here she felt huge and clumsy beside the small, fine-boned teachers.

Shyam was evidently a very political person; he was secretary of several organizations and Margaret noticed that he contrived to ease himself into every possible photograph. He clearly improved his relations with schools by bringing a foreign visitor to admire them; Margaret suspected that this was the real reason for all the school visits.

They returned to the camp for lunch and afterward set out for Saltora, a small town south of Tiluri. Here they took tea with the district police officer, picked up a friend of Shyam's, named Mrs. Mukherjee, and her father and drove on south and east. They stopped frequently in settlements and villages to inquire after chickens for the camp larder, but without success.

After some miles, they came upon a group of road workers digging earth from areas close to the road. They dug rectangular excavations, leaving a little bit in the center of each so that their overseers would recognize the original ground level and see how much work had been done. The earth was carted in split-bamboo baskets and scattered on the dampened roadway where, on their knees, the workers patted it in place by hand. The exquisite slowness of the process was fascinating; Margaret again realized that time had no place here; one year—or ten—to fix a road, it was of no account. She prepared to take a photograph of the hand-finishing process, and a group of women and girls promptly stopped work, perched themselves on a pile of rocks, and started to sing; in their brilliant saris, they looked like flowers in a rock garden. They were small dark people, wearing distinctive heavy brass anklets. Their faces, too, were distinctive, their noses broader and flatter, their lips fuller than those of the general populace.

"These people," said Shyam, "are Santals." The Santals are an aboriginal tribe. About three thousand years ago, India was invaded by light-skinned Aryan hordes from southern Europe and Asia Minor. They drove the endemic darker-skinned population southward and enslaved those who remained; thus began the Indian caste system. Some tribes, including the

Santal woman carrying coal,
gouache, 1991.

Gonds of Madhya Pradesh, the Todas of the Nilgiris, and the Santals of
Bengal took refuge in the forests and the hills and kept themselves separate
over the centuries, largely by obeying strict marriage rules. If they married
outside the tribe, they were outlawed. The cataclysmic political upheavals
endured by India in the twentieth century had begun to erode the Santals'
isolation, but in 1964 the tribe was still essentially apart ethnically, socially,
and culturally.

They passed more Santal road workers as the jeep lurched southward. In
the coming days, Margaret saw Santals collecting stone to rebuild a washed-
out bridge north of Tiluri. And in an open-pit coal mine near Asansol, Santal men used picks to loosen rock or dirt or coal while women, like caryatids
in perfectly draped homespun saris, toted heavy loads in bamboo baskets on
their heads. (From memory in 1991, Margaret completed a gouache painting
of one of these women, with the coal mine in the background.)

Sri Khirod and Shyam suggested they visit some Santal villages—scattered throughout Bihar and West Bengal—and Margaret agreed with enthusiasm. They reached the first village on their route and parked the jeep.
Shyam disappeared for a time on his quest for chickens.

In comparison to Hindu settlements—which were shabby and grimy, with cattle and other livestock roaming freely and messily—the Santal village was tidy and clean. Houses were constructed with smooth, uncluttered, curving lines, not unlike Native American pueblo homes. The walls were whitewashed, some decorated with paintings and graffiti. On one low white wall a cat, sleek and aloof, stretched its black length.

Cattle stood in stalls, some with curtains across the doorways. Shyam explained that cattle are not sacred to Santals and therefore may be restrained. Large round brass vessels held the villagers' water supply and in the courtyards were ledges with scooped-out depressions to hold these containers. Cooking stoves were baked clay structures with no sharp corners. Outside the village was a grove of trees, and Margaret's guides, although somewhat vague about specifics, indicated the grove was sacred to the Santal villagers.

In the 1940s, William Archer, an English official, lived and worked among the Santal people, learned the Santali language, and made a collection of their sensuous poetry. His book *The Hill of Flutes* describes Santal religious practices. He explains that each Santal village has its sacred grove in which dwell nature spirits, or *bongas*. The Santals believe in a creator, sometimes identified with the sun, who allots each person a term of life. But the bongas —some malign, some benign—direct and influence every aspect of their lives; all ceremonies and festivals relate to bongas. Margaret was struck with the parallels between bongas and the *kachina* spirits of southwestern Native Americans.

They continued south, and the farther they went, the more tidy were the Santal villages. They then came to an area that Sri Khirod Roy described as no man's land. He announced, "There is so much land that no one is living here. Such sceneries are very *cheerful*." English is spoken by anyone with education in India, so language should have been no problem, but the two guides' English threw Margaret at times. As well as interesting use of words such as this "cheerful," an "f" sounded like a "p." They told her that the reason it was taking so long to find chickens was because many "poke pestibles" had taken place. When she looked puzzled, they kindly repeated it a little louder: "*Poke Pestibles!*" "Ah—folk festivals!" She got it. A village shrine contained a small clay statue; the guides said it was a dy-tee. She looked at it closely; it was crude but unmistakably equine. She said with diffidence, "A horse?" Shyam agreed equably. Many little horses graced courtyard shrines in both Santal and Hindu villages. "Dy-tees," they affirmed again, smiling gently. At last she got that too: a deity.

They turned toward Susuna Hill, and a troupe of monkeys melted off into the woods. At the bottom of the hill stood a small temple; a natural spring emerged from a tiger-head gargoyle and splashed into a small paved court. The light was strange, unearthly. (On the way home from South Africa, Margaret and Ned had briefly visited Greece. This place—its light, its atmosphere—made her think of Delphi.) Offerings of fruit and flowers—to a dy-tee, no doubt—lay on a slab of rock.

Behind the temple, a path led up the steep hill. Mrs. Mukherjee and her father gave up first, then Sri Khirod, while Margaret and Shyam trudged doggedly on until they reached a spur of the hill and looked out over a view of cultivated fields and trees, then sat in long grass and let the breeze cool their faces.

By the time they had come down the hill and driven to Jadarpur, the next village, the light was fading. Jadarpur was a fairly large Santal village that reminded Margaret of the ancient Hopi village of Walpi, which sits on top of a mesa in Arizona. Jadarpur's setting was not as dramatic or wind-swept as Walpi's, but it had the same sculptured, organic effect. To Margaret's frustration, it was already too dark for photography.

Shyam led the way into a spotless courtyard. Four or five water buffalo stood in a thatched shed, motionless except for steadily ruminating jaws and the occasional flip of a tail to dislodge a fly. The sweet hay smell of cattle filled the air. Shyam talked briefly with an old man, who nodded and climbed a ladder under the conical thatch of an open-sided structure. He stirred out a flock of pigeons, which wheeled around the courtyard and flew away with a great clattering of wings. The old man reached up into the cone and, bearing two live squabs, came down the ladder. Shyam took them, tied them up in a handkerchief, and stowed them in the jeep. Margaret looked at the wriggling bundle doubtfully, thinking of the number of mouths to be fed.

They were a good thirty miles from the camp. Along the way, they made several more stops at other Santal villages—no chickens; the guides' faces grew gloomy. But then it seemed they left the festival area, and in the next villages, Shyam's negotiations were successful. The plaintive peeps of the squabs were joined by a swelling chorus of clucks and squawks.

It was now dark, and Margaret began to feel uneasy. It was getting so late, and Ned would certainly be anxious. She imagined him fidgeting, pacing, the creases of his forehead deepening. At home, he hated for her not to appear exactly when expected; in a land of leopards, tigers, bandits she could just imagine his worry. Sri Khirod and Shyam were obviously unconcerned and determined to do everything on their agenda.

The jeep stopped. Another school—the Gogra junior high. Chairs and a table were brought, and after introductions to several teachers and administrators, Sri Khirod, Mrs. Mukherjee, and Margaret sat in pitch blackness for three-quarters of an hour while tea was prepared. Shyam and Mrs. Mukherjee's father wandered off to chat with a group of men. Tea came at last, together with little cakes and—praise be—an oil lamp. The tea was welcome; Margaret had not realized how thirsty she was. By lamplight, she was shown the school's cultural club with its small library and was requested to inscribe a visitor's book. Finally, the school officials presented her with two paper dahlias.

They made two or three more chicken stops and paused briefly at Kanthal to watch a Hindu religious gathering. It was set up in country-fair style; booths of all kinds were arranged around a brightly lit central area in which men danced and drummed, watched by a crowd seated on the ground.

To the final faint peeps from the squabs, they at last drove into the camp. Margaret was exhausted and hungry. She hurried out of the jeep, sure she would find a distraught Ned; by now he must be imagining every kind of dire accident. However, although one of the institute scientists had indeed set out in another jeep to look for them in case they had broken down, nobody else appeared to have noticed the lateness of their return; they were all—including Ned—busy discussing their own adventures.

The next day—Sunday—Shyam and Sri Khirod turned up mid-morning in the jeep. Margaret climbed in, and they set off northward to visit a small Hindu village, Tetulia Rakh, where basket makers were producing the ubiquitous baskets; these were strong and light, of scutched (beaten and shredded) bamboo and were used for every sort of carrying. Shyam maneuvered a basketmaker to one side and asked Margaret to photograph him "making" a basket. The basketmaker's face was a picture of disdain.

They returned to Tiluri, where Margaret was introduced to Shyam's wife and children. She also met his mother, who looked disapproving, her expression unrelentingly dour. Social niceties taken care of, Margaret was taken to watch a silversmith at work and they dropped in briefly at the local weavers' society. Today, her guides were evidently taking seriously her request to see arts and crafts.

After lunch and visits to two Hindu temples, Margaret was driven to a tile factory situated south of Saltora. Many local houses were roofed with curved tiles, and now she saw how these were made: three men worked a tile press, tamping lumps of clay until they were flat; a man in nothing but a loin cloth folded the flattened sheets over his thigh and trimmed them with a sharp knife; the result, a tile with a distinctive curve.

Also near Saltora, a potter was throwing pots on a wheel—a wagon wheel—on the ground. To make it spin he stirred it with a stick so that it whirled on its hub. With apparent ease, he squatted in what looked like an impossible position, one knee up, the other leg stretched out beside the wheel. Leaning forward, he plopped his clay onto the flat disk in the center of the revolving wheel and raised a pot; he sliced it off when completed, then set the wheel going again, managing to raise three pots from one lump of clay. Nearby, a woman squatted with a supply of his pots— utilitarian but quite elegant—that had been rendered leather-dry over a slow fire. With a rounded stone, she gently massaged ashes into the inside of the pots to toughen the clay, then placed them in a brick kiln fueled with dried dung.

On Monday morning (January 20), the first destination was Jhahurbana, a Hindu weavers' village. Both men and women were weaving, working on wide looms—simple but functional—set up under thatched roofs, with hollowed-out depressions for the treadles and the weaver's feet. Before being transferred to the looms, warps were being stretched on frames under trees. One woman was weaving a brocaded pattern; a small woman stood above the seated weaver and plucked the warps as if they were the strings of a harp. Once again, Shyam had to have his picture taken; Margaret snapped him "helping" a woman working on a white sari with vivid blue borders. Saris are traditionally woven all of a piece—the ancients had a taboo against seams in a garment—and are bordered on both ends and down one side. "Saris worn by women doing heavy work are pulled between the legs and tucked in at the waist to form a sort of baggy trouser," Margaret commented. "Women do not lift the skirt of a sari to walk upstairs—or even to climb on the arm of an airplane seat to reach the luggage bin!"

They drove on to Kulabahal, an almost deserted Santal village. A few men threshed rice using a homemade husking machine, and behind the houses a group of children and elderly men and women gathered pulms— fruit a little like crab apples but in vivid shades of yellow, green, and orange-red. There was a school near the village; Margaret faced the visit with resignation. Shyam stopped at the next village to pick up a very beautiful woman in an indigo-purple sari. He introduced her as his "sister-in-law."

Tuesday, and it was Saltora again, and more tea with Mrs. Mukherjee and her family—Mrs. Mukherjee announced her intention of accompanying them on the day's expedition, and soon Shyam's "sister-in-law" appeared and did likewise. They drove south and west to Jorhira and visited a multipurpose school. And then to a Santal rice factory at Jhantipahari, where the manager proudly showed off enormous boilers. Vast quantities of rice had been boiled and spread out on a cement court to dry. Women turned this creamy mountain with pusherlike tools. In a sorting room, other women tossed dried rice in baskets woven from rice straw and picked over the grain by hand for husks and stones. A man was twisting rice straw into a coil of rope; another worked a machine like a see-saw—first one end, then the other thumped into a pile of grain, grinding it into rice flour.

At this town, yet another school—a senior basic girls school, where the headmistress showed them an exhibition of handiwork and gave Margaret a handkerchief made by one of the students. Margaret was very hungry and was relieved when the headmistress showed them into one of the schoolrooms to eat the packed lunch the camp cooks had prepared for them.

Before they left, the women in the party needed to use the bathroom facilities. "I waited for half an hour," said Margaret. "The bathroom was at the end of the garden and occupied. We women stood around, uncomfortable, and lost for topics of conversation. When at last, the occupant emerged, I trotted thankfully down the garden, opened the door and looked in . . . a bare cement floor with a drain around the edge. I had to creep back ignominiously and ask Mrs. Mukherjee what I was supposed to do. She told me kindly that I was to use the drain. Such basic cultural differences can make for difficulties."

On then to Kennjakura, a ringing, clanging settlement where 150 families supported themselves by making brass objects. Each open-fronted shop had a forge with hand-worked bellows, and a lathe operated by pulling on a string. Margaret purchased a plate and, feeling in a shopping mood, a gold and deep rusty brown cotton sari from the local weavers' society for herself. Inevitably, the Kennjakura High School awaited their visit and inspection. Then once more they headed back toward the camp.

As they approached the Santal village of Jirrha, a man came out to the roadside and waved the jeep down to inform them that a dance ceremony was in progress a short way off the road. Sri Khirod turned off the motor, and they heard drums. The man led them across rice fields to a flat patch of ground where dancers and drummers were performing. The drums—some beaten with sticks, others with hands—were hollow wood with a pattern of strings to hold the heads tight. The whole village had turned out to participate or watch, and around the perimeter of the festivities were tables laden with attractively displayed edibles.

To one side, a pot smoked lazily. One by one, the male dancers sniffed the smoke, and after only a few moments they fell backwards in a trance. Two men stood by to catch them as they fell, and to drag them ungracefully to chairs under a little canopy; there, two women fanned them and fussed over them. Shyam informed Margaret, "These men are possessed by Marang Buni, the Santal's only goddess." Meanwhile, a group of women in white saris with marigolds in their black hair occasionally danced and sang, very demure, very restrained.

"A fellow clad only in a rather baggy and grimy white loin cloth shepherded people around and kept them in order." Margaret said, "He carried a branch—it looked as if he had just plucked it out of a tree and he waved it about. Toward the end of the proceedings, he became quite wild, spinning round and round with his branch, but I did not see him sniff from the pot. He seemed to be too busy the whole time to do so.

"A small goat had been tied up to one side throughout the proceedings. He was miserable and scared, and he bleated pitifully. The moment of sacrifice came; he was imprisoned between two stakes and his head was lopped off with one blow of a large knife wielded by the fellow with the branch. He died with a leaf in his mouth. . . . The male dancers rushed forward to drink his blood. It was strong stuff for me and my guides knew it was time to leave."

In *Hill of Flutes* William Archer describes different ceremonies but none that fits perfectly with Margaret's description. The *Baha* festival is a fertility rite lasting several days; girls dance with flowers in their hair, and three mediums become possessed by *Maran Buru* ("Marang Buni?") and two other influential bongas of the sacred grove, one of whom is the Lady of the Grove. The priest in charge of the ceremony holds a branch from a sal tree and communicates messages by waving it. He sacrifices a fowl, and the mediums devour its hot blood. However, the *Baha* festival is held in March. Perhaps this was part of the *Sohrae* harvest celebration or was a lesser festival, incorporating some of the features of the Baha.

Time to leave the ceremony—and also it was time to leave the camp. The party returned to Calcutta to regroup for the sight-seeing part of the Indian odyssey. This tour was designed to continue exploration of relevant fossil localities and sites of geological interest, while taking in some of the ancient wonders of India. The party included Pamela Robinson, several institute geologists, and two drivers. Carefully planned by Prashanta and Rani Mahalanobis, it was all at Indian Statistical Institute expense.

The first stop on the tour was New Delhi. There on January 26, Indian Republic Day, Margaret and Ned watched, from grandstand seats, an impressive parade, complete with gorgeously caparisoned elephants, military uniforms, and traditional costumes of all kinds. The Colberts shivered in inadequate clothing as a wind with a memory of snow on its breath whistled down from the high Himalayas. After the parade had passed, they attended a garden party at the presidential palace, where Margaret was dazzled by the saris; in rich, jewel-colored silks and cottons, they looked wonderful, even when wrapped around the more than ample brown waists of dignified matrons.

From New Delhi they visited the Taj Mahal at Agra and the nearby city of Fatehpur Sikri, the palace of which is preserved as a museum. (The city was founded in the seventeenth century but abandoned for lack of water after less than twenty years.) In the evening, the party was nearing New Delhi, sight-seeing en route. "I hated to keep people waiting while I took photographs, but I saw this wonderful scene and I just had to take it," said Margaret. "Silhouetted against the light, a handsome Brahma bull stood beneath a tree. It was perfect. I raised my camera to take this once-in-a-lifetime shot—and he started to urinate. I waited—and that was my mistake. He went on and on and on. Everyone in the party laughing . . ."

They flew to Bombay, from where they visited the Ajanta and Ellora caves, in which people in the sixth century A.D. had carved wonderfully intricate and detailed temples out of volcanic rock. How it was done defies the imagination—because basalt is, as Ned put it, "as hard as the hinges of Hades."

Next, the group flew into Nagpur in central India and took a camping trip into the back country of Madhya Pradesh for the paleontologists to work in the Triassic sediments along the Pranhita and Godavari rivers; two Land Rovers, each pulling a trailer loaded with food and field and camping gear, took the party into the back country. They came to a river and a ferry too small and uncertain to take both vehicles at once. Margaret crossed with the first Land Rover and sat on the bank to wait, idly watching the swirl of the muddy water.

"Wavelets were breaking over a mud bank close to shore, and little pieces of fern, twigs, and leaves were getting hung up on the mud. I watched a particular piece of fern. The wavelets started to wash mud over it, and at the same time, swirled mud up from below. It sat there for several minutes, and then a wave broke it loose and it bobbed off downstream, enclosed in a neat mud envelope. I realized this was probably why botanical fossils (or fish, insects, or other critters)—are found enclosed in concretions, and why they come in such neat oval packages. I'm sure everyone knows this, but I actually saw it happening."

Madhya Pradesh, in east-central India, is the home of the Gonds. (Eduard Suess, an Austrian geologist of the late nineteenth century, first postulated the existence of a southern supercontinent, and named it Gondwanaland for the Gonds.) Like the Santals, the Gonds are an aboriginal tribe and have kept themselves separate. A small Gond village was located in the jungle a few miles away from Sironcha where the party was staying overnight. One of the institute men went to the village to ask if they would be willing to dance for the visitors. They agreed, and early next morning a group of about fifty arrived prepared to perform. In *Digging into the Past*, Ned describes the scene:

> The men [were] clad in loose white clothing accentuated by very baggy pants, wearing turbans on their heads, in many cases with a long peacock feather sticking up out of the turban to serve as a waving guidon, and around their waists leather belts to which were attached many little globular bells. The women . . . were clad in very short tight skirts extending down only about half way to the knees, with red bands around the lower part of each skirt, and each woman wore a short-sleeved blouse or perhaps an abbreviated little shawl, pinned together over the left shoulder. They wore a profusion of beads around their necks, and every woman had a little square mirror below her chin, hanging by a cord around the neck. Each of them had a silver ring through the left side of the nose, and almost all of them wore long red, white, and black streamers of yarn, two on each side suspended from a band around the head. . . . The two leaders of the group were prosaically clad in khaki shorts and shirts and each of them carried a big, black umbrella.

As they began to dance, a throng of several hundred Indians gathered to watch. The Gonds had kinky hair, dark, copper-colored skin, and their features looked like a mix of Australian aborigine and black African. They walked the fourteen or so miles from their village overnight, and then proceeded to dance all morning. Some men played clarinet-like woodwinds, some small drums, and the music was punctuated by the deep notes of a drum so huge it needed two men to carry it. When the paleontology party decided they must be on their way, the smiling dancers surrounded the vehicles and accompanied them down the road, still making music.

From Sironcha the party drove west across country to the village of Bhi-maram, about ninety miles north of Hyderabad, in the state of Andhra Pradesh. The Indian Statistical Institute had asked Raja Reddy if he and the village would host the paleontological party while they hunted further Gondwana fossils nearby. Raja Reddy was a tall, handsome man with very dark skin; thick, wavy, black hair; and an interest in geology. A small tent village was set up on the outskirts of the village, but Raja Reddy invited Margaret and Ned to stay at his home.

Raja Reddy's father had been a blacksmith. A story was told of how he was walking along a road and was set upon by a pair of bandits. He simply picked them up—one under each arm—and carried them to the police station in the next village. This legendary figure had founded Bhimaram; in carefully calculated numbers, he had gathered together people skilled in the trades and crafts necessary for a community to be viable and largely self-sufficient.

Shortly before the Colberts visited Bhimaram, the village had been awarded a prize for progress, under the aegis of Raja Reddy, who had initi-ated a program employing the local people to grow corn and rare exotic vegetables. With some pride, Raja showed them fields of corn, growing way above his head. The hospital in the village, however, was a sloping dirt area, with a thatched roof supported by corner posts—again, the mind bog-gled at how it must be in the rainy season.

Raja Reddy and his wife were both college graduates, and their house was full of books. His wife was reticent and self-effacing, but she came out of her shyness to show Margaret how to wear her sari. Later, Margaret put it on by herself, and when she appeared in it, Mrs. Reddy and everybody else present politely smothered their mirth. She had wound it backwards, so that her left arm was free instead of her right. "I put it on widdershins, instead of deasil!" said Margaret, the lover of good words.

Beyond the boundaries of Bhimaram, the countryside was quite wild. Leopard pawprints were visible on the Reddy property one morning. A few days before the Colberts' arrival, the big cat had leapt over the Reddy gar-den wall and made off with a dog. One evening Raja Reddy came in with the news that he had seen a tiger on his way home, and he suggested a tiger hunt. After dinner, Margaret and Ned, plus three institute geologists—Sohan Lal Jain, Tapan Roy Chowdhury, and Supriya Sangupta—piled into Raja's Land Rover. They roared off into the blackness of the jungle; every-body was very cheerful, and the Land Rover was loud. They racketed along through the forest, peering through the blackness, hoping to see the reflection of tiger eyes in the headlights. Startled and unidentified birds fluttered out of their way, a fox slipped across their path, and once the bulk of a sambar deer loomed close, but they saw no tiger.

The next destination was Hyderabad, and Margaret stayed in the home of Justice P. Jaganmohan Reddy and his wife while Ned and the field party drove off in the Land Rovers once more to work in the back country. A distant relative of Raja Reddy, Justice Reddy was chief justice of the High Court of Hyderabad. (Later he was to serve on the Supreme Court of India.) He was an imposing and distinguished figure, but his family of three grown children treated him with cheerful lack of respect, arguing energetically with him at mealtimes. His wife, Pramila, held up her own end of the discussions with quiet dignity; she was a striking woman, with a diamond stud in her nose.

Justice Reddy and Pramila were to visit the Colberts in Leonia in the late 1960s; Denis and Matthew (George and Jenny's small sons) were staying with their grandparents at the time. Justice Reddy kept the boys enthralled recounting how he used to go to school by elephant. It was like a school bus, he told them. The elephant went around and picked up the children one by one, and they all strove to avoid the back seat because when the elephant sat down to let them off, the other children fell on top of the child in that unfortunate position. Denis, aged six, whispered to Margaret: "This is a very interesting conversation!" Matthew, who was four, leaned against Mrs. Reddy's knees and gazed fixedly up at her, entranced by the diamond in her nose.

Raja Reddy had accompanied Margaret to Hyderabad, and he took her on several sight-seeing tours into the countryside, including a trip south of the city to see the Nagarjunasagar Dam on the Krishna River. It was still under construction, destined to be the largest masonry dam in the world. From a distance the hundreds of workers looked like insects crawling over and around it. At the bottom of the largely completed face of the dam, Raja Reddy invited Margaret to climb one of the bamboo ramps that leaned against it. She took off her shoes so she could use her toes to cling to the bamboo slats. Up these steep and slippery ramps, women carried mortar in baskets on their heads and, in groups of four, men carried slabs of the bluish rock from which the dam was constructed, slung on ropes between them. The dam was almost entirely built by hand. Margaret's experience was like watching the pyramids under construction.

Upstream of the dam were the ruins of an ancient Buddhist monastery—or university, because it was where people had come to learn from their gurus. It would be flooded when the dam was completed, but plans were in place to move the most precious archeological remains and artifacts onto an island and to build a museum around them. These included a very early *stupa*. Raja Reddy explained that when Buddha's disciples asked him what kind of memorial he wanted when he died, he replied that he wanted none—that he wanted to vanish like a bubble. The Nagarjunasagar stupa's spherical shape was covered with big pieces of iridescent, airy jade stone. It looked indeed like a heavenly bubble. (In 1977, on the Colberts' second visit to India, they saw the dam finished and operational and visited the museum. Margaret was very glad to have seen the monastery and the artifacts in situ.)

Raja Reddy took Margaret to attend a trial where Justice Reddy was sitting. "We sat down and watched lawyers and a confusing number of unidentifiable witnesses speak. We left after about half an hour, and I asked Raja Reddy what language they had been speaking. It had sounded fast and sing-song. He looked at me, puzzled. 'Why, *English!*' he said. I was very embarrassed." Indians have over the years developed different pronunciation and word usage, as she had found out with her guides in West Bengal; and, as Ned said, "Now there's a generation of Indians who learned English from Indians who learned English from Indians!"

When Ned came out of the field, Justice Reddy made arrangements for the Colberts to go and visit the palace of the Nizam of Hyderabad. The Nizam was one of the last of the Indian princes. After Independence, princes were granted life tenure, but when they died, their descendants became commoners and their estates reverted to the government. The Nizam had been one of the richest men in the world, and Justice Reddy had been his lawyer.

The palace had been built and accoutred at the turn of the century. The entrance hall was big, and square, two stories high, with stairs going up one side and across the far end. Beside the stairs and along the wall below them were stuffed dogs, pets of the Nizam that he could not bear to part with. Many of these had hinged heads that nodded in the slightest breeze. Against the other wall, opposite the stairs, was a mechanical band; inside an enormous glass case were genuine instruments, arranged ingeniously so that they would play; the Colberts' guide assured them that it worked.

They were shown a splendid bedroom in which all the furniture—including the bed—was made of cut glass. A room with great windows overlooking formal gardens and a view to the city of Hyderabad in the distance contained an immensely long table with chairs lined up on each side of it. Margaret counted ninety-four chairs. She said to the guide, "This must be the banquet room." "Oh no," said he, "this is the breakfast room."

Hyderabad saw the end of the field work. The Colberts' next destinations were purely for sight-seeing. Professor Mahalanobis had asked Margaret if there was any place that she would particularly like to visit. She remembered her mother's description of Darjeeling and asked if a trip there would be possible. Anything was possible for the professor. They flew up from Calcutta, the only non-Indians on the flight. As they approached the mountains, the flight attendant told them Mount Everest was straight ahead, and they could come up to the pilot's cabin to view it. The bearded pilot, a Sikh, wore a large turban. From the cockpit could be seen the vast range of the Himalaya, blue, purple, white, weather streaming from the highest peaks; Everest itself, its silhouette familiar, its romance and aura intact. In Darjeeling the clouds had rolled in and they were able to see little of the mountains. But otherwise the town matched satisfyingly Kate Matthew's 1920s description.

A final stop in the last week of their Indian stay was made in Benares. Benares and the Ganges could not, according to Professor Mahalanobis, be missed on a tour of India. But Margaret rather wished it had been missed, for there she contracted dengue fever. For several days she suffered aching joints and head, diarrhea, and a high fever. By the time she saw a doctor back in Calcutta, she was practically over it. The doctor came into her room each day and asked, "And how many motions have we had today?" Margaret longed to answer, "I don't know about you, Doctor, but for myself I can say . . ."

When Margaret and Ned returned to India for the 1977 Gondwana Symposium held in Calcutta, they visited Hyderabad again. The trip coincided with Justice Reddy's seventieth birthday, and they attended a large party in his honor. By then, Justice Reddy had retired from the High Court and had become chancellor of Osmania University, the big university in Hyderabad, a campus made beautiful with water gardens and flowers.

They were invited to visit the Hyderabad Zoo, where the director personally conducted them around the exhibits. It was very crowded; the director was proud of the zoo's popularity and enthusiastic about cooperation with other zoos around the world in progressive breeding programs. In one big natural-habitat enclosure, he pointed out the pride of Indian lions, extinct now in the wild. The creatures lay yawning and torpid, in the manner of all lions. Unlike African lions, which lose their spots by the time they are twelve months old, Indian lions retain shadowy freckles and flecks all their lives. The director very much wanted the lioness to get up and show herself off. Although it was not feeding time, he had a keeper go and fetch a food cart, but the lioness just blinked; she would have none of it.

They were followed around the zoo by a bizarre personage who had flowing white hair, a heavy beard, strange tattoos on his face, a cloak thrown around his shoulders, and bare feet. Margaret nudged Ned. She was thinking: A madman? A priest from an ancient cult? "We kept glancing behind us—he was always there. The director seemed unconcerned. Suddenly, from under the cloak, the apparition whipped out a Hasselblad! He was the official zoo photographer."

To both Colberts, the experiences of India were unforgettable. As distinguished visitors, they recognized that they had been largely shielded from the poverty, dirt, and disease of the subcontinent. Rags and beggars, weeping sores and hunger could not be completely avoided, but time obscured the unacceptable. To be cherished in memory were the hospitality, the Mahalanobis generosity, the lasting friendships with the Reddy families.

For Margaret, woven through each recollection of India are the colors (burnt umber, chocolate, gold, and rust; violet, indigo, ultramarine, crimson), the smells (turmeric, smoke from dung fires, coriander, cattle), the artisans (potters, weavers, brass and silver smiths, makers of musical instruments). She remembers a black cat on a white Santal wall, and the marigolds—marigolds everywhere, decorating temples, black hair, Ghandi's tomb in Delhi, more temples. The blooms recalled the blaze of orange careening over her father's garden in Hastings-on-Hudson.

❧ 18 ❧

Australia

It was no more expensive to fly east than to fly west, so the Indian Statistical Institute flew the Colberts home to the States via Australia. This particularly suited Ned; after what he had seen in South America, South Africa, and India, he was finding it harder to hang onto his skepticism about the ancient supercontinent and continental drift and harder to believe in the alternate theory that animals had wandered to the different areas the long way around across land bridges. But before he could finally climb down off his fence and join the team of the "Drifters," he had a few more questions. He had long wanted to observe for himself Australian Gondwana fossil localities—on the east coast, in Tasmania, and in Western Australia.

After a three-day stopover in Thailand, the Colberts flew to Sydney and then to Melbourne. From Melbourne, they took a trip to the Grampians, a range of hills to the west of the city. They found no fossils, but they wandered through a forest of spicy eucalyptus trees and came upon a spiny anteater, or echidna. The monotremes (duck-billed platypuses and echidnas) are primitive egg-laying mammals and are of great interest to vertebrate paleontologists, who consider them living mammal-like reptiles, or, perhaps, reptile-like mammals. The spiny-coated beast moved slowly over the ground, and Ned gently picked it up and turned it over. It looked like a large, elongated hedgehog, with enormously long and heavy claws, no teeth, and the tiny eyes of a creature that spends a lot of its time below ground. It lay torpid in Ned's hands, but when he put it down, it dug itself into the forest floor right there, at his feet, at an indignant and astonishing speed.

In Hobart, Tasmania, Margaret and Ned were met by an American couple, John and Bette Cosgriff. John was on a fellowship in Tasmania, studying

Triassic amphibians and reptiles. Bette was a graduate of the California College of Arts and Crafts in Oakland, so she and Margaret had plenty to discuss. The two couples went to the southernmost tip of Tasmania and into a dark and brooding forest. If the nearly extinct Tasmanian wolves still existed, they would be there, hidden among the almost impenetrable underbrush, as would the fierce-looking Tasmanian devils. Neither creature showed itself, however.

They picnicked in a cove and looked out across a leaden sea that they knew rolled uninterrupted until Antarctica; as if to keep her in mind of this, Margaret found a dead penguin on the beach. Small, round, gray crabs scuttled sideways out of her way, causing a ripple effect across the expanse of sand. On the rocks at the edge of the tide she found oysters, and picked them up and ate them immediately, "like a Cro-Magnon lady," said Ned.

Triassic reptiles, dinosaurs, and other fossils of interest had been found in Queensland, so the Colberts bade the Cosgriffs farewell and flew on to Brisbane. The Great Barrier Reef, with its abundance of living creatures, was a lure even for a hunter of fossils, and Ned decided he could spare the time to visit it with Margaret. They took a small plane to Gladstone, north of Brisbane. The aircraft circled above white coral-sand beaches, and the southern end of the Great Barrier Reef; from that height, the reef appeared as a string of islands, many of them atolls with bright turquoise centers, set in water crystal clear with stripes of different blues. They saw a ship, wrecked and sunk years ago, clearly visible from the air. Heron Island, their next destination, was a green dot of land, sixty miles out from Gladstone.

A launch took them out to Heron Island the next day. The trip took several rough hours, but Margaret gritted her teeth and survived. Among the trees close to the beach, they camped overnight with a group of people. After dark, sea turtle eggs buried in the sand began hatching; somebody put a flashlight in the water, and the baby reptiles swarmed toward it.

A marine research station is based on Heron Island, and there they met Miss Goh, a zoology student from Kuala Lumpur. With Miss Goh and snorkeling equipment, Margaret set off to explore the reef, but first she asked at the research station about sharks. A voice of authority told her not to worry: "They don't come inside the reef, except very occasionally on cloudy days." The sky was indeed rather gray, but nobody at the station seemed perturbed. The two women waded into the warm sea.

"We started out kicking with our fins, but decided we would do better if we poled ourselves along with stout sticks. That way we would be less disturbing to the denizens of the reef. It was thrilling—the underwater seascape, the multicolored, multi-shaped fish and other creatures. We breathed through our snorkels and floated lazily along, poling against the white sandy bottom.

"Because it was indeed a cloudy day, we looked around every once in a while for sharks, and by and by we spotted five. They were inside the reef. We were about halfway between the shore and the reef, and both Miss Goh and I decided immediately we'd rather be in shallower water. We used our fins to travel fast. When we were about knee deep, we stood up, breathing rather hard, and looked again. One shark had come after us—perhaps our splashing fins had attracted him. He was about five feet long—he could take a good chunk out of us. We stood there, our sticks raised like cudgels and our snorkels pushed up. . . . Evidently that was enough to intimidate him. He made a U-turn and swam away."

The journey back to Gladstone was even rougher than the way out, and it was raining a little. The launch could not make it in across the reef to fetch the passengers. A lighter had to take them out to the launch in batches. Ned and Margaret were in the last lighter load, which was a blessing. The launch wallowed and heaved waiting for the lighter, and by the time the Colberts were off-loaded onto it, many people were already seasick. Margaret, for once, was fine—she hung onto a stanchion above her head for the whole journey; thus she stayed upright and let the boat roll under her as much as it wanted to. She even felt well enough to enjoy a pod of dolphins frolicking alongside the launch as it lurched toward the mainland. She went ashore very tired, but not sick.

From Brisbane, Ned departed for Western Australia, and Margaret started for home, flying via Sydney to Wellington on the North Island of New Zealand. A tour bus took her to Auckland via some of the sights of the island and then, more than ready to stop traveling, she boarded a plane for the States.

⁓ 19 ⁓

Flagstaff

It's time, my dear, it's time! it's peace the heart requires;
The days are flying past, and with each hour expires
A little bit of life.—and yet, not knowing whether
We swift, perchance, may die, we plan our life together.

This world holds little joy, but peace there is, and scope;
Long have I entertained an enviable hope:
Long I, a weary slave, have contemplated flight
To some far-distant home of work and sheer delight.

— *Alexander Pushkin, translated by Margaret Colbert*

Ralph Minor died in the late 1950s, and the house on Cedar Street in Berkeley reverted to Betty, Margaret, and Bill. Both Ned and Margaret loved the Spanish house; with its warm red tiles and white stucco walls, its fond memories, and the northern California climate, it seemed from a distance of time and space the ideal place for retirement. With that idea in view, they bought out Betty and Bill's shares in the property.

"Retirement itself was anticipated with pleasure and much discussion by both of us," said Margaret. "Regrets at leaving Leonia were tempered by the fact that most of our longtime good friends had already moved away. In addition, the air and water quality were deteriorating. Ned was anxious to retire."

Since the early 1950s, Ned had used the Museum of Northern Arizona as a base for his summer operations; it was ideal for his Triassic studies, and he had established good relationships with staff members. When the museum director, Edward (Ned) Danson (father, incidentally, of Ted Danson, the actor), suggested to him that office and laboratory space at the museum could be his if he were to consider retirement to Flagstaff, the idea was very interesting. He sounded out Margaret.

Margaret loved the Southwest and knew Flagstaff in the summer: dry air, hot sun from deep blue skies, afternoon thunderstorms building from spectacular towers of cloud, brilliantly starlit cool nights. But winters? The town is seven thousand feet above sea level. Its winters are bitter cold and deliver formidable quantities of snow. It occurred to them both that they should give a Flagstaff winter a test run. Ned had accumulated months of vacation time, so he took leave of absence from the American Museum of Natural History and Columbia for the whole winter of 1967–68.

The Museum of Northern Arizona leased the Colberts a little house. Ned settled in to write *Men and Dinosaurs*, an account of famous dinosaur hunters and their discoveries. Margaret took over a museum guest apartment as a studio, set up her easel, and settled in to enjoy the luxury of uncluttered blocks of time for her own creative work. Housekeeping duties were cut to a minimum, the distractions and commitments of life in Leonia were absent, and the telephone did not ring. She had no illustrating commissions to eat up hours. Ideas bubbled up; she had time to give expression to philosophical concepts, and time to experiment in different techniques. It felt like self-indulgence, and it was joy.

"I painted an African woman, with her elbow on her knee, her chin in her hand, and a small boy peering through the space formed by the angle of her arm. . . . My idea was the challenge that the younger generation poses to the older. The technical challenge I set myself was fascinating: I had discovered the delight of painting with an ordinary kitchen sponge, and for this painting, I approached it like a printer doing color separations for reproduction of a colored picture. Yellow first—I did everything that was to be yellow, and then everything that was to be red, and then blue; colors were mixed directly on the canvas to achieve greens, oranges, purples, etc. And, of course, it was black when all three colors were together. The composition had to be very strong because fine detail is not possible with a kitchen sponge. I made a small sketch to work it out, and then I worked freehand. It was difficult to think of the colors ahead. Faced with a blank canvas, it was tricky to think of everywhere that yellow should appear—the small highlights for instance. I only cheated a little, touching it up with a brush here and there."

Another painting, also done with a sponge and acrylics, Margaret titled *Continental Drift*. With this, she allowed herself to mix her colors on a palette, rather than using only the three primary colors directly on the canvas. The painting represents the continents of South America and Africa, with the diagonal split between them. But South America suggests a man, his ear and neck and shoulder in silhouette; Africa is a woman facing him, trying to say something to him, trying to get him to listen: "It was a statement about women's relationships with men."

Margaret painted a portrait of Ned that winter. Ned looked at the finished painting and announced that yes, it was indeed the official way he looked, but he did not care to have it hanging around the house. Perhaps he looked at it and saw what he had not acknowledged in the mirror—that he no longer looked quite the young man he still felt himself to be.

As for the climate, both Ned and Margaret loved wintering in Flagstaff. Almost every day they were able to eat their lunch outdoors, even with deep snow on the ground and the ambient temperature way below freezing. When the sun was out—as it so often was—its heat was burning and intense. They were both energized. In the spring they returned to Leonia, the decision made to move to Flagstaff. Although Margaret had no reservations about Arizona, putting the Berkeley house on the market and finally cutting all ties with her mother's home was not easy for her.

Ned answered the telephone one evening in August 1968. Bill Breed, a geologist from the Museum of Northern Arizona, was calling to say that a group of doctors had bought a tract of land along Schultz Pass Road in Flagstaff and had subdivided it. A piece of land almost in the back yard of the museum was available for sale. Ned was too busy to get away, so it was up to Margaret; she caught the first available flight to Flagstaff, a little timorous at the responsibility.

Even in the heat of August, the two and a half acres looked wonderful: a meadow of grasses, sagebrush, and wild flowers—Indian paintbrush, penstemmon, scarlet gilia—loud with bees and hummingbirds. Grasshoppers popped from the dry grasses with rattlesnake crackles and spread brief wings for flight. The land was outside and above the city of Flagstaff, its elevation about 7,200 feet. Behind it to the north, the San Francisco Peaks formed a glorious backdrop. They thrust perfect cones into a dark blue sky, rising steeply from geologically recent lava fields. Their flanks were clothed with aspens and ponderosa pine trees, which spilled all the way down the slopes to Schultz Pass Road, spicing the air with vanilla. Margaret had told Ned when they first talked of retirement that she would consent to live anywhere with him as long as she had at least three pine trees; she laughed, for here were scores of pines, the wind hushing in their branches. The laboratories of the museum research center were across the road and about a quarter of a mile away, behind two round holding tanks for the city's water supply. In the nearest tank floated a pair of mallards. In the desert heat, it was delightful to see any water, albeit of such a constrained sort. Margaret bought the land without hesitation and flew home.

Before he was drafted into the military, their son Dan had completed a liberal arts bachelor's degree at Columbia University. After Vietnam, he returned to Columbia to do a degree in architecture. His parents approached him about designing the house; he was enthusiastic, so they described their needs and desires, and Dan drew up plans. As he was still a student, a licensed architect had officially to approve and accredit the design; Flagstaff architect Jack Daly examined Dan's plans and made almost no changes. Margaret said, "He consulted with us only about minor details, such as where we would like to find electrical plugs and switches, what sort of tiles we would like on the floor, and so on."

Events moved fast. For the sake of prudence, before the foundations were laid, a well was drilled, hitting an ample supply of clean, clear water. Building began in the fall of 1968. It was strange living so far away and not seeing or knowing what was happening. Through the fall, "while Nixon was being elected," and into the winter, Ned constructed a foamcore model of the house from the plans, with Margaret's help. The sculptor in Margaret needed to see things in three dimensions, and the model helped both of them to modify and adjust details. "It was a nice experience, building the house," Margaret said. "The contractor and the architect had built many homes together, and they were good, and very pleasant. Our son Philip got involved. He put in some of the final woodwork and installed wires for a sound system and other specialized things."

In March 1969, Margaret and Phil drove out from New Jersey to inspect the house. They stayed in one of the guest apartments attached to the museum research center. One night a late storm dumped three feet of snow all at once; winter wonderland notwithstanding, getting across to the house was a problem. Phil had the brilliant idea of borrowing snowshoes from Bill Breed, but the snow was light and powdery, and Margaret's feet sank, snowshoes and all, to the knees. When she pulled a foot up to take a step, it was mounded with a great load of snow that had suddenly become less light and

The Flagstaff house, 1990s.

powdery. She finally arrived at the house, breathless with laughter and an-noyance, and she and Phil walked into the kitchen. They heard a faint scrabbling noise coming from the flue over the kitchen stove; investigation turned up two mice that had somehow gotten in there and were caught on the screen. Phil captured the little creatures, found a box for them, and kept them fed and watered. When the time came to go home, Margaret flew because she did not feel up to another long road trip. Phil drove back to Leonia, carrying the mice with him. He had not changed; as had been his habit when he was a child in Leonia, he was still a rescuer of small and helpless wild creatures.

To advertise the Leonia house, Margaret made a card with a photograph of the house taken from the back, with azaleas in full glory. She described the space and added "Wonderful Neighbors!" She said, "I think the neigh-bors sold the house. And when prospective buyers came to view it, there was the Chambers stove that Ralph Minor bought for me." The house sold easily.

Moving was a different matter. The Colberts had lived in the Park Ave-nue home for thirty years; and the packing and sorting of thirty-years' worth of belongings and clutter, the decisions of what to take and what to leave or dispose of, were a nightmare. Charles and Grace Cole were out of town, and they loaned their home to Margaret and Ned for two weeks. It was a boon not to have to live in the chaos of packing crates, but living with the Coles' treasures had its drawbacks, in particular the collection of kachina dolls that hung all the way down the stairway wall: "I wouldn't want to have to dust those little feet forever."

Margaret and Ned moved into their Flagstaff home in July, and Ned was installed in his position as honorary curator of vertebrate paleontology at the museum. In October, he left for Antarctica.

In the winter of 1967–68 Peter Barrett and Ralph Baillie of The Ohio State University found a piece of fossil bone in the Transantarctic Mountains. The men carefully wrapped the two-inch, 250-million-year-old fossil in toilet paper and placed it in a cookie can labeled "Bone." When they landed in Christchurch, New Zealand, customs officials viewed it with alarm and impounded it in a freezer; New Zealand does not permit introduction of meat products to the country.

Back in the States, Ralph brought the scrap to Ned for identification. Ned was beside himself—tiny as it was, it was diagnostic. It was a fragment of jaw bone, and because its articulation surface was intact, Ned was able to establish that it was amphibian and that it had the characteristics of the early Triassic amphibians known as labyrinthodonts. If the theory of continental drift and the previous existence of Gondwanaland were true, Antarctica was a key element, an essential piece to lock together the geologists' jigsaw puzzle of Gondwanaland. What was needed was Antarctic fossil evidence to link Triassic rock sequences found in all the southern continents—those rocks and fossils that Ned had been exploring for years. Someone had to go back to the area and look for more fossils.

Led by geologist David Elliot of The Ohio State University, a National Science Foundation expedition was launched in the winter of 1969–70 to follow up on the Barrett-Baillie bone. Ned was the obvious choice of paleontologist to go on the trip; however, he had to be persuaded. At sixty-four he was too old, he protested, but the NSF and David assured him that he would be looked after. He recounts his adventures in detail in *Digging Into the Past*. Here it is enough to say that at Coalsack Bluff in the Transantarctic Mountains, the expedition found fossil fragments of land vertebrates, including an incontrovertibly diagnostic fragment—part of a jaw and a tusk of a mammal-like reptile, the marker fossil, *Lystrosaurus*.

Communications with the Antarctic were abysmal; letters from Ned came through at very infrequent intervals and arrived out of sequence and in bunches. Very occasionally radiotelephone messages were possible through ham radio operators, but this was frustrating at the least and at times disturbing. (This state of affairs has only very recently improved for "ice widows and widowers," with the advent of electronic mail and advanced telephone technology.)

Bill Breed from the Museum of Northern Arizona was also on the Antarctic expedition, so Margaret and his wife, Carol, kept in touch and shared what little news they received from the south. They both received radiophone patches from their husbands intimating that a momentous find had been made, but nothing could be announced until after the NSF had cleared the information. The men had to be circumspect over the radiotelephone because news by that source is fair game to anyone with a suitably tuned ham radio. Margaret and Carol, sworn to secrecy, met at a museum party and watched each other fending off the eager questions. "Well, how are they doing?" "Have they found anything?" "Is there news?" They smiled and nodded and hedged, but could only say that they believed some sort of fossil had been found.

One morning Carol called Margaret with the news that there was a squib in the *Daily Sun*, the local Flagstaff newspaper. The item picked up from the Associated Press stated in a column barely an inch long on the back page that fossils had been found in Antarctica. Ned Danson, indignant that the news had been treated in such a casual fashion, called the newspaper and asked if they were aware that two people from Flagstaff were on that expedition, and whether the story did not merit more enthusiastic treatment. The *Sun* duly called Carol and asked her to come to their office to be interviewed. She agreed to go and called Margaret to go with her. Margaret agreed, but she was reluctant and annoyed to be summoned downtown. Surely, she thought, it would have been more appropriate for reporters to have come to them. At the office, the paper sat the two women in front of a Christmas tree, and a reporter with notebook and pencil asked them solemnly, "Tell me, what is going through your minds with your hubbies away at Christmas?" "That," said Margaret, curling her lip, "was the limit of their interest in the story." Meanwhile, the *Lystrosaurus* find was on the front pages of major newspapers all over the States and in Europe.

After Ned returned, Margaret worked on a model of *Lystrosaurus*. The sculpture measures about sixteen inches in length, and eight inches in height. A dozen casts of this restoration were made, each one individually hand-colored by Margaret, and each one different. Nick Hotton of the Smithsonian remarked that it is "the only restoration of *Lystrosaurus* that does not look like a coffee table draped with an alligator skin." The models have found homes in several American universities, including The Ohio State University (in the Byrd Polar Research Center), and in a couple of universities in New Zealand. One is in the geology department of the Museum of Northern

*Margaret's
model of
Lystrosaurus,
1970.*

Arizona. Two were used as part of a display on continental drift (plate tec-
tonics) in a travelling exhibit, "Creativity: A Human Resource," which
was sponsored by the Standard Oil Company of California and its Chevron
Family of Companies; the show toured the country from 1980 until 1983,
after which it was established as a semipermanent exhibit at the Pacific
Science Center in Seattle. (One of the remaining models is a treasured
possession of David Elliot and the author. It lives among plants and rocks
in the hearth of their Columbus, Ohio, home.)

∿ 20 ∾

"A Place of Work and Sheer Delight"

The house on Schultz Pass Road grows comfortably from the landscape. Its wooden siding is stained an odd donkey brown that melds perfectly with crushed lava, Flagstaff's excuse for soil. Although it is not large, the home gives an impression of spaciousness. Its construction is frame on cinder block, and it feels cool inside, as if it were adobe or old stone—an impression helped by the dark red brick downstairs floor.

The living-dining room has a cathedral ceiling. It is furnished sparingly with comfortable modern chairs and rugs. At the south end, a floor-to-ceiling cinder-block fireplace sports a seven-foot hanging of appliquéd wild flowers—a creation of Ned's. In the winter, a whimsical hanging designed by son Charles takes its place. A huge window on the west side lets in cool, green light filtered through the ponderosas. The north end holds the dining table and chairs and has sliding glass doors onto a narrow patio, across which bounce chipmunks and showy Abert's squirrels to feast off the birdseed left each day in the hollow of an old stump. Flashes of iridescent blue herald the presence of a Steller's jay in the closest big pine, while pygmy nuthatches run headfirst down the trunk of this tree and swarm over a suet feeder like so many gray mice.

On the east side of the room is a small cozy area Margaret and Ned call their kiva. It has a sunken floor, benches with comfortable cushions on two sides, bookcases on the third, and a second fireplace on the fourth. It is a perfect area for up to four or five people to gather to chat or read, especially in the winter months.

Upstairs, Margaret has a studio/bedroom, and Ned a study/bedroom. An indoor balcony overlooks the living room, but, with an eye to energy

173

Scratchboard Christmas card, Steller's jays.

conservation, this can be shut off from the rest of the house during the winter. Some of Margaret's paintings and drawings hang in the upstairs hallway. One upper room was designed as a guest bedroom but is now a subsidiary sitting room, with television and several armchairs; from this room, sliding glass doors lead to an outside balcony on which, at noon on a sunny winter's day—even with the temperature in single digits, snow on the ground, icicles hanging from the gutters—it is possible to sit in dark glasses and shirt sleeves and worry about sunburn.

Entry to the house is through a lobby with a glassed-in herbarium containing green plants and cactuses. A sturdy chair—a brainchild of Margaret's—stands against the stairs in this hallway. The Colberts had brought to the house a pair of Queen Anne chairs that had been in Margaret's family, and one of these had stood in the hall. Son Charles was married in 1982, and he and his wife, Agatha, looked so longingly at the antique chairs that

Margaret decided they should have them. But a replacement in the hallway was essential—a chair was needed to sit on to remove boots or to change shoes. In the late 1970s, a grand specimen of a *Pentaceratops*—a dinosaur built somewhat like a huge rhinoceros, with a tall bifurcating bony frill behind its head—was found in New Mexico. The fossil was brought to Flagstaff and prepared in the Museum of Northern Arizona. Margaret sculpted a miniature restoration of the beast, a model about eight inches long and three inches tall, and had it cast in bronze. While working on the frill, she saw—with her special ability to see—that it would make a fine chair back. She went to see Bill Burke, a friend in Flagstaff who makes beautiful wooden furniture and mandolins, and asked his advice. Together they melded the two ideas of Queen Anne and *Pentaceratops*; the result is a stout design in golden wood, with an impressionistic frill forming the back, and ponderous legs curving and reminiscent of Queen Anne.

"And then I learned to do needlepoint well enough to do the chair seat." It is rare to find fossil plants in the same block as a fossil creature, but the New Mexico *Pentaceratops* came with a lot of leaves, twigs, and sticks in the matrix. All the plant remains were identified by a paleobotanist. "So I restored these plants to their modern equivalents and made a collage of leaves. I used that for my pattern for the seat of the chair. Paleontologists usually get the joke and laugh when they see it, and that pleases me. Other people tend to look at it and wonder."

In the Flagstaff house Margaret at last had a real studio—a large room with good north light, ample work surfaces, a sink and running water, and lots of shelves and storage space. She could work on a regular basis in the daytime, rather than catching odd moments as they flew by. Ned was not "underfoot"; for him "retirement" was a relative term. Most mornings he trudged over to the museum research center, where he continued to study and describe fossil specimens, and to write books. He no longer took off in the summers on field trips, although he still traveled regularly to Ghost Ranch to run the summer paleontology seminars, and Margaret usually accompanied him there.

Margaret's Flagstaff years have been very productive. Her interest in different crafts has led her down many paths, and she has explored a variety of media. She said, "I pursue something hard until I really know how it works, and then I pursue something else. If I had stuck with one medium, I might have become much better at that particular art form. But I am being myself when I am a 'dilettante.'" With such multidirectional knowledge, teaching was an obvious option, but, "I've done little in the way of teaching and I don't enjoy it. It seems a shame with what I know, but I can never get it together to present to other people. I'm not that clear-headed."

Sculpture, her major at art school, continued to be a favorite art form. As well as modelling restorations of extinct beasts (which she liked to do as a prelude to an illustration), she worked on free sculptures for their own sake: for example, the terra cotta portrait heads of George and Jenny's sons, Denis and Matthew; and the Thembu couple of her South African travels. As an alternative three-dimensional medium, she tried wood carving and enjoyed it until her wrists would no longer take the pounding.

A clay model of which she was particularly fond she called *Letting Go*; a slab-style piece, it depicted two mature hands, with forearms supported on the elbows. "One hand was clasped with the thumb inside as a baby would hold its hand; the little finger and ring finger of the other were still curled loosely, the middle and index fingers uncurling, and the thumb free. The whole made a kind of rolling composition." Margaret commented, "It might have been more popular here in Flagstaff if I had made it more realistic. But I wanted it to be a sketched idea."

A local lack of understanding also occurred over a small cast-ceramic model that had been inspired by a life drawing done some years earlier in Leonia. About four inches high, a female figure is seated on a nautilus shell. An Arizona chapter of PEN (International Association of Poets, Playwrights, Editors, Essayists, and Novelists) Women rejected it from even entering a competition. Margaret was somewhat put out. "The group let in pseudo-artists, quilters, knitters. . . . Maybe they thought I was one of those women who is 'into ceramics,' meaning I had bought the cast and decorated it. Perhaps I had not made it clear enough that it was my own original design." It was not in her nature to contest their decision, however.

When first in Flagstaff, Margaret took a short course in card weaving. She had used a regular loom in art school, and understood the fundamentals of weaving. Card weaving really intrigued her. For one thing, the loom was small and very portable. The warp was threaded through a series of three-inch squares of cardboard, each punched with asymmetrically placed holes. The shuttle was manipulated as the cards were turned in a fixed order; intricate mathematically precise patterns emerged. Margaret wrote:

I like to turn the cards and see
The patterns dutifully rise
In sinuous lines; to set them free

So hidden nuances surprise;
To regiment the dark and light
And march them off to left or right.

Who first devised this way to ring
The changes on the vibrant warp?
What mental twists did genius bring
To fashioning this silent harp?
Ah! for the music it subtends
I greatly thank you, unknown friends.

She explored every aspect of card weaving. In addition to the inevitable plethora of woven belts (for which she also designed and patented a simple but ingenious metal "buckle" so that they could be fastened neatly at the waist without a cumbersome knot), she devised "sculptural" three-dimensional weavings. One of these was a whimsical wall hanging inspired by the two winter mice rescued by Philip when the house was being built: two life-size gray mice scramble on a circular "screen," which was woven in a narrow strip with slits, so that it could be opened like a net. She joined the Weaver's Guild and was invited to give a demonstration and a talk about her card-weaving ideas in Phoenix at a meeting. And then, "I suppose I ran out of ideas and of people to give belts to, and now the little loom just sits idle."

For a time, needlework and embroidery were consuming interests. Designing and making special needlework presents for special people was a great pleasure. The arrival of grandchildren—and then great-grandchildren—inspired her to produce some unusual and witty gifts.

For instance, there was *Couch Potato*, made for great-granddaughter Mari, daughter of grandson Denis. Couch Potato is two lightly stuffed quilted cushions zippered together. They are made of potato-colored velour on the outside and warm flannel on the inside. The eyes of the potato are randomly embroidered quilting knots. It is intended as a snug place to put feet on a cold day or perhaps, since cold days are uncommon in California, as a receptacle for special treasures. The pull for the zipper is a potato bug, and Margaret found perfect fabric for the insect—Madras striped in the correct colors. For the legs she used round elastic wrapped in silk, and she fastened them to a fabric potato leaf in such a way that the bug could be moved around.

She invented a simple method to do appliqué. "It's shamefully easy. I buy that cloth from the fabric store that's sticky on one side when you iron it with a warm iron, and I trace my design onto that. I cut the piece out, then pin the cloth that I want to appliqué onto its nonsticky side, and cut around evenly, a little bigger than the pattern piece, and clip the curves and corners. I take my iron and turn all the edges in so that the appliqué "patch" is now exactly the right size and shape, with the edges turned under and stuck in place. If I have two colors that are going to line up against each other, they are cut out of the same piece of sticky stuff, so they fit perfectly. Then I pin all the pieces onto the background, iron them so that they stick, and then stitch them in place. The sticky stuff is very light and adds negligible bulk or weight."

With this ingenious method, she designed a quilt. Overall, it was a Flagstaff scene, and it was divided into squares. She proposed to the Flagstaff PEN Women that each member appliqué one square; the whole could be assembled to complete an unusual quilt. "But the members must have believed it would be too much work. They were uninterested." This was a disappointment. (Recently, however, Margaret explained the process to daughter-in-law Agatha and showed her the Flagstaff design—Agatha was intrigued and began the task herself.)

The Museum of Northern Arizona has an outstanding collection of Native American archeological artifacts, a great many of which are in storage. Margaret borrowed some of the objects—mostly Hopi and Navajo treasures such as pottery and kachina dolls—and started a series of paintings of them. "I painted them quite realistically. I thought it a neat way to be able to look at some of those beautiful things that were otherwise stored out of sight. Nobody has to worry about their getting broken—and they don't have to be dusted!" Living with the Coles' kachinas for the two weeks before the move to Flagstaff had left its mark.

In 1984, at the suggestion of art curator Kathryn Chase, a retrospective exhibition of Margaret's work was arranged by the Museum of Northern Arizona. Kathryn Chase and her assistant went to the Colberts' house, looked over what was available, and selected the material they wanted to show. They chose work in a variety of media: paintings and drawings, jewelry, ceramics, her three-dimensional card-weaving pieces. Margaret was delighted, especially as they left her almost nothing to do; the museum did all the mounting, the labels, the hanging, and the necessary short biography. The only task required of Margaret was to appear at the official opening and to be suitably charming and friendly—which she could do. "Everyone who didn't know what else to say about my work," said Margaret, laughing wryly, "came up to me and said how *versatile* I was, and how *talented*!" The exhibition was hanging for a couple of months and was a success.

Apatosaurus *scratchboard illustration,* The Year of the Dinosaur, 1977. (*Courtesy of the Museum of Northern Arizona Photo Archives, Flagstaff, Arizona*)

Birgitte Urmann, a friend of Margaret's, and herself an artist said, "Her retrospective show blew me away. She has such a wonderfully intelligent and quirky mind!" She added with a slightly wicked chuckle, "And hardly a dinosaur in sight!"

Professional illustrating jobs continued to come Margaret's way. In 1974 she illustrated *Journey onto Land,* by Coleman J. Goin—an expert on amphibians—and Olive B. Goin. "It was an interesting little book, but it didn't sell." It was produced originally in paperback, and at least at that time, paperbacks received no reviews, which may have contributed to its poor showing.

Her retrospective exhibition included a portrait bust of Coleman Goin, holding one of his favorite frogs. "He was not exactly a handsome man, but his face was very pleasant. He had a withered arm and I'm sure some people who didn't know him will look at the bust—which is down to the waist— and say, 'Well, she didn't get *that* arm right!'" The bust was cast in bronze in Santa Fe.

She undertook two major tasks for Ned: *The Year of the Dinosaur,* published in 1977; and *Dinosaurs: An Illustrated History,* published in 1983. An entire issue of *Plateau,* a Museum of Northern Arizona publication, also published in 1983, was written by Ned. The issue, titled *Dinosaurs of the*

Colorado Plateau, contains skeleton drawings, scratchboard illustrations, and three full-color paintings by Margaret. The cover of the magazine is a color photograph of her little model of *Pentaceratops*.

In the late eighties, Ned was working on his autobiography, *Digging Into the Past*, published in 1989. Margaret enjoyed doing simple and whimsical pen-and-ink drawings for the chapter headings. She looked through her sketch books and photographs for inspiration. For instance, "From our first Brazilian adventure I found a sketch of Fausto and his shovel. For the chapter about Brazil in the book I used his boot and his silhouette and the procession of ants carrying their leaves."

Many of the scratchboard illustrations in *The Year of the Dinosaur* are of the gigantic, long-necked, amiable-looking herbivore, *Apatosaurus* (one of the brontosaurs). Several years after the book was published, Jack McIntosh of Wesleyan University found that the type of skull that had for years been accepted as the correct one to go with the brontosaur skeletons actually belonged to *Camarasaurus*. After much painstaking resorting of bones and studies of associations, he found the correct skull for *Apatosaurus*. Thus, many of Margaret's illustrations in *The Year of the Dinosaur* are, as she put it, "of wrong-headed dinosaurs." This is an example of the sort of good-faith mistake that is made repeatedly and without question, until it becomes part of the dogma. Such mistakes occur in every science and can be much more serious than a wrong-headed dinosaur.

In 1986 a traveling exhibition was organized by the Natural History Museum of Los Angeles County and sponsored by the Natural History Museum Foundation. It opened in February in Los Angeles in conjunction with a symposium at which invited speakers—artists and scientists—addressed important new dinosaur restorations and discussed interpretations of paleozoology and paleoenvironments that collaboration had made possible. The focus of the exhibition, "Dinosaurs Past and Present," was to illustrate how drastically ideas of dinosaur appearance, mobility, and behavior have changed over the years. After Los Angeles, the exhibition went to the Denver Museum of Natural History; the Philadelphia Academy of Sciences; the Smithsonian Institution, Washington, D.C.; the American Museum of Natural History, New York; and the New Mexico Museum of Natural History, Albuquerque. In Canada it went to the Tyrrell Museum of Palaeontology, Drumheller, Alberta; and the Royal Ontario Museum, Toronto.

The exhibition featured 121 paintings, drawings, and illustrations by many artists, going back to nineteenth-century illustrators (Benjamin Waterhouse Hawkins, C. L. Greisbach, F. Berger, among others), and included well-known artists of the early and mid-twentieth century such as Charles Knight, and Charles Whitney Gilmore. The illustrious list of modern artists included Margaret Colbert. Sylvia Czerkas, herself an artist and fossil hunter, was guest curator of the exhibit, responsible for selecting the artists and their work. Three of Margaret's scratchboard works from *The Year of the Dinosaur* were chosen: "Patience in the Rain," "Contest for Dominance," and "Poling in Shallow Water." The title of the latter piece refers to the text in *Year of the Dinosaur* where Ned describes dinosaur tracks that show just toe marks. He figured the animals were in the water, not truly swimming, but pushing off—poling—with one toe at a time.

A two-volume book was published in 1987 consisting of articles based on the presentations at the symposium. The book has the same name: *Dinosaurs Past and Present*. Sylvia Czerkas and Everett Olson are editors of the volumes. In the introduction, John M. Harris writes: "A new generation of artists, working within the framework of rigorous analyses provided by their scientific colleagues, has helped redefine our understanding of these fascinating animals. The lumbering giants envisaged by the artists of yesteryear have ceded place to dynamic creatures, both large and small, that are now shown posed naturally in realistic settings."

However, earlier artists such as Charles Knight often depicted their dinosaurs in very dynamic modes. The American Museum of Natural History has on permanent exhibition one of Knight's paintings, completed in 1897, that shows a pair of squabbling *Dryptosaurus*; one creature is airborne in the heat of battle, the other writhes sinuously. This idea of mobile dinosaurs went into disrepute during the first half of the twentieth century. Robert T. Bakker says in his article "Dancing Dinosaurs," also in *Dinosaurs Past and Present*: "Dinosaurs were [considered] evolutionary deadends—lumbering, swamp-bound, cold-blooded behemoths that managed to rule the earth only because the worldwide habitat was a steamy tropical jungle." But, "Fossil footprints show that dinosaurs cruised at warm-blooded speeds. Marks left by ligaments and muscles show that dinosaurs had great power at shoulder, elbow, hip, and knee. The design of dinosaur vertebrae and back muscles provided many giant herbivorous species with the capacity to rear up high in the foliage. Pound for pound most giant dinosaurs were stronger, faster, and more maneuverable than the rhinos and elephants of today."

A major argument is still in progress as to whether or not dinosaurs were warm-blooded, and it may remain an enigma forever. This controversy runs parallel with whether or not modern birds are descendants of dinosaurs. Such arguments keep the paleontological artist on her or his toes: illustrators of paleontological scenes are aware that a current composition is based on current information, and that next year or month, a scientist—a paleozoologist, a paleobotanist, a paleoecologist—may stumble on information that invalidates their labor. For example, in the 1850s Benjamin Waterhouse Hawkins carefully illustrated *Iguanodon* with a stubby horn on his nose. A few years later, it was established that the hornlike object associated with *Iguanodon* fossil skeletons was actually a digit—a "thumb spike"—of the forelimb. Similarly, scientists still vacillate about the arrangement—and therefore the function—of the back plates of the familiar *Stegosaurus*: Did they stand upright? Or did they droop parallel to the beast's flanks? The artist illustrates them according to the theory of the month.

Ancient land forms and climates are likewise open to question. They are vital to understanding how an animal existed—how it would have moved and interacted with other creatures—in a particular environment. Paleoecology is a young science, and ideas and interpretations of evidence change frequently. When Margaret started to work on her murals, arguably the most important—certainly the most visible—works of her career, these factors were crucial.

∽ 21 ∾

The Murals

Apart from the obvious fact of scale, murals pose challenges to a restoration artist that differ from those faced when illustrating a book or a magazine article. Book illustrations are used by authors to demonstrate or emphasize particular facets of the animals involved. The artist naturally seeks to make a pleasing composition, and adds backgrounds that are not incongruous, but the illustration is directed by another individual. In a paleontological mural, animals are the central features of the work, but plants, land forms, and a suggestion of climate are also very important. The museum or other public building that commissions the mural will specify in general terms what they want illustrated, but then the artist is on his or her own. Responsibility is not shared with an author; it rests with the artist. To offset this burden, the artist has a measure of freedom to create a work of art.

Margaret wrote in a biographical sketch she was asked to submit with one of her commissioned murals: "All restorations of plants and animals are based on careful studies under the expert guidance of [my] husband and other well-qualified advisors. None pretends to be the last word, but aims at being 'state-of-the-art.' Stacks of zoo and field sketches, photos taken on trips to many parts of the world, and of course good library references augment some knowledge of anatomy and the experts' advice. But the whole must be realized in three dimensions in the artist's mind before it can be convincingly rendered—and that is where the delightful challenge lies in this type of work."

Whenever possible, Margaret modeled her animals before painting or drawing them. Her models were usually plasticine (oil-based clay) over an armature. But when it came to the murals, time constraints prevented her from modeling every creature. "I had to crowd in so many animals in the sort of composition I was asked to do. I had to add up all I knew about them, turn them around in my head in three dimensions, and paint them from that. Even with so many creatures, the composition had to make some kind of sense—the beasts had to be reacting to each other in some way, not just standing about, all four feet planted on the ground." Her modus operandi was to prepare a watercolor sketch to scale and then to modify it as necessary as she painted the full-scale surface.

Margaret's first mural was a small one done for the Museum of Northern Arizona, painted soon after the move to Flagstaff. This was done in acrylics on a panel and was part of a series done by another artist.

"It was done in a style that I would not have chosen to use—it's kind of slick—but it needed to fit in with the others," she said. "Barton Wright was curator of the museum at the time. He wheeled out acrylics for me on a little cart and they were all perfectly dry—the tubes all pinched and sad. I said to him, 'Your tubes are twisted and dry.' His jaw dropped for a moment. But then he understood that I was not being personal, and he got me some paints I could use!" The painting shows an early Triassic scene, some 240 million years ago, with giant crocodile-like phytosaurs. It was in the geology section of the museum for many years but is now in storage.

Also in the early 1970s, Margaret was asked by Big Bend National Park to paint a mural of Eocene mammals, including *Hyracotherium,* and *Diatryma,* which lived in that area about fifty million years ago. Big Bend is on the lower reaches of the Rio Grande, in the southwest corner of Texas, bordering Mexico. The climate there is extreme: the summers are blisteringly hot, and the winters quite cold. The mural was to be housed in a small, glass-fronted adobe-like building, the floor of which was the site where the fossils had been found. A previous mural there had been destroyed by vandals; the building was some distance from the main park headquarters and visitors' center and could not be monitored twenty-four hours a day.

Margaret and Big Bend officials consulted Barton Wright on how to paint the mural so that it would withstand the temperature extremes. Wright suggested they experiment with exterior house paint on Formica. The Formica was glued to a plywood backing, then sanded to give a surface that would take the house paint. The mural was installed, and the experimental technique seemed to be working well as far as the climate was concerned. But before long, the vandals were back. They attacked both the building and the mural. Before it was totally destroyed, the painting was removed to a storage place in the park headquarters. Unfortunately, it is no longer possible to view

Eocene scene; Big Bend National Park mural, early 1970s; housepaint on Formica; approximately 9 x 6 feet. (Courtesy of the National Park Service and Big Bend National Park, Texas)

it; all Margaret has left of this mural is a black and white photograph and—to give some idea of its color—a faded slide of the back views of two scientists working in front of it.

Her next commission, however, has enjoyed a far better fate. The fossil logs that litter Arizona's Petrified Forest National Park come from the Triassic Chinle Formation. A 1930s diorama by Paul J. Fair formerly displayed at Petrified Forest (and now mounted at the Painted Desert Inn) reflected what Charles Camp of Berkeley knew of the Chinle flora and fauna. It shows only phytosaurs (*Rutiodon*) in a wet and steamy habitat, in which grew giant *Araucarioxylon* conifers, cycads, and ferns.

Since that time, new interpretations of the fossil record and multifarious fossil finds of both animals and plants have shed fresh light on the region's prehistory. It is now known that the middle to late Triassic was a time of transition, when early labyrinthodont amphibians, dicynodont mammal-like reptiles, phytosaurs and other thecodont reptiles were evolving in and out of the picture, or dying out in favor of the dinosaurs. As has been mentioned, the nineteenth-century paleontologist Edward Drinker Cope found *Coelophysis* fragments in New Mexico. These were the first dinosaur remains found in the Chinle Formation, but it was Ned Colbert's 1947 discovery of the *Coelophysis* "quarry" at Ghost Ranch that put the little dinosaurs on the map.

Mary Jean Taylor and Margaret at work on the Petrified Forest mural, 1977–78.

The Park Service recognized that exhibits in the Rainbow Forest Museum and Visitors' Center at Petrified Forest needed to be updated to reflect the new knowledge of the Chinle biota and the new interpretations of its climate and land forms. In the mid-1970s, they commissioned Margaret to paint a mural to be a centerpiece at Rainbow Forest Museum. She was chosen for the task not only because she could paint and was known for her meticulous work, but also because she collaborated closely and efficiently with Ned, the acknowledged expert on the subject.

Margaret's Petrified Forest mural measures sixteen feet by four and was painted on one panel. The geology department at the Museum of Northern Arizona made space for her to work in a large room—in which the one drawback was "the music people had to have blaring all the time!"—and she had a little help with routine "donkey work" from a volunteer friend, Mary Jean Taylor. People drifted by and often stopped to watch what she was doing. "I listened to advice from everyone who came by—even from children and nonscientists. What they had to say gave me a notion of what people's reaction would be to the painting. The scientists kept me from going astray and becoming too fanciful. When I started the mural, I put in a volcano. Petrified Forest has a lot of volcanic ash mixed in with the fossiliferous beds and I thought it would be de rigueur to have a volcano, preferably erupting. A geologist came by—someone who, Ned said, had the right answers about the geology—and he said 'No volcanoes!' They had been further north than Petrified Forest. So I took my brush and simply wiped out the volcano. What power!"

The mural was completed in 1978, and Margaret and Ned hired a school bus and a driver to move the painting to Petrified Forest. They opened the emergency exit at the rear, slid the panel down the central aisle, and sat on each side of it to prop it up on its way to the Rainbow Forest Museum.

Whimsical as always—and perhaps iconoclastic because the National Park Service is a staid institution—Margaret composed verses to describe her work. She titled it "The Unpetrified Forest."

This is the forest, primeval and green,
Just as I fancy it might have been seen
If you and I, safe in our own Time Machine
By pressing the switch marked "Triassic" had been
Transported in *time* without leaving this *place*.
Some two hundred millions of years in the space
Of a second have vanished and left not a trace—
A sizable chunk, you'll agree, to erase.

A slow, muddy stream hosts some creatures exciting—
Metoposaurs toping and phytosaurs fighting*—
A gaggle of dinosaurs leaving in haste
Though the scales of their tails wouldn't be to the taste
Of placid *Placerias*, or I'll eat my hat.
(I know my anomodonts better than that.)
Of three kinds of thecodonts, *Desmatosuchus*,
Though spinily mild, is the most apt to spook us.
But then, *Typothorax*, seen here in the distance,
Could meet any foe with passive resistance.
Two *Hesperosuchus*, more agile and thinner,
Are foraging fiercely for something for dinner
While gnashing their teeth, which are sharp past belief
As one poor wee phytosaur found, to his grief.
If mammals live here, and we think that they might,
They're tiny and shy and would come out at night.
Since birds, grass, and flowers have not yet appeared
To grace this fair planet, to us it seems weird
That mosses and ferns form the forest-floor cover
Where insects aplenty hide, creep, jump, and hover.
Both tree-ferns and cycads with tropical green
Remind us that this is a warm, humid scene
While tough equisetums along the stream's course
Are kin to the horsetails. (I must say, some horse!)

The Rainbow Forest Museum mural, 1978; oil. (Courtesy of the Petrified Forest Museum Association and the Petrified National Park, Arizona)

Above all this medley of life types riparian
Tower some pines of a type araucarian
Awaiting, with luck, vivid reincarnation
As agatized logs for our own delectation.

So now we'll begin to retrace our time-trip
And, reaching for "Recent," command that our ship
Whisking us back from Triassic adventure, re-
Turn us intact to our own native century.

*Oh well, if you must—that's a lungfish he's biting.

Margaret offered the verses to the Park Service to use as a legend, but they turned them down in favor of a formal description.

The metoposaurs were large labyrinthodont amphibians; *Placerias*, a lumbering dicynodont mammal-like reptile, with a beak and conspicuous tusks, built like a tank; *Desmatosuchus* and *Typothorax*, impressively armored low-slung thecodonts; *Hesperosuchus*, a nimble light-boned bipedal thecodont predator. The "gaggle of dinosaurs" was of course a small herd of *Coelophysis*; Margaret allowed her imagination some play with the little dinosaurs and portrayed them clad in stripes—not unreasonable when modern reptile coloring is considered. They are leaping away from the center of the painting, their tails held high for balance. Margaret surmised that phytosaurs may well have behaved like modern crocodilians; she depicted one

Rutiodon guarding its den, from which emerges a cluster of babies. One of the hatchlings has climbed on its parent's head, another is coming to an unfortunate end in the mouth of a *Hesperosuchus*.

Since the time of the Fair diorama of the Petrified Forest, knowledge of the flora had also expanded. Margaret painted *Araucarioxylon* (from which the Petrified Forest logs—"agatized for our delectation"—originated), cycads, and ferns—as had Fair. She added tree ferns, scouring rushes (extinct horsetails), and club mosses (lycopods).

In a chapter in *Dinosaurs Past and Present* (1987) by David Gillette (titled "The Age of Transition; *Coelophysis* and the Late Triassic Chinle Fauna"), a description of Margaret's landscape points up the amount of care and attention to background detail that went into the mural, and Margaret's understanding of geological processes:

> The landscape ranges from open water to dry uplands, with an overall open character in the vegetation. The misty swampland of the earlier interpretation [the Fair diorama] has been replaced with a drier habitat. The substrate is entirely sedimentary, consisting of red and buff muds and silts presumably deposited by prior wanderings of the river. A few rocks are evident along the shoreline, suggesting lag deposits let down from older Paleozoic formations or episodes of higher-stream velocity when larger sediments could be carried in the stream load.
>
> Where roots of the giant conifers have stabilized the soils, river erosion has cut resistant banks with vertical slopes along the shore, but elsewhere the slopes are gentle, grading from quiet backwater to isolated pools, muddy swirls with mud cracks and dry, higher slopes. Much of the landscape is barren and open, reminiscent of semi-arid tropics.

Margaret with her jury piece for the New Mexico Museum of National History mural contract, 1984.

David Gillette was to play a vital role in Margaret's next major mural project. In 1984, the New Mexico Museum of Natural History was nearing completion in Old Town, Albuquerque. A Triassic mural was proposed for the brand-new museum. Gillette was at that time the museum's curator of vertebrate paleontology, and he wanted Margaret to paint it. Local artists were not happy about a woman in her seventies from another state getting the job, and there was considerable feeling among experts and scientists about who could be trusted to do it right. Several artists, including Margaret, were each asked to submit a small full-scale sample of what they proposed to put in the mural. Gillette arranged a panel of disinterested people to judge the samples, and to his relief and great pleasure, the panel gave Margaret the commission.

The work was to portray the biota from the Chinle Formation of northern New Mexico, and this time Ned was included in the contract in an advisory role. "We worked together in the geology department of the Museum of Northern Arizona," said Margaret, "and once more benefitted from lots of free advice from expert and nonexpert kibitzers."

The design was ordered on eight panels that could be displayed either as a continuous whole or separately, so no tails or other unexplained bits of beasts could cross the dividing lines. The New Mexico museum furnished the panels, marine plywood supported by wooden frames and primed with three coats of gesso. At this point Margaret experienced what she described as "a little difficulty." The panels had been constructed by a skilled carpenter, and it had been an exacting job. They were eight feet tall and four feet wide, according to the original museum specifications. The museum art director then changed his mind and requested them to be seven by three feet. "That shouldn't bother you," he said blithely to Margaret. "The proportions are the same." Not by Margaret's arithmetic; not only had the panels to be started from scratch, but she had to redesign. "I should have been hard nosed and rewritten the contract—proportionally!" she said.

Planning and preparing the design took six months; the process included decisions as to which animals and plants to include, and which should predominate. Ned presided over the fauna; Dr. Sidney Ash from Weber State University in Ogden, Utah, was a great help with the flora.

"I squared off my color sketch and transferred the drawing to the panels, which had been squared off in proportion with chalk lines. For this I used a brownish, thinned-down oil paint, referring to published material and actual fossils where possible to avoid that 'copied' look and to keep the drawing fresh and lively. Many changes entered into the process as expert advice dictated and as the composition demanded. I used Windsor Newton oil paint for its well-known reliability."

Margaret acquired an assistant in the form of a young fine-arts graduate of Northern Arizona University, Louise Waller. "I said to her, 'You name your price per hour, and name your hours, and come and do donkey work.'" She and Margaret worked together very happily, painting mainly in the mornings—when the light was best. Louise was pleasant and thoughtful, and very good; she put hours in whenever she had time, and "She was always good-tempered when we had to wipe out something and start over." Overall, the two women put in over eight hundred actual painting hours. The project took (not counting the six-month preparation period) the better part of a year, and work was interrupted a couple of times for trips to which Ned and Margaret were committed. The mural was completed in 1985 and was first displayed to the public at the January 1986 museum opening.

Of the final mural, Margaret recalls:

We portrayed a world without grass or flowers or birds. We know that there were tiny mammals, but the evidence is so scarce that we can't make a good guess as to what they looked like. That is why the only mammal represented in the mural is disappearing down his burrow with only a bit of a furry tail to indicate his presence. The fishes shown were part of a large number known from fossils of the region. There were horseshoe crabs very much like those we see today, but inhabiting fresh water. The rest of the fauna, except for insects not too different from our modern dragonflies and cockroaches, were reptilian. Only one of them,

Detail of the Albuquerque mural, Postosuchus, *1985; oil. (Courtesy of New Mexico Museum of Natural History, Albuquerque, New Mexico)*

Coelophysis, was a dinosaur. They made their livings in many different ways. Like modern reptiles they were not soft and cuddly, but probably had their own kind of patterned—sometimes rather terrifying—beauty.

A total of fifty-seven creatures appear in the mural. Some are, of course, multiple examples of the same species—for instance, there are six *Coelophysis*, but the numbers of different species are considerably expanded from those of the Petrified Forest mural. It was decided to include a small gliding reptile—behind which hangs a tale. Bob Salkin (the friend who had modeled Margaret's design for the Society of Vertebrate Paleontology logo in metal in 1942) was a high-school shop teacher in a depressed area of Newark, New Jersey. He was also an avid amateur paleontologist, and once a year he presented a fossil program for fifth graders. After a class or two, he took the children out in the field, guaranteeing that each would find at least one fossil. In 1960, three of his students were exploring a quarry in North Bergen, just across the Hudson from Manhattan. One of the boys picked up a piece of black shale with a fossil in it. Bob Salkin examined it and recognized it as something different, so he took it to Ned Colbert for identification. The shale came from the upper Triassic, and the fossil was indeed something different. It was the first specimen found of a little creature that Ned named *Icarosaurus* after the legendary Greek fellow—Icarus—who flew too close to the sun and melted the wax securing his wings. The four-legged creature was only about four inches long from chin to pelvis (its tail was missing) and very delicate. It also had wings, which were formed from ten ribs each side, elongated and straightened, presumably to provide a framework for stretched skin—like bat wings, or more relevantly, like those of a modern far-eastern gliding lizard, the draco.

Although *Icarosaurus* fossils had not been found in the Chinle Formation, Ned thought it highly probable that the little reptile would have been around, so he deemed it appropriate that Margaret include it in the mural. In the left-hand outside panel, the reptile appears tucked on the side of a tree, while another glides away from the upper branches of an *Araucarioxylon*.

In one of the center panels of the mural, a large thecodont carnivore props its bulk against a giant fallen log. This predator has been studied and named *Postosuchus* since the completion of the mural. It owned a skull as large and terrifying as that of *Tyrannosaurus* and grew to at least twenty-five feet in length.

Paleoecologists and geologists had been arguing back and forth in the decade since the completion of the Petrified Forest painting and now believed that the Triassic landscape and climate must have been somewhat different from that portrayed in the earlier mural. Margaret as "the eyes of the paleontologists" illustrated the current wisdom, and David Gillette (*Dinosaurs Past and Present*) describes her interpretation:

> The landscape is changed, with little barren ground and several considerably more complex habitats [than in the Petrified Forest mural]. *Araucarioxylon* forests dominate both lowland and upland habitats. Tree ferns and scouring rushes are abundant, set in habitats quite apart from the giant conifers. Open spaces are occupied by cycads and ferns. Uplands, the source areas for the bountiful supply of mud and silt that collected in the Chinle lowlands, are clearly visible in the distance. The meandering river has deposited a litter of clam shells and piles of water-soaked logs on its shore. In one bend, the river has eroded into a steep bank where its channel has been incised into its older sediments.

The clear blue sky of the painting and the mixed habitat, he continues, suggest quite dry conditions, "perhaps subtropical with limited seasonality." The Gillette article describes the paleontological transition observed in the Chinle Formation and the growth of knowledge from the 1930s to

Detail of the BBC painting; phytosaur, foreground; stegosaur, background. (Courtesy of the British Broadcasting Corporation, London)

the 1980s. It is illustrated with details of the Paul J. Fair mural and excellent color reproductions and details of both the Petrified Forest and the Albuquerque murals.

For a while, the demand for enormous murals subsided. Commissions for two lesser jobs arrived in the late 1980s. Farish Jenkins, a Harvard professor, found a tiny Triassic mammal, *Dinnetherium*, and requested a small watercolor restoration of the creature. The second commission was from the British Broadcasting Corporation. Emissaries from the BBC arrived, asked Margaret to paint a Jurassic landscape, then disappeared for a couple of months. When they returned, Margaret presented them with a mural complete with suitable dinosaurs disporting themselves on the meandering banks of a river under a showery sky.

"They brought their television camera into our living-room and photographed the painting. Michael Andrews pulled his money belt out, extracted what I'd asked (it was something like eight hundred dollars), and gave it to me in cash. 'Thank you,' I said. And that was that." The BBC owns the rights to the mural, but did not take it to Britain. It now hangs in the Ruth Hall Paleontology Museum at Ghost Ranch.

David Gillette and his then wife, Lynett, coordinated the development of this museum at Ghost Ranch, which opened in 1989. At one end, this small but excellent museum contains a large block from the *Coelophysis* quarry. This block had been lowered into position by a huge crane before the museum hall was completed. At the last minute, it was feared the hole left in the roof was not going to be big enough to admit the block, but it slid in with an inch or two to spare. (The roof of the museum was added afterward.) A gallery is arranged around the block so that visitors can watch as preparators painstakingly remove matrix, flake by flake, to expose and extract bones of the little dinosaurs.

At the opposite end of the hall is a diorama. A reconstructed skeleton of a gigantic *Rutiodon* phytosaur bares its formidable teeth against a curved painted background. David and Lynett Gillette and Ghost Ranch wanted Margaret to paint the background mural of the diorama. It was a formidable task; the very size was daunting. "I made a design," Margaret said, "but I was afraid I would not be able to finish painting the mural if I started. I was also not prepared to get up on a ladder to do it. Through a roundabout way, we heard of a Seattle couple, named Hitchcock. They have made a business out of making small pictures big. They can take a postcard and blow it up as big as a room, and they create enormous billboards, murals for bank buildings, and suchlike. The Ghost Ranch folk approached them and they agreed to do the job—and at a special price because Ghost Ranch is nonprofit and such a worthy cause."

Margaret's sketch was four feet long and eighteen inches high. The Hitchcocks blew it up to the required size of thirty-two by twelve feet. "They measured things off to scale and drew them freely, a little like 'painting by numbers.'" Margaret worked with them throughout the process. As they pursued the task, it was evident that some parts of the design did not work well when blown up to size, and appropriate changes were made. Because it was curved, the sides appeared foreshortened from the front, and so the design had to be modified to accommodate that. "They even put in a couple more critters," said Margaret. "All told, we had a lot of fun. Ned, of course, was there too, lending his scientific know-how."

The finished background is an evening scene, twilit and watery, with the appropriate Chinle fauna and flora. "Lynett, the curator, wanted to have the eyes of the phytosaurs in the painting shining as alligator eyes do at night. I said to her, 'But who's going to be holding the jacklight in the Triassic?'"

Lynett's idea was not completely nixed. Margaret's mural was not ready to install by the time of the museum-opening celebration, so behind the *Rutiodon* reconstruction there would still be a blank wall. A couple of keen amateur paleontologists from Albuquerque, Peggy and Wilson Bechtel, came to the rescue. Volunteers for the New Mexico Natural History Museum, they had worked with David Gillette on excavating the seismosaur—the biggest dinosaur yet found. Peggy Bechtel was an artist, and to hide the blank wall, she climbed on a ladder and slapped on a sketchy and playful mural. For the phytosaur eyes, she used fluorescent paint. At the opening ceremony, the lights were doused—and the reptilian eyes gleamed with suitable menace.

"I felt terrible when we had to black out Peggy's jolly mural to put mine up. But it had to be done, and she said she did not mind at all."

Rather than paying her for her labors, Ghost Ranch endowed a scholarship fund in the joint names of Ned and Margaret. Each year this enables a schoolteacher to come to the ranch to learn about the geology and paleontology of the region.

∽ 22 ∾

Company and Family Matters

Visitors come to Ned and Margaret not only to relish Colbert company, but also to explore the Flagstaff environs. With "Flag" as a base, it is possible to drive from alpine meadows to desert moonscapes in an easy hour or two. Among attractions within reach are the South Rim of the Grand Canyon, Sunset Crater, Fairfield Snowbowl for winter skiing, Meteor Crater, Petrified Forest National Park and Painted Desert, and Anasazi ruins including Wupatki and the cliff dwellings at Walnut Canyon. The Colberts entertain a steady stream of relatives, friends, and professional colleagues from all over the world. Visits from their five sons and their families are, of course, high points; the "boys" have pursued an interesting variety of careers and lifestyles.

George had been interested in maps since he was a child. He enjoyed the detail and the pinning down of exact locations. Ned arranged for him to meet Ricky Harrison, whom Margaret called the "Grand Old Man of Mapmaking." Ned knew Harrison because he came frequently to the American Museum of Natural History, where maps were in constant demand. Rather than returning to college, George joined Harrison as an apprentice. He helped the mapmaker with the donkey work, tried to make some order out of Harrison's chaotic work style, and at the same time learned to make maps.

George and Jenny still live in New York, where George works as a freelance cartographer out of their home, chiefly creating maps for books. He has also worked on projects with another mapmaker, Guenter Vollath; together George and Guenter drew all the maps for the *Smithsonian Guide to Historic America,* a series of books for the various regions of the United States, published in 1989.

Jenny obtained a master's degree in education, and then spent many years as a Montessori teacher. She now works at New York's Covenant House, an organization that takes in homeless young people.

George and Jenny's first son, Denis, was born in 1961. He was a cheerful and lively boy, with a mass of freckles that he considered a serious affliction. He grew out of freckles and developed a bent for foreign languages. At Earlham College in Richmond, Indiana, he studied Japanese and, soon after graduating, married a Japanese American from Hawaii, Susan Ogawa. The couple had a bright and bouncy daughter, Mari—a first great-grandchild for Margaret and Ned, and the child for whom Margaret made "Couch Potato." Denis and Susan divorced when their baby was quite small, but Susan and Mari have kept in touch with Margaret. Denis joined the intelligence branch of the military, where he could use his languages. Margaret occupies a special place in his affections. He wrote in a 1993 letter:

Grandmother would take me by the hand and walk through the woods of Greenbrook Park, near Leonia. She would spend time on my three-year-old level of wonder at the world and would pace herself so that she got as much appreciation out of a ladybug crawling across a twig as did I. Not only that, but she'd show me how to *look*, and how to observe such things on both an artistic and scientific level. In short, she taught me to *see* the awesome grandeur of nature, of the world, of life.

Grandmother on a drive through New York State on a crisp very bright autumn day. . . . Every time the car came around a bend she would sharply inhale, in awe of the maple trees, the lavish orange and red leaves. She was visibly moved by the glory of autumn. Sitting on her lap, I was very aware of her joy, and felt moved more by her reaction than the event. [Back at the Leonia house] Grandfather in his very methodical way raked the fallen leaves into a neat pile. Grandmother came out and invited me to smell the leaves, and to pick out a nicely colored one to take into the house.

Matthew was born in 1963. He was a round-faced child, quieter than Denis. The two children spent several summers in Flagstaff, and, used to young male creatures, Margaret had no problems keeping them occupied and happy. She noticed that Matthew was becoming a perfectionist, a tendency she recognized he must have inherited from her. As she had done with all her sons, with varying degrees of success, she tried to teach him his great-grandfather's maxim—*There are a lot of things that need to be done that needn't be done well.* "I gave him a lecture and included the quote from my father. Matt put his head on one side and said, 'But I don't see anything wrong with perfection.' And I couldn't answer that." Matthew delighted his grandfather by becoming a vertebrate paleontologist.

It was no secret that Jenny had always wanted a daughter. Margaret used to shop with her in New York before the move to Flagstaff, and Jenny often drifted toward the little-girls' departments, and wistfully fingered pretty dresses and frilly nonsense. So the arrival of "Little" Margaret in 1978 was a particular joy for Jenny. Grandmother Margaret made a tiny portrait ceramic head of the infant, about two inches high, and wondered how she would cope with a girl child.

Little Margaret stayed with her grandparents for several summers in a row, and at first all went well. The summer that she was ten, Margaret, Ned, and Little Margaret stayed at Ghost Ranch while Margaret worked with the Hitchcocks on the enlargement of the Ghost Ranch mural. The child came to the museum every day and watched, enthralled as Margaret's original sketch escaped its bounds, spread, and grew. As she edged toward her teens, however, her summer stays became difficult. Margaret and Ned sensed the child was restless and unhappy, and they did not know how to help her. Unlike her brothers, who had been happy away from the concrete jungle of New York, Little Margaret was a child of the city. Her grandparents were mystified by her dyed pink hair and her tendency to change clothes many times a day. Food was problematic, because Little Margaret did not like what her grandparents ate, nor when they ate it. Trying to please her became physically and mentally exhausting for Margaret, and she and Ned decided the summer visits were counterproductive to their relationship with the child. With sadness, and a feeling that they had failed despite a lot of effort, they told George and Jenny in the spring of 1993 that they thought Little Margaret had outgrown Flagstaff. A translation of a German poem that Ned Manning had set to music kept coming into Margaret's mind:

The rosy glow of summer
Is on thy dimpled cheek,
But in thy heart the winter
Is lying cold and bleak.
But things will change hereafter
When years have done their part;
When on thy cheek be winter
And summer in thy heart.

She said wistfully, "I hope the summer comes to her heart before too much winter touches her cheek."

George is a confirmed city dweller and feels he must stay in New York to be close to his publishers. Nonetheless, he has been a fairly frequent visitor to his parents' home, sometimes with Jenny, sometimes alone.

After three years in Copenhagen, and a somewhat abortive sojourn in Israel at a Danish kibbutz, David and his wife, Edith, returned to the States. David finished his bachelor's degree at the University of New Mexico in Albuquerque, then completed a Ph.D. in Scandinavian languages at the University of Washington in Seattle. The couple decided to make Seattle their home. David continued to study and research Danish literature and folklore. He made a collection of Scandinavian Christmas songs that he hopes will be published. However, steady employment in his chosen field has proven impossible, and he had to look elsewhere for a job. He wanted to do something useful for humanity, so he took courses in nursing; he now works on the cancer floor of the Swedish Hospital in Seattle.

"Before the move to Seattle," Margaret said, "Edith had been doing small but perfect tapestry weavings. David sometimes designed for her." But in Seattle, Edith began to suffer from arthritis, and she could no longer weave. She took nursing courses at the same time as David but her condition prevented her from working. Ned and Margaret visited them in Seattle in the spring of 1974 and again in the fall of 1994: "Edith has a great sense of humor, and she's a good cook. . . . But she has never wanted to be involved with us or anyone else of Dave's family. She is polite but has remained detached." This, coupled with the fact that she and David have taken in numbers of stray animals—which cannot be abandoned—has meant that she has never visited Flagstaff, and David's visits have been rare.

Philip followed David to Wesleyan University and studied biology. For a short time, Ned hoped that this son at least would follow in his paleontological footsteps. But at the end of his junior year in 1960, Phil decided to take a break and spend a year bicycling around Europe. He stayed in youth hostels and took odd jobs to put food in his mouth. For several months in 1961 he was in Germany, taking language courses and cycling his way to Berlin. That summer, the mass exodus from the East was in progress, and Russian tanks were grinding along the border. Curious, Phil walked into the eastern sector, where a young East German approached him and told him that he wanted to cross to the West on his motorcycle and figured he would have a better chance with two aboard. He asked Philip to ride out with him. The pair got across the border with no hassle. The Berlin Wall was thrown up very shortly afterward, on the night of August 12 and 13. Margaret and Ned were glad that they heard of Phil's adventures only after they were over.

He returned to the States to finish his degree, then taught at a Connecticut school for a year after he graduated. But he was restless and found it hard to settle into a regular job. An urge to travel and see more of the world had entered his system; he decided to join the Peace Corps. After training and learning the Nepalese language, he spent three years in Nepal, teaching general science in schools. This was frustrating because the students wanted to learn only in order to pass tests; he wanted them to learn because the subject was intrinsically exciting—consequently he diverged at times from the strict syllabus. It became a point of contention, and toward the end of his tenure the students almost resorted to riot tactics when he continued to try lifting them out of their preoccupation with examinations.

Otherwise, Nepal was a grand experience. Phil had already learned to love mountaineering in the States, and the Himalayas posed ambitious challenges. He made several ascents with native Sherpa guides, including two previously unconquered high peaks. Again, Margaret was grateful that she heard of his exploits only in retrospect.

While he was on the subcontinent, Phil took a trip down into India. Ned and Margaret engineered an introduction to Raja Reddy. Raja and his wife went to the railway station and Philip emerged from the train barefoot because his shoes had been stolen en route. Raja Reddy told Ned and Margaret that they recognized him immediately; they were looking out for a person with a worried expression just like Ned's.

Nepalese culture and values conditioned Phil to life with few material belongings. It put him out of tune with American "civilization," and he has never settled into a regular career. He has followed his enthusiasms and lived a full, adventure-packed, exciting, but impecunious life. He has been many times to Antarctica as a mountaineer and a base manager, driven a bus in Seattle, and captained a fishing boat to Alaska. True to character, Philip appears in Flagstaff out of the blue and at irregular intervals. His parents feel lucky when they catch him on the wing. He may be flying by Flagstaff on the way to a hang-gliding adventure somewhere or perhaps returning from climbing the cliffs of the Grand Canyon. But when he comes, he stays for several days and discussions are lively. Margaret finds a particular joy in Phil's company and conversation, in his insights and introspections. He challenges her to examine her own values and beliefs.

Daniel had two unsuccessful marriages. Margaret put the blame on architecture, at least for his first marriage. "It was not the first marriage that architecture destroyed," she said. Dan works extremely hard and puts in outrageous hours. At times, he becomes burned out and depressed, doubtless uncomfortable to live with. Margaret had been fond of his first wife and knew that Dan was crushed when it ended. His second marriage was brief, stormy, and unhappy.

After he qualified as an architect, Dan worked for a time for a big firm, but he had ideas that could not be accommodated within the framework of a large company, so he launched out on his own. For the last several years he has contracted almost exclusively with Manhattan's Dooney and Burke, makers of handbags and other fine leather goods. Projects have been varied, from designing a log cabin in Utah for one of the partners, to remodeling the firm's Madison Avenue premises, to designing a new outlet in the Trump Tower. The Dooney and Burke association has been good; aside from wrestling matches with the New York City bureaucracy, Dan has been able to focus his energies on design rather than on where the next contract is going to come from. Lately, his interests have veered away from architecture and into interior design.

In 1982, Dan married Catherine Clinton in New York. Catherine taught women's history at Harvard for several years, but she left when the tenure hurdle stymied her. She writes on her subject—specializing in the nineteenth-century South—and her books are successful enough for her not to worry about another university appointment. Dan and Catherine live in Greenwich, Connecticut, with their two boys: Drew, born in 1985; and Ned, born in 1989. Drew shows signs that he has inherited his grandmother's talent, and certainly her whimsy. Aged seven, he sent her a book he wrote, titled "My Best Dog." He had drawn dogs of different sizes and shapes, engaged in various interesting pastimes, with a few suitable words in his bold, lopsided hand.

On Charles's thirty-second birthday in 1978, Margaret again burst into rhyme:

Before you embark on your thirty-third annum
Some versification is clearly prescribed
No need to eat worms, dear, however they can'em,
Try, rather, champagne, with some caviar imbibed.
Then soup and roast beef, some asparagus, buttered
A salad of fresh avocado between
All this and dessert (some spumoni, uncluttered?)
To celebrate being just twice sweet sixteen!

Charles studied art history at the University of Chicago for his undergraduate degree. He had been an average and dutiful student all through high school, but at Chicago he found his niche and took fire. Harvard accepted him for graduate work, and he won an expenses-paid trip abroad to study Renaissance art. He was in Italy for close to two years and traveled all over Europe. After he graduated from Harvard (marching in the procession to receive his diploma sporting a red armband to protest the war in Vietnam), he taught for a year at Southern Illinois University at Carbondale. He now teaches history of American art at Boston College, at Brandeis University, and at Boston University. He has become fascinated with phrenology, the pseudoscience that started in the early nineteenth century, which was not only concerned with bumps and hollows on skulls and the supposed seats of various emotions and facilities, but also spawned a whole philosophy. Given access to Harvard's outstanding collection of phrenological writings, Charles has studied the effects of this once-respectable discipline on the art of the period.

When Charles met Agatha Piedmont, a medical doctor, she was working at Tufts University. Margaret said, "He called us and said, 'I'm going to get married. Her name is Agatha, but she pronounces it Agatha.' And he described her brown hair and blue eyes." They were married in 1982. For some years, Agatha has specialized in muscular dystrophy and has introduced innovative treatments and equipment. Lately she has become increasingly interested in alternative medicines as adjuncts to conventional medicine. "She is wonderfully sensible and open-minded, both in medical and in other respects." Charles and Agatha visit Ned and Margaret frequently and have also joined them several times at Ghost Ranch when Ned has been teaching summer seminars there.

A memorable visit was that of George Haas, who had been on the "Four Continents" trip to the American West in the summer of 1965; he was a professional colleague of Ned's and a good friend and came to Flagstaff to visit the Colberts in the summer of 1972. George was a large man, a bear in thick glasses. He and Ned had been born in the same year, as had Llew Price of Brazil—1905, they decided, had been a vintage year for paleontologists. He was a professor of herpetology and paleontology at Hebrew University in Jerusalem. Born and raised in Austria, George had emigrated to Israel in his late twenties and took an active part in the nation's struggle for existence.

In the fall of 1965, George had guided the Colberts through his adopted land. He was an outstanding guide, possessed of an encyclopedic knowledge of archeology, botany, and the history of his country. He took them to

Jerusalem, Tel Aviv, Ashdod, Ascalon, Beersheba, Shivta in the Negev Desert; En Gedi on the shore of the Dead Sea, where Margaret found thistles that she used in a linoleum-cut design for that year's Christmas card, and stunted trees bearing luscious-looking round fruit—Dead Sea fruit—that were nothing but dust inside. They were entertained at a kibbutz near Tiberias on the Sea of Galilee, an agricultural community striving to build a new way of life while Syrians on the Golan Heights lobbed occasional shells in its direction; the kibbutzim accepted the shells as part of life—annoyances like wasp stings or hail. George led the Colberts through Upper Galilee, and then back to the shores of the Mediterranean at the northern end of the country: Acre, Caesarea, and then the Carmel Caves where, in a banana grove, they ate ripe fruits off the trees; and where Margaret came upon miniature cyclamen growing as wild and profuse as violets in the eastern United States. "When I came back from Israel, I made a painting of the mouth of the cave at Carmel, with a gnarled leafless olive tree, and the cyclamen. In the background, I indicated a road with two Israelis on bicycles—'cyclemen'—a sort of visual pun."

George Haas had been an unforgettable host, and the Colberts wanted to celebrate his visit to Flagstaff. They planned a party for him. It was to be attended by the museum geology department, geological faculty members from the University of Northern Arizona, and sundry friends and neighbors.

Margaret came back from town where she had been to pick up last-minute provender. Ned was standing on the doorstep waiting for her, and she knew at once that something dreadful had happened. He came over to the car and told her that he had received a telephone call from San Diego; her sister Betty and brother-in-law Nick had been killed. They had been exiting a freeway and a car driven onto the ramp in the wrong direction had hit them head-on.

The party was to begin in an hour or so. To cancel and inform everybody seemed a more insurmountable task than to let the party happen. "It was even a nice party. I carried on, somehow, going through the motions of being a hostess. I was numb—in shock, I suppose—and nothing felt real."

The funeral was the following week. Margaret attended but declined to see Betty's body. "I wanted to remember her as she was when she was full of life. And she is still alive to me today—my mother too. I constantly bring them into my thoughts, thinking what I should tell them, wishing they could see the lovely things that I enjoy."

Aunty Em had been living with Betty and Nick in San Diego since the death of Ralph Minor. She was ninety-eight years old. For one of her last birthdays, Margaret wrote:

Oh enviable is our Anni-Em:
In our whole family's bright diadem
The cynosure today, the brightest gem.
For you have spanned time upon this earth
That's let you mine the riches of your worth
And polish through hard work and healing mirth
Your own intrinsic self. The gifts of wit
And courage for us others have been lit
With inspiration of achievement. It
Is no small thing we thank you for today
But makes April the fifth a time to say,
Thanks just for being you, your own dear way.

Em died in 1973, aged ninety-nine.

By 1980, the volume of visitors caused Margaret to issue an ultimatum. Said Ned, "She threatened to leave if we didn't build a guest house." Margaret explained, laughing, "I was tired of the two of us dragging beds around in order to accommodate guests."

At first they considered a separate guest house. Then Dan suggested an addition to the existing house—using the east wall as a common wall, but keeping the two areas separate, with their own entrances, their own latchkeys. He drew up plans, and the result, completed in 1981 by the same contractor who built the house, was so well done that the new structure gives little hint that it is an addition. The annex, the addition, or the apartment, as it is variously called, gives flexibility to hosts and visitors alike and eased the wear and tear on Margaret imposed by a surfeit of guests.

⌒ 23 ⌒

New Zealand: The Third Eye

It was mid-February 1980, and Margaret and Ned were flying, white knuckled, into Wellington, New Zealand. The aircraft bucked viciously. Out of the window, Margaret watched the wing twist out of sync with the body and wondered how it stayed attached. They were losing height fast—suddenly they were in a valley between two ridges. Out of foaming water, sharp rocks reached for the plane's belly, and then they were thunking into the runway, bouncing off, juddering to a roaring thankful halt . . . . Margaret had been holding her breath. Ned looked as shaken as she felt. "Whew! Don't want to have to do that again," he muttered. They entered the terminal in time to hear that the authorities had closed the airport to incoming traffic; their flight had been the last to risk a landing.

Ned had come to New Zealand to attend the Fifth International Gondwana Symposium at Victoria University in Wellington, New Zealand. Margaret looked forward to a tour of South Island after the meetings were over. She wanted to see the west coast: Milford Sound with its five-thousand–foot peaks rearing straight out of the sea; the rain forests; the glaciers of the Southern Alps.

But, the best-laid plans . . . In 1965, Chuck Landis of Otago University in Dunedin on the South Island had spent a day and a half on Stephens Island. He was doing field work for his Ph.D. dissertation on the Permian rocks of South Island, New Zealand. While he waited for a launch to come and pick him up, he poked in a casual fashion at the conglomerate rocks just below the landing stage, and found a two-inch-long piece of fossil bone. It looked as if it might be from a vertebrate. If it was, it was a first in that particular rock formation. The fragment was packed off to Ned Colbert for identification. It was very worn, but Ned thought it could well be a Triassic reptile. After he had finished examining it, Ned gave it to the American Museum mailing department and asked for it to be packed up and returned to Chuck in Dunedin. A parcel indeed arrived at Otago University, but it contained the wrong fossil. Efforts to locate the real Stephens Island bone have been in vain.

In 1979 Chuck Landis took sabbatical leave from Otago, and he and his wife, Carolyn, spent some months in Flagstaff, where they became good friends with Ned and Margaret Colbert. It occurred to Chuck that a return trip to Stephens Island with Ned in tow might yield further fossils. As Ned planned to attend the New Zealand Gondwana Symposium in 1980, Chuck contacted Hamish Campbell of the New Zealand Geological Survey at Lower Hutt, and Hamish offered to organize an expedition to the island.

And so it was Margaret found her anticipated trip to the scenic glories of South Island superseded. She swallowed her disappointment and gamely agreed to go along.

Stephens Island in Cook Strait is one crag among a jigsaw-puzzle of crags that constitute the northeast tip of South Island. It is just over a mile across at its widest dimension, and half a mile wide, and juts to a height of about 920 feet. Bounded by steep cliffs, it is uncompromising and unwelcoming. It is also a home of the tuatara, the "lizard" (which is, of course, no lizard) with three eyes.

Tuataras were common on the New Zealand mainland until the middle of the nineteenth century. Introduced feral cats, pigs, and rodents, and human encroachment on their habitat brought them to the edge of extinction. They are now confined to a few islands off the northeast coast of North Island and to Stephens Island. They are strictly protected by the New Zealand government; permission to visit the reptiles on Stephens Island is not easily obtained.

However, Hamish arranged for a small group of people to go to Stephens after the meetings in Wellington were over: Chuck Landis, Mike Johnston (of the New Zealand Geological Survey in Nelson), Dr. R. Goellner (a herpetologist from the St. Louis Zoo in Missouri), Ned and Margaret, and Hamish himself. Andy Cox, an officer of the New Zealand Wildlife Service, accompanied them, chiefly to ensure that no government restriction regarding the tuataras was transgressed; he also was knowledgeable about the reptiles.

Everybody was to congregate at the Admiral's Lodge, a hotel in Picton on the northeast mainland of South Island, on the evening of February 25. Margaret and Ned had planned to make the trip from Wellington to Picton by

Tuatara Christmas card, linoleum cut, 1980.

air, but flying was out of the question because of more bad weather. Instead, they took a large ferry; the trip took over three hours. Dog-tired and queasy, they arrived in Picton at about 11:30 P.M. At the Admiral's Lodge—for six New Zealand dollars a head—they were able to snatch less than three hours of rest. At 3:45 A.M., they were awakened to go to the wharf, where they boarded a government lighthouse tender, the *Enterprise* (provided free), and set off at 4 A.M. on the six-hour crossing to Stephens Island.

Those six hours were an eternity; it was very rough, especially the last two hours when they were in open water. Everybody was seasick, with the exception of Chuck Landis, who was clearly enjoying the ride. Between waves of nausea, the others glared at him in deep dislike. With admirable prescience, Margaret had pocketed airsickness bags from the plane they had taken into Wellington, but she did not have enough—she and Ned had to share one. Dr. Goellner disappeared into the boat's toilet and locked the door, not emerging until they arrived at Stephens Island. (Margaret photographed him on arrival looking luminescent green; later she mailed the snap to him in St. Louis with a note on it: "Getting there is half the fun.")

The waves were running from the south and the landing spot, on the south side of the island, was still in shadow at 10 A.M. The island loomed above them, dark, forbidding, and impossibly steep. There was no beach or wharf. The lighter circled sickeningly many feet below a concrete platform. To get onto the island, a small derrick swung a tea chest—a large wooden box—into the lighter. Two people at a time climbed into the chest and stood clutching the hawser while the derrick operator—who turned out to be the lighthouse keeper, Gary Schroeder—waited for the precise moment when the boat hung precariously on the top of a swell. With consummate skill, he then snatched up the flimsy chest with its passengers, and wound them up. Hamish wrote in a 1994 letter from Bangkok, Thailand: "It all seemed terribly treacherous and foolish—to all of us. But it worked." He added, "Margaret never showed any hesitation or apprehension." This may have been because by that time, she cared little what happened to her, just as long as she got off that boat. She remembered the young son of friends in Flagstaff puzzling when he was small about how people and animals stayed put below the equator; she was no longer sure of the answer.

From the platform, an inclined railway took the baggage, but people had to walk. A grassy track led steeply upward seven or eight hundred feet and then climbed further across the top of the island to the lighthouse and the keeper's cottages. At the top of the steepest part of the climb, they were met by Anne Schroeder, Gary's wife; and Diane Smith, the wife of the assistant keeper, Brendan. The two carried a large thermos of tea and some crackers; Margaret had never been so grateful for a cup of tea in her life.

Hamish wrote: "The climb to the lighthouse was long and steep. It was slow going. I remember Margaret being concerned about Ned on occasions, but she herself showed her normal calm, quiet, stoical disposition." Ned, it should be remembered, was seventy-five, and Margaret herself sixty-nine. Anne and Diane walked up the hill with Margaret. "Every now and then," Margaret said, "one or the other of them would say something like: 'This is where I like to stop and look at the view.' *Very* tactful." They passed by some cattle. The mind boggled at the thought of bringing a cow in on the tea chest. Close to the lighthouse, some geese and chickens wandered, pecking at the short grass.

The group was put up in an empty house with electricity, a refrigerator, and a gas cooker. They had brought their own food, organized by Hamish at a cost of eight New Zealand dollars a head, and their own utensils. First things first; everyone took a much needed nap—they were all exhausted. Hamish, with a migraine, was in particularly poor shape, and he collapsed in his sleeping bag on a couch. "I remember Margaret fussing over me, mak- ing sure I was comfortable and bringing me food (goodness knows from where)," he wrote.

Tuataras are nocturnal. When the sun went down, the visitors sallied forth armed with powerful flashlights. They could hear the reptiles croak- ing. They sounded like frogs. They found the first one in a ditch—an adult, about two feet long. It had orange spots that looked like lichen on its skin; these Andy Cox identified as clusters of mites. By the time it was completely dark, the creatures were emerging by the dozen from their burrows, waddling around, apparently unconcerned by the flashlight beams, which provided sufficient light to take photographs. They had "frills" consisting of a jagged row of "teeth" from the top of their heads to the tips of their tails, dewlaps, long claws, and liquid eyes. Margaret was captivated: "Tuataras are beautiful. They have nicer proportions than many reptiles." They came in all sizes; some were almost three feet long, but the smallest were perhaps five inches, or even less. Several of the tiny ones still had their "egg teeth"—the spikes on the tips of their noses to help them break the hard shells of their eggs—which would disappear within days of hatching. The skins of the beasts came in a variety of colors, although they were all the one species, *Sphenodon punctatus*. They shed their skins like snakes as they grow, and the difference in color was probably a function of the age of the skin. The creatures were catching and eating giant crickets with three-inch-long legs.

On each reptile's head, the third eye was visible as a flat spot. The pineal eye is found in some other reptiles, but it is best developed in the tuatara. It has no iris, but it does have a lens and a vestigial light-sensitive retina. Sockets in the top of the sculls correspond to the orbits in the skull behind functioning eyes. The tuatara is a hangover from the time before the dinosaurs, the sole survivor of an order of reptiles called beak-heads, Rhynchocephalia, that became extinct during the Jurassic.

On Wednesday, February 27, the men went off to look for fossils. Margaret had a full day to spend sketching and talking to Diane Smith and Anne Schroeder and her children. She was able to absorb a little of the day-to-day lives of the "castaways."

The lighthouse still had its original equipment, intact and functional in case the modern electronically controlled system that had superseded it broke down. With the new equipment, the lighthouse keeper no longer had to leap out of bed every hour to tend the light.

The Schroeders' two young children, a boy and a girl, were being educated with home lessons, supplemented with radio programs. These well-worked-out programs were broadcast by the New Zealand government educational authority to supply the needs of many children scattered around the country in remote locations far from schools. Gary Schroeder, like many people in lonesome places, was quite a talker. "Wonderful to listen to," said Margaret, "but his accent was so strong, and he talked so fast, he was a little hard to follow."

She explored the habitat of the tuataras in the daylight. They had almost all vanished at sunrise—although she did find one or two wandering about. Their burrows were in soft loamy soil under a canopy of low stunted

Coprosoma trees. The reptiles often share their burrows with petrels: the birds live in them at night, the reptiles by day. The tuataras dig them in areas where the topsoil has been loosened and turned and manured by the birds to a depth of up to two feet. Margaret watched the slate-gray and white petrels wheeling about, then heading off for their day's fishing and shrimping.

The geologists returned in the evening, pleased enough with their work on the island. They had found no further trace of vertebrates, but had turned up a cache of invertebrate fossils in the Stephens Formation. On his way back to their lodgings, Dr. Goellner found a dead juvenile tuatara. He put it in the refrigerator, intending to take it back to the States.

Pat Aston, the skipper of a private launch from French Pass, had arranged to arrive at 8 A.M. on February 28 to pick up the party "provided," he had said, "that no southerly or sou'wester was blowing." Thursday dawned fair and calm, and so the visitors said their farewells to the Smiths and Anne Schroeder, turned off the power in their borrowed home, and made their way back down the long climb to the landing stage. Gary Schroeder climbed up to work the derrick. The voyagers were let down in pairs. Instead of the tea-chest system, each person placed one foot in a loop of rope and held on for dear life while they were swung out over the water. However, this time the boat waited quietly to receive them, rolling almost imperceptibly.

On the two-and-a-half-hour trip to French Pass, Skipper Aston served tea and biscuits, the sun shone, and the sea was kind. A small pod of dolphins kept them company, riding the boat's bow wave. They were about an hour out, when Dr. Goellner disturbed the peace with an anguished cry— he had forgotten his tuatara.

As they approached French Pass, a dark, long-necked bird flew low over the water toward them. With rapid wing beats, it circled the launch and then perched on the rail. The skipper explained it was his tame cormorant, that it always came out to meet him.

A minibus awaited their arrival with a driver from the New Zealand Geological Survey in Nelson. Hamish found a telephone and called the Schroeders to warn them that a dead tuatara would soon be festering in the refrigerator, and then the group was driven back to Nelson, from where they would catch their respective flights onward. The road sometimes took them close to the ocean and the rugged coastline, and sometimes it dipped into the rain forest, so Margaret at least tasted what she had looked forward to: tree ferns, gnarled and twisted branches of moss-covered trees with epiphytes in all the crotches, small bright birds, exuberant life falling over itself in the lush, dripping green.

~ 24 ~
Of Boats, Babies, Birds

Four years later, in 1984, a series of paleontological meetings in southern Germany and in Oslo gave the Colberts an excuse to cross the Atlantic one more time. The first conference was in Tübingen, south of Stuttgart; they had been there nineteen years earlier, for a conference before their journey through Israel. And then Venice: a wealthy Venetian businessman, Giancarlo Ligabue, had invited them to his city, paid their way from Tübingen, and put them up in a good hotel.

Venice in September—the sun was still hot in the daytime, but the evenings were cool and the stifling humidity of high summer had gone. Margaret wandered the narrow back streets, beside the dark oily water of side canals. Here, away from the grandeur of the dying city, people actually lived: lines of limp laundry stretched across the water between buildings; multitudes of skinny cats, in T. S. Eliot's words, "no less liquid than their shadows"; exuberant scarlet geraniums in window boxes; caged canaries singing loudly to the sun, which touched only the upper windows of the houses. The air was heavy with garlic, olive oil, and an underlying dank, marshy smell of water laced with sewage. She thought suddenly of Aunt Peggy and the rotting seaweed of Portsmouth. "Puff mud!"

Giancarlo Ligabue was interested in science and had contributed money to the founding of a natural history museum in Venice. He was acquainted with the director of the Paris Museum, Professor Taquet—a colleague of Ned's—and was underwriting a program for that museum. Through Taquet, he had persuaded Ned to write a chapter in a book about dinosaurs he planned to publish. Ned obliged, and *Sulle Orme Dei Dinosauri* by Bonaparte, Colbert, Currie, et al., a coffee-table volume in full color, appeared in 1984.

212

With a phalanx of other guests, the Colberts spent the day of the historic Regatta Storia at Ligabue's palace on the Grand Canal. The water carnival has been staged annually since medieval times. Situated almost directly opposite the red awnings of the reviewing stand, the palace was in a perfect position to view the affair in comfort and in shade. Very old, ornate boats were brought out of storage once a year for the event. They were reminiscent of the bucentaur (*bucintoro* in Italian), the lavish galley that from the twelfth century until well into the eighteenth carried the Doge of Venice onto the Adriatic Sea each Ascension Day, symbolizing Venetian maritime supremacy. The boats were like outsize gondolas and were rowed by up to two dozen people standing up and facing forward. Carved dolphins, prancing horses, or female figures graced the prows of the craft, and their oarlocks were also carved wood. Tableaux were staged on the boats—here the Doge of Venice, there St. Mark's lion—and the costumes of the participants and the oarsmen were from the fifteenth century. Some of the boats trailed long swags of dark red velveteen in the water. Some carried musicians who favored Corelli, Vivaldi, and trumpets. The regular gondolas and other utilitarian boats were also dressed up for the occasion. The show left an impression of gaiety and opulence, color and light, set against the shabby elegance of the sinking palaces.

Later in the day, races were staged. Instead of double sculls, they had double gondolas. And the big old boats raced with teams of muscular oarsmen straining at the long sweeps. They even had a women's race, which, said Margaret, "was no doubt a very modern invention."

It was almost unheard of for Ned to take a holiday, but, after the Oslo meetings, he stayed still and enjoyed the several days of a canal boat trip. Twenty-four passengers boarded the *Wilhelm Than* in Göteborg, Sweden. Their route followed the Göta River and crossed the expanse of the lake of Vanern, and then the boat slipped into the Göta Kanal. Completed in the 1830s, the canal still ships a quantity of goods and traffic. It was so narrow that in places it was possible to pluck leaves from trees as they passed. The numerous locks were about eighteen feet wide; the beam of *Wilhelm Than* seemed all of seventeen feet, eleven inches. The skipper slid her in each time, with never a jolt—although the boat did have rows of fenders on each side, in case of misjudgment. The passengers disembarked as the boat locked through, and Margaret marveled each time at the speed with which water poured in to fill a lock and raise up the boat and rushed out again to lower the level for the next vessel. The locks were worked by hand, with a large ratchet. Through fields, woods, and small towns, woods, fields again, "the wake of the boat made all the reeds on the edge bow as we went by," said Margaret. The Göta Kanal took them to the Baltic Sea and they sailed north, up the convoluted coastline, to finish their voyage in Stockholm. The boat was well appointed and comfortable, the food served smorgasbord style and delicious, the water smooth. For those few days, the Colberts let the world slide by. It was civilized and wonderfully relaxing.

Between the Tübingen and Oslo conferences was a meeting devoted to discourses on *Archeopteryx*; it was held in the Bavarian town of Eichstätt, south of Nürnberg, on one of the tributaries of the Danube. Eichstätt is a town of seventeenth-century gabled houses, paved and cobbled streets, baroque churches and halls, and it is surrounded by quarries from which is cut Solnhofen limestone. Quarrying has been the local industry for centuries. In earlier times this fine-grade limestone was used for lithographs; today it is used for interior and exterior ornamental facing stone. Even now, the stone is quarried by hand because blasting shocks it; the stonecutters take out very slender slabs, working with hammers and sometimes heavy pliers.

The Solnhofen limestone was laid down in the Jurassic period. In the 1860s, an extraordinary fossil was found between two of the thin slabs. The creature had teeth in its elongated jaw and a long, bony tail, but the perfect imprint of feathers established it as a bird rather than a reptile. It was named *Archeopteryx*. The fossil was so well preserved and so strange that doubt was cast on its authenticity; birds were not supposed to have arisen until after the Jurassic, and the discovery upset some paleontologists' theories. (Even quite recently, Fred Hoyle, the controversial British astronomer, suggested the remains were of a chicken in cement; this pronouncement did little for his scientific reputation.) A few other *Archeopteryx* specimens have been discovered in the Solnhofen. John Ostrom of Yale (who had been a student of Ned's at Columbia) found a partial skeleton in a museum in Holland that had been for years classified as a reptile; he recognized it as another Solnhofen *Archeopteryx*.

In paleontological circles, a battle still rages between those who believe birds descended directly from dinosaurs similar to *Coelophysis* (whose hollow bones and hind-limb structure gives credence to the idea) and those who believe that birds and dinosaurs shared a common ancestor and developed in different directions. *Archeopteryx* is crucial to scientists on both sides of the argument. It also enters into the debate over whether and when dinosaurs became warm-blooded.

After the Eichstätt talks, the paleontologists were taken to see the quarries. "As we approached," said Margaret, "we heard 'tonk—tunk—tenk—

A nest of hatchling Mussaurus, *illustration from* Discovering Dinosaur Babies *(1991) by Miriam Schlein.*

tink, going up in tone. The stonecutters were chipping off the edges of the stone, and as the pieces fell off, the sound went up the scale." Fields of scarlet poppies surrounded the quarries.

Eight years later, Miriam Schlein, a New York writer of children's books, with over eighty titles to her credit, asked Margaret to collaborate with her and illustrate a book on *Archeopteryx*. Schlein's books are well written and carefully researched. In many of them, she strives to educate and excite young readers in aspects of natural science. Joan McGrath in the second edition of *Twentieth Century Children's Writers* (1983) wrote of her books: "Schlein's especial talent is her ability to explain while entertaining. Hers are works of charm and simplicity that have stood the tests of time."

Margaret had already illustrated Miriam's 1991 *Discovering Dinosaur Babies*, an account of the dinosaur eggs and hatchlings that have been found. The book explains what scientists have been able to determine about the way different dinosaurs cared for their young. It is a scientific report at a child's level. Margaret enjoyed working with Miriam, and the book was right up her alley. For the more than twenty full-color illustrations, she used gouache. Her son George designed a map at the beginning of the book. Margaret dedicated her contribution to the book to "my good friend Ned, who helps me keep these animals plausible."

The *Archeopteryx* book was to be a similar book of serious science for young children, and Margaret was enthusiastic about the project. But she had been having trouble with her eyes. Glaucoma and cataracts were taking their toll. The cataracts had been successfully removed, but the glaucoma, especially in her right eye, was stubborn. However, after treatments of varying degrees of unpleasantness, and with regular medication in the form of eye drops, the situation had stabilized. Before she agreed to tackle the project, Margaret asked her ophthalmologist if he thought she would be irresponsible to take on such a task. Would she be able to complete it? He gave her the go-ahead. Miriam was delighted; she, too, had enjoyed the previous collaboration, and Ned was an invaluable resource.

Margaret began work on a model of *Archeopteryx*. From pictures of reconstructions of its skeleton, and from available literature, it is estimated that the creature must have been about the same size and shape as a modern roadrunner. Fossils have revealed that it had feathers along the length of its tail, which was long and reptilian—unlike the nub with which modern birds are left. From the structure of the breastbone, or "keel," it was evident that it was not a brilliant flier and probably did little more than glide; the bones and muscles would not have been strong enough to support any serious flapping of wings. Its wings, however, were formed from modified phalanges ("finger" bones), like those of modern birds. At each "wrist," the vestiges of three other digits were manifested in long curved claws. These were a puzzle. They seemed big enough and strong enough to be functional, but in that position their function is obscure. Paleontologists now believe they helped the creature climb trees and that it scrambled up to gain height, then used its wings to glide down. Its legs were well muscled, and the three middle toes were elongated and had powerful claws, particularly the center one of the three.

Margaret's *Archeopteryx* model is in a flying—or gliding—pose. She used *papier-mâché* and "Liquitex" modeling compound over an armature of light wire. Its feathers are rice paper with pine-needle shafts. Its claws came from a sliced-up black plastic ink bottle: "That bottle had exactly the right curve in its square corners," she explained, finding it not at all extraordinary that she could perceive that in the intact bottle. It has beads for eyes. The image of the roadrunner kept popping up, and she submitted to its urging and gave the model a tuft of real feathers on its head. As for color, Margaret felt that for once, no holds were barred. Feathers of modern birds come in all colors—why should not *Archeopteryx* have been brilliantly hued? She chose blues, shading from a light jade-blue on its underparts to darker, almost teal on its upper surfaces. The flight feathers and tail feathers are burnt orange—an earthy shade of coral. The completed model hangs over Margaret's studio bed. John Ostrom has tried to coax it away from her; thus far she has resisted all blandishments because she feels the model is not sturdy enough for public display.

Margaret had plans and preliminary sketches for many paintings in the book. In one picture she planned to incorporate an age-old wooden statue that she saw in Dollnstein, one of the Solnhofen quarry villages. It depicts a man carrying a stone cutter's saw in his right hand, a mallet over his left shoulder, and a little rucksack on his back. For the table of contents page, she resuscitated her 1958 drawing *Turning the Pages of Geology*, and this time she executed it in full color; the unfolding strata underlaid a landscape evocative of that around Eichstätt, including the red poppies. Two possible designs for the cover of the book were completed, both in quite dark, vivid colors: one shows *Archeopteryx* shinning up a tree, using its claws; the other has the bird standing in an almost heraldic pose, tail rampant.

And then in the winter of 1992–93, Margaret started to feel discomfort in her neck. It grew steadily more painful. Standing at her easel with a raised paintbrush became torture. X-rays and probings by doctors revealed osteoarthritis in the cervical vertebrae, for which nothing could be prescribed except rest. Margaret gave herself a week or two off painting, but it was not enough; the pain came back as soon as she began work again. With a publisher's deadline hanging like the sword of Damocles, she called Miriam and told her with great regret and disappointment that she was not going to be able to do the *Archeopteryx* project after all.

She was quite disconsolate. She had painted through and around many ailments—through surgeries, through shingles, through a terrifying interval after a Flagstaff specialist told her she had lymphoma (which turned out to be mononucleosis), and through chronic intestinal miseries. To be defeated by a stiff neck was an indignity.

~: 25 :~

Completing Circles

June 1993, Ghost Ranch, New Mexico: The window of the adobe cottage is open and admits a cool breeze, although the sky is cloudless and the sun hot; sweet, insistent bird chatter from tall cottonwoods; the braying of a distant donkey; the *pht-pht-pht-takataka* of a sprinkler system in a field of alfalfa; the smells of laid dust, sage, juniper . . .

Margaret and I sit on spartan chairs before a low table strewn with notebooks, paper, pens, paper clips. We have talked of journeys taken; of childhood and old age; of parents and relationships; of sons, grandchildren, great-grandchildren; of living, and of dying. We have laughed a lot. And we have cried. It is intense, this probing of a life; I have learned much, but her dark brown eyes never give everything away. Her habits of self-control and self-discipline, of graciousness and humility are strong; this, after all, is Margaret. She takes off her glasses—a gesture I recognize as a prelude to another tale, another memory. She tells her story, stops once to point out the black-headed grosbeak that has landed on a low fence . . . The tape recorder hums.

Ned is out in the desert with students, one of whom is Miriam Schlein, here at the Colberts' urging; she is overwhelmed by the landscape—but also by the Ghost Ranch bugs. The instructors with Ned are Lynett Gillette, David Gillette, and Sid Ash. Lynett, curator of the Ruth Hall Paleontology Museum, is the organizer of the paleontology seminars. Dave returns to Ghost Ranch every year from Salt Lake City and his new job as state paleontologist of Utah. Sid is the paleobotanist from Weber State University who in the past has helped Margaret to "keep the prehistoric plants plausible," in particular, in the Albuquerque mural.

*Ann Elliot and
Margaret at Ghost
Ranch, 1993.*

Interest in the Ghost Ranch paleontology program has grown steadily, and a number of people return to take part in the seminars a second and third time. The new director of Ghost Ranch, Joe Keesecker, has continued where Jim Hall left off and encourages secular programs of worth.

"If you stay long enough at Ghost Ranch, your past seems to turn up," Margaret says. Already this year, Mickey, a good friend and widow of Charles Bogert (one of Ned's colleagues from the American Museum) has visited, bringing greetings from the daughter of Alice Sharp, the Leonia potter. A niece of Tom Ierardi was here with her husband: "She must have been one of the little kids running around our yard in Leonia." Artist Cecily Colbert, granddaughter of Ned's brother Herschel, dropped by; she lives and works in a small village not too far away from the ranch. ("Cecily does very interesting ceramics—fine art rather than useful pots. She used to have a studio in Los Angeles, and Ned and I visited her there. She had a roomful of large pencil drawings, beautifully done, in an unusual technique of her own—but they were all erotic subjects. Ned and I looked and did not know what to say. We both went rather pink.") And then, out of the blue, New Zealanders Chuck and Carolyn Landis appear. The Colberts have not seen them since the trip to Stephens Island, thirteen years ago.

The grosbeak has flown and the volume of bird song diminishes as the sun begins its dip westward.

Time telescopes as years pass, and aspects of life come full circle. The New Brunswick Museum in Saint John decided in the early 1980s to reinstate a paleontology section, and a young paleontologist from Ontario, Randall Miller, was hired to organize the effort. In the basement of the museum Randy unearthed George Frederic Matthew's collections and became interested

Ned and Margaret at
Ghost Ranch, 1993.

in his work. Randy Miller spent a year or two sorting out the collections and then arranged an exhibit. He made contact with members of the Matthew family and invited them to come to the opening of the show in 1987. Most of the family were able to attend, but "Bill and Gladys, Ned and I could not manage it that year, so we put it off until 1988 and then went together. We had a great time."

Randy Miller has a strong interest in education: with his wife, he initiated a program to foster interest in earth sciences and fossils in the New Brunswick schools. Margaret designed at his request a sequence of drawings, like a strip cartoon, to be used as a teaching tool: George Frederic Matthew and her father Will as a child are depicted setting off on a fossil hunt; Will finds the giant trilobite; they hammer it out of the rock and bring it home to study; Grandfather George Frederic writes at his desk, describing the creature, and names it—*Paradoxides regina*, in honor of Queen Victoria.

Although advancing years have meant travel is less simple than it used to be, Margaret and Ned eagerly seize excuses to visit back east. The East-Coast sons—George, Dan, and Charles—arranged a grand party for Margaret and Ned's golden wedding anniversary on July 8, 1983. It was held at the farm in Rhode Island, which is still owned and cherished by Tom

Charles, Dan, Phil, Dave, and George. The Colbert "boys" at the Rhode Island farm for Margaret and Ned's golden wedding anniversary, 1983.

Nichols, Betty and Nick's oldest son. A lobster feast with all the fixings took place under a big walnut tree near the house. All five sons were there— the first time the seven Colberts had all been together for many years.

(No hurrahs took place for the sixtieth anniversary in 1993. "We are saving those," said Margaret, "for our seventy-fifth!")

A journey to the east coast in 1991 was undertaken with the express purpose of visiting family—Charles and Agatha; Dan, Catherine, and the two little boys; George, Jenny, and Little Margaret; Bill and Gladys Matthew, and several of their offspring and grandchildren. Margaret and Ned were tourists, complete with cameras and sore feet. It was early fall, and the Catskills were touched with brilliance here and there. Further north, in New England, the trees edged into their full autumn glory.

The pilgrimage included a visit to Hastings-on-Hudson. The house at 65 Edgar Lane was now painted white, the tiled roof replaced with shingles, the third-floor balcony missing. Most of the rampaging vines and wisteria had gone. It looked very tidy, and rather naked. At the back of the house was an elegant swimming pool. The rest of the grounds were overgrown, and two or three other houses had sprouted on the land. Margaret and Ned knocked on the door and were invited inside by the owner. Interior differences were more marked and its smell was no longer of home. Nonetheless, in spite of all the inevitable changes, the house was achingly familiar.

They went to Rhode Island and the farm. *Alice Through the Looking Glass* was still there, if a little dulled. When Aunty Em's paper stencils finally began to disintegrate, Margaret asked Louise Waller (the artist friend who had assisted her with the Albuquerque mural) to recut them in mylar; they were too good to lose, and now they are permanent. Dan used them for his son Drew, so Alice and her friends also romp around a house in Greenwich, Connecticut.

Physical contact with family members is perforce sporadic, given the distances that must be traveled and the pressures of busy lives. With the exception of Dave in Seattle, who has difficulty getting away, the sons manage visits to Flagstaff at least once a year, and one or other of the families almost always contrives to be with Margaret and Ned at Thanksgiving and Christmas. Meanwhile, the telephone lines are frequently humming between the older Colberts and their offspring and other relatives and good friends. Margaret finds a particular joy in contact with the grandchildren and great-grandchildren.

The late winter and spring of 1993 brought a long visit from grandson Denis and his family. Denis had left the army in 1990 and moved to Japan, where he worked for almost three years. There he met and married Kazumi. He had difficulties with his job, as he came to realize that his employers were less than honest. In addition, cultural differences made trouble in his home life; his wife's mother assumed the customary powers accorded Japanese mothers-in-law and tried her best to rule their household. Denis telephoned Margaret from time to time for support and advice. "Grandmother would always lend me her ear," he wrote, "and often helped me put things into perspective in a very tender way. Having raised five independent, bright, energetic, and sometimes horrible boys, Grandmother is an old hand at conflict resolution. Kazumi, with her limited English ability, felt comfortable enough with Grandmother to call her long distance from Japan and ask advice."

Denis came back to the United States at the end of February 1993 with Kazumi and their two children—four-year-old George and a little girl, Micah (pronounced "Meeka"), aged eighteen months. The little family stayed in the Flagstaff annex. Denis decided to rejoin the army, and after some weeks moved to Monterey and the army language school there, planning to learn Korean. Kazumi and the two great-grandchildren stayed on in Flagstaff until May. Of this time, Denis wrote:

I was deeply impressed at how much focused attention and *quality* time Grandmother was able to spend with my children, especially George. Grandmother and George quickly established a daily ritual of taking a little nature walk around the garden, and then spending time reading. Grandmother instilled George with a love and respect for the Hopi Indian culture, especially the Kachina dolls. When

George arrived here in Monterey on May 4th, he knew no less than twenty-five kachina names, and maybe half a dozen or so in the native Hopi: "See, Dada, this is *Powamu,* the bean kachina."

In Japanese kindergarten school, the teacher would tell the children, "Now, class, here's a piece of paper. Hold your pencil so, and copy this duck." The end result was fifty *identical* ducks. If George embellished his duck using his imagination, the teacher tore it up and told him to try again. Grandmother thought that kind of art instruction was education in a low form. But she saw a positive aspect. George holds his pencil very well, he colors carefully within the lines, and has an attention to detail. In Japan George began to dislike art. Grandmother turned his imagination onto the paper.

George was learning English fast, but as Margaret said, "All Micah has to do is say "Mm? mm? mm?" and she gets what she wants—in any language!" Kazumi was learning fast too, and Margaret was amused: "Denis asked her one day to get him a cup of coffee. She said very sweetly, 'No, you get it. This is America.'"

Ned and Margaret love the home on Schultz Pass Road, especially for hosting family and friends, but once in a while they talk about leaving Flagstaff and moving to a retirement center close to one of the sons. So far, there is no imperative to do so. But sometimes Margaret worries that if she became sick, she could not look after Ned; Ned worries that he might become sick and not be able to look after Margaret.

April 1994: Margaret will be eighty-three this month. Ned has his eighty-ninth birthday in September. He no longer finds it quite so hard to slow his pace to match Margaret's, although his energy level is still remarkable, and he will once again be an instructor at Ghost Ranch in July. He is winding up a book about the little dinosaurs of Ghost Ranch, and Margaret is illustrating it for him. The pain in her neck has diminished enough to make this possible. She has begun driving again—the arthritis had prevented that for many months—and is eager to attack a list of projects that have stacked up.

Her eyes, however, are a worry: the glaucoma has seriously reduced her field of vision, and it is exhausting to have to move her whole head along a line of print to read. For years, she and Ned have taken turns to read to each other before bed. Now Ned does all the reading. She can still do scratchboard drawings and can work with a brush, but pen-and-ink has become too difficult. Tomorrow is her monthly appointment with the ophthalmologist, and Margaret is convinced the specialist will suggest more laser surgery on the right eye to reduce the mounting pressure. But she has decided to dig her toes in. Surgery has been tried more than once; it did little good and was unpleasant—she will have no more of it.

Ned's worried look intensifies.

"I'm coming with you to see him," he declares.

"Why?"

"I want to hear what he has to say. I want to know what the options are." He mutters that for such a visually centered person blindness would be a catastrophe.

"But whose eye is it, anyway?"

"Yours . . ."

"Well, then, keep out of it!" She is flushed. "I know you want what's best for me, but I think I know what's best for me!" To soften what has sounded harsh, and because she sees he is hurt, she adds, "*Dear*."

From the annex next day, I hear their car return from the appointment and I go to the garage, anxious to know the outcome. Ned is unpacking groceries from the trunk of the car. He straightens and turns upon me a beaming face: "She's inside—I'll let her tell you." Margaret is stashing orange juice in the refrigerator. She tells me the pressure in both eyes is down almost to normal. A new prescription of drops she has been applying for the last month has worked—no surgery. She is light of step, and the offending eyes sparkle. She and I share a beer and toast Ned, ourselves, and all ophthalmologists.

The "endless Sabbaths" of her childhood in New Brunswick may be partially responsible for Margaret's rejection of "formal" religion. She has given it a lot of thought, but her perspective is thus: "Here I am, in my eighties, a person without religion—or at least, any religion so far established. I simply cannot accept the 'supernatural,' knowing what (admittedly little) I do know of this ever-amazing natural world. I am grateful to have been born into a time which offers so much in the way of knowledge. I cannot see any virtue in 'believing' that which I do not think is true."

For Philip, she expanded on her personal philosophy of life, and there can be no better way to end this chronicle of Margaret's life thus far:

> How can one arrive at a satisfying view of life? Well, there are various routes, and religion is one of them. But to lots of us, the religions that exist are so untenable intellectually that they cannot satisfy. Perhaps religion at its ideal best has always aimed at offering a larger view of life, a world view to which the individual can relate, and thus build a sense of his own identity out of which he can act.

It seems to me that science is now offering raw materials from which modern man's world view may be built into something truer and more satisfying than ever: astronomy and physics for a frame; all the studies of the natural world for an appreciation of some of the possible routes that life may follow; anthropology for a broad platform from which to understand society; and history, natural and human, to lend the dimension of time. And the chinks can be filled in with one's own individual experience of life—at least provisionally.

I am not advocating the "larger view of life" for the attitudes expressed in (for instance), "The vastness of the universe makes human aspirations seem trivial," or, "What will it matter a hundred years from now?"—though these attitudes are sometimes salutary—but rather for the fact that, with growing comprehension of the real world, patterns emerge, and even the small acts which make up daily living become important, precisely as tiny bits in a larger picture.

You will laugh, but my "first commandment" to myself has become, "Let phenotype express genotype,"—which is just a fancy way of saying, "Be yourself." Although other animals do it easily and with natural grace, for us it has become difficult exactly because of our specialization in adaptability. There are so many ways in which we can meet a given situation that we get confused and choose solutions which are no solutions, or which exact terrible penalties—or both! However, I am *not* advocating untrammeled instinct and impulse, for these are, after all, only part of what makes up a human being.

To live we all must have an environment to fill our needs, plus a commitment—even if it is only on the level of instinct satisfaction. It seems to me that, for thinking man, emotional commitment must ultimately be to life itself, and I believe that we are all so committed. We can contemplate, intellectually, a lifeless world, but I cannot imagine anyone who would desire it.

And now I will tentatively suggest that if we recognize this commitment, and accept the laws of the universe under which we must operate, and learn to see ourselves for what we are, we acquire the strength to accept and absorb our mistakes, and to behave in general in due proportion to our place in the pattern of life as we see it. Thus life, and inanimate changes too, become a proving-out of the potentialities inherent in matter. And a darned fascinating drama it is.

~: *Bibliography* :~

Reference Sources

Archer, William George. *The Hill of Flutes: Life, Love, and Poetry in Tribal India: A Portrait of the Santals.* Pittsburgh, Pa.: University of Pittsburgh Press, 1974.

Bakker, Robert T., "Dancing Dinosaurs." In Czerkas and Olson, eds. 38–69.

Bonaparte J. F., E. H. Colbert, P. Currie, et al. *Sulle Orme Dei Dinosauri.* Rome: Erizzo Editrice, 1984.

Campbell, Hamish J., A. C. Coleman, M. R. Johnston, C. A. Landis. "Geology of Stephens Island and the Age of Stephens Formation." *New Zealand Journal of Geology and Geophysics* 27 (1984): 277–89.

Carpenter, A., and T. Balow. *Enchantment of Africa: Lesotho.* Chicago: Children's Press, 1975.

Colbert, Edwin H. *Digging Into the Past: An Autobiography.* New York: Dembner Books, 1989.

———. *Men and Dinosaurs: The Search in Field and Laboratory.* New York: E. P. Dutton, 1968.

———. *William Diller Matthew, Paleontologist: The Splendid Drama Observed.* New York: Columbia University Press, 1992.

Cook, James H. *Fifty Years on the Old Frontier.* 1923. University of Oklahoma Press, 1957.

Crichton, Michael. *Jurassic Park.* New York: Knopf, 1990.

Czerkas, Sylvia J., and Everett C. Olson, eds. *Dinosaurs Past and Present,* Vol. 1. Seattle: University of Washington Press, 1987.

Gillette, David D., 1987. "The Age of Transition: Coelophysis and the Late Triassic Chinle Fauna." In Czerkas and Olson, eds. 132–52.

Godden, Jon, and Rumer Godden. *Shiva's Pigeons: An Experience of India.* New York: Knopf, 1972.

Russell, Dale A. "Models and Paintings of North American Dinosaurs." In Czerkas and Olson, eds. 114–31.

A Selection of Publications in Which Margaret Colbert's Illustrations Appear

Camp, Charles L. *Earth Song.* Palo Alto, Calif.: American West Publishing, 1970.

Colbert, Edwin H., 1935. *Siwalik Mammals in the American Museum of Natural History.* Transactions of the American Philosophical Society for Promoting Useful Knowledge, New Series, Vol. 26. Philadelphia, Pa.

———. *Millions of Years Ago.* New York: T. Y. Crowell, 1958.

———. *The Age of Reptiles.* New York: Norton, 1965.

———. *The Year of the Dinosaur.* New York: Charles Scribner's Sons, 1977.

———. *An Illustrated History of the Dinosaurs.* Maplewood, N.J.: Dembner, 1983.

———. *Dinosaurs of the Colorado Plateau.* Plateau 54, 2 & 3 (1983).

———. *Digging Into the Past: An Autobiography.* New York: Dembner, 1989.

———. *William Diller Matthew, Paleontologist: The Splendid Drama Observed.* New York: Columbia University Press, 1992.

———. *The Little Dinosaurs of Ghost Ranch.* New York: Columbia University Press, 1995.

Czerkas, Sylvia J. and Everett C. Olson, eds., 1987. *Dinosaurs Past and Present,* Vol. 1. Seattle: University of Washington Press, 1987.

Goin, Coleman J. and Olive B. Goin. *Journey Onto Land.* New York: Macmillan: 1974.

Schlein, Miriam. *Discovering Dinosaur Babies.* New York: Four Winds Press, Macmillan, 1991.

✌: Index :~